Globalization and Contestat

Globalization is undoubtedly the great overarching paradigm of our era. However, there is still little agreement on what globalization actually 'is' and some do not accept that it 'is' anything at all.

This new book addresses the contestation of globalization by the anti-globalization movement. To contest is to challenge, to call into question, to doubt, to oppose and to litigate; this study shows how globalization is 'contestable' in many different ways and how the counter-movements we have seen emerging over the last decade also 'bear witness' on behalf of an alternative human future. Ronaldo Munck presents an overarching framework that allows us to understand how globalization and its contestation are inextricably bound up with one another. This volume insightfully explores a number of case studies, including the Battle of Seattle in 1999; the World Social Forum; peasant internationalism and environmental movements and reactionary movements including the US Patriot movement, Islamic fundamentalist movements and other nationalist movements.

This text will be of great interest to all students and scholars of international relations, politics and of globalization and global governance in particular.

Ronaldo Munck is Theme Leader for Internationalisation, Interculturalism and Social Development (IISD) at Dublin City University, Ireland.

Rethinking globalizations
Edited by Barry Gills
University of Newcastle, UK

This series is designed to break new ground in the literature on globalization and its academic and popular understanding. Rather than perpetuating or simply reacting to the economic understanding of globalization, this series seeks to capture the term and broaden its meaning to encompass a wide range of issues and disciplines and convey a sense of alternative possibilities for the future.

Globalization and Contestation

The new great counter-movement

Ronaldo Munck

Routledge
Taylor & Francis Group

LONDON AND NEW YORK

First published 2007 by Routledge
2 Park Square, Milton Park, Abingdon, Oxon OX14 4RN

Simultaneously published in the USA and Canada
by Routledge
270 Madison Ave, New York, NY 10016

Routledge is an imprint of the Taylor & Francis Group, an informa business

© 2007 Ronaldo Munck

Typeset in Garamond 3 by
Florence Production Ltd, Stoodleigh, Devon

British Library Cataloguing in Publication Data
A catalogue record for this book is available from the British Library

Library of Congress Cataloging in Publication Data
Munck, Ronaldo.
  Globalization and contestation: the new great counter-movement/
Ronaldo Munck.
     p. cm. – (Rethinking globalizations)
    Includes bibliographical references and index.
  1. Anti-globalization movement – International cooperation.
  2. Globalization – Social aspects.   3. Globalization – Political
aspects.   4. Social movements – International cooperation.
  5. Protest movements – International cooperation.   I. Title.
  JZ1318.M8586 2007
  303.48'2 – dc22   2006020731

ISBN10: 0–415–37655–6 (hbk)
ISBN10: 0–415–37656–4 (pbk)
ISBN10: 0–203–96237–0 (ebk)

ISBN13: 978–0–415–37655–6 (hbk)
ISBN13: 978–0–415–37656–3 (pbk)
ISBN13: 978–0–203–96237–4 (ebk)

For Agustín Tosco and the workers and
students of the Cordobazo of 1969, who taught
me that another world was necessary.

Contents

Preface

Globalization is undoubtedly the great overarching paradigm of our era. Globalization casts its glow over all human processes and endeavours. Yet, there is still little agreement on what globalization actually 'is' and some do not accept that it 'is' anything at all. While this book addresses the complexity of globalization and its contestation by the anti- or counter-globalization movement, it is well to bear in mind the etymological meaning of the word 'contest'. The *Oxford English Dictionary* (*OED*) defines 'contestation' as 'an assertion contended for' (from the Latin *contestatio*). To contest thus means to challenge, to call into question, to doubt, to oppose or even to litigate. But it can also be derived from the Latin word *contestari* (*testis* meaning witness), to signify 'bearing witness'. Thus, globalization is 'contestable' in many different ways and the counter-movements we have seen emerging over the last decade also 'bear witness' on behalf of an alternative human future.

What I propose is a new paradigm or framework that will allow us to understand how globalization and contestation (or anti-globalization, to put it crudely) are inextricably bound up with one another. Writing just when the long post-war boom was looming on the horizon, Karl Polanyi foretold a great expansion of the free market but also a great social counter-movement that he saw as 'the one comprehensive feature in the history of the age' (Polanyi 2001: 80). For Polanyi, capitalism was moving towards 'an attempt to set up one big self-regulating market' (Polanyi 2001: 70), nothing less than a global economy where the market ruled supreme. However, there was a counter-movement from within society to protect itself from the anarchy of the market. Powerful social movements and institutions would emerge in a veritable 'double movement' to check the actions of the market and reinstate human interests over those of a utopian market economy. My basic thesis is that we are not now witnessing a 'clash of civilizations' (Huntington 2002) at a global level but, rather, a clash between the free market and society.

Chapter 1 introduces the great globalization debate, a complex social, political and cultural phenomenon as much as it is about economics. While opinions are still sharply polarized in terms of the benefits or downside for humanity, its importance as a new matrix for our era is undisputed. We examine the paradigms in contention, the ways in which it is changing the world around us and the critical problem of 'governance', that is, how free market expansion can be managed and made sustainable. This chapter also introduces the Polanyi problematic – the tension between free market expansion and societal reaction – that frames the analysis of the great counter-movement against globalization emerging in recent years. My basic argument is that the Polanyi problematic – duly 'scaled up' for the era of globalization – provides us with a powerful yet subtle optic for examining the intertwined processes of free market expansion and societal reactions to it.

In Chapter 2 I introduce the various approaches to social movements underlying the 'contestation' element of my title. This is also the second element in Polanyi's 'double movement' of free markets expanding and society reacting defensively to protect itself from its effects. Thus, we examine the various theoretical paradigms, such as the resource mobilization approach versus those theories stressing the role of large-scale structural and cultural change as well as identity politics as a basis for mobilization. That leads me into the distinction between the 'old' social movements, such as those of labour and nationalism, versus the 'new' social movements such as the environmental and women's movements. The next section explores the distinctions and relationships between 'progressive' movements for social change and those that seemingly articulate a 'reactionary' response to globalization today. To simplify we need to understand the 'bad' as well as the 'good' social movements. To conclude I offer some Polanyian perspectives on globalization and social movements to complement and answer the Polanyi problematic raised in Chapter 1.

In Chapter 3 we turn from social movement theory to a brief historical overview of transnational social movements that did not begin, of course, in 1999 in Seattle when the global media detected an anti-globalization movement. Modern capitalist society – and the expansion of the free market as its driver in particular – has always generated counter-movements. We explore the politics of scale and why some forms of contestation have taken local, national or transnational form. The time frame adopted is that of the First and Second Internationals (1870–1919) through to the rise of the 'global civil society' in the 1990s. We could parallel this time frame with the first and the second wave of globalization. What were the limits and the achievements of labour internationalism in Europe prior to the inter-imperialist carnage of the First World War? Was the communist internationalism that followed the Bolshevik Revolution of 1917 merely a façade for Russian state interests? Was the colonial revolution simply about nationalism or did it contain elements of transnational solidarity? Finally, what is the significance and what are the prospects of global civil society today and the new cosmopolitanism its proponents advance?

Chapter 4 takes up the story of the contemporary counter-globalization movement, which many symbolically associate with the 'Battle of Seattle' in 1999, when protests prevented the World Trade Organization (WTO) from reaching a conclusion. But Seattle did not spring out of a clear blue sky and we trace the much longer lasting and generalized revolt against neoliberalism, especially in the global South. The symbolic importance of Seattle does, however, provide us with an opportunity to analyse the 'meaning' of the counter-globalization movement. Some of its sequels were carnivalesque at least in terms of the tactics used by those contesting globalization as we know it. What had this got to do with the land struggles of the indigenous people in the Lacandón Forest in a remote region of Mexico, later to become known as the Zapatistas, that potent symbol of global economic solidarity? This chapter explores the various theoretical perspectives developed since Seattle to account for the widest ranging set of transnational protests since the global revolution of 1968. Are these movements simply attempts to 'civilize' globalization and make it more socially accountable or are we at the start of another great anti-capitalist revolt comparable to that at the start of the twentieth century?

Chapter 5 moves from the street demonstrations of Seattle (1999), Genoa (2001) and Edinburgh (2005) to the transnational political arena, such as the World Social Forum that first met in Porto Alegre, Brazil in 2001 to proclaim that 'another world is possible'. We also examine the way the women's movement has developed a formal transnational political presence, symbolized by the Beijing UN Conference on Women in 1995. The other main area to be considered is the transnational human rights movement that has flourished greatly in the era of globalization. In spite of their distinctive dynamics the human rights movement, the women's movement and the World Social Forum are all exemplars of the way transnational social movements have created a space for themselves on the global political scene. What does this mean for the future of movements seeking to foment positive social transformation? Has the transnational level of political activity transcended the national scene as some globalists believe? In brief, we need to cast a retrospective look on transnational political fora to consider what their achievements and limitations are.

Chapter 6 turns towards what we might call 'local transnationalism' by which I mean social movements that have an international orientation but which seek to 'embed' themselves in local communities. The environmental movement was the first to coin the phrase 'think globally, act locally' quite early on in the development of globalization as we know it. This is also the movement that has probably been most successful in creating an impact on the 'mainstream' agenda. Workers' organizations have often subscribed to internationalist ideologies – 'Workers of the World Unite!' – but in practice most workers' struggles have been local in character. And peasants, as workers on the land, have been most rooted of all in the locality and the community, yet today there is an active transnational peasants movement

known as Vía Campesina (The Peasant Path). What do these apparent contradictions mean for a critical theory of globalization and contestation? Is the
'new localism' an adequate response to neoliberal globalization? How might
social movements combine action on various scales of human activity to best
advantage? I would essentially argue that local struggles for human emancipation are as much a part of the contestation of globalization as are the
headline-grabbing events such as Seattle 1999.

Chapter 7 turns to a topic that is too often ignored by the optimistic globalizer and global civil society advocates, namely that of the
literally reactionary social movements. These react in different ways to
the complex patterns of internationalism created by globalization. They are
anti-globalization not from a counter-globalization perspective but more
often on behalf of a conservative mythical past. We examine the various
nationalist reactions to economic internationalization. Many ostensibly
progressive counter-globalization movements are also nationalist in essence.
Then we turn to the far-right Patriot movement of the US which is also
opposed to globalization but from a perspective totally different from
that of the Seattle 1999 protesters. But maybe working-class 'common
sense' in the US can go either way? Finally, we examine in terms of reactions to globalization the militant Islamic 'Jihadists'. Was the attack on the
Twin Towers and the Pentagon an attack on globalization? In conclusion,
we examine the fraught question of whether these reactionary movements
can be considered akin to 'new' social movements or whether they are simply
backward-looking retrograde formations.

And so to the concluding Chapter 8 which returns to the Polanyi problematic of Chapter 1, seeking answers on the basis of the analysis and
description of the great counter-movement of our era. To what extent
can social forces and social movements constrain the free market and strive
for democracy? What is the relationship between progressive and reactionary
social counter-movements? This chapter (re)examines our broad themes of
globalization and contestation under the rubrics made famous by Michael
Hardt and Antonio Negri's books: *Empire* and *Multitude*. Are these terms
adequate for the complex new realities unfolding? My own understanding
of the issues is explored in a reworking of Polanyi's theme of the double
movement through which the market expands into the social sphere but
society reacts back in diverse ways. Finally, what are the prospects for the
counter-globalization movement that have been the subject of this text?
I try to summarize what we have learnt in our various explorations above
and project some of the possible scenarios emerging for the construction of
a more democratic world.

The overall argument of this book is that the Polanyi problematic
provides, potentially, a complex and dialectical framework for an understanding of globalization and contestation, but it does require concretization
in my view. In the first place, it points us towards the dilemmas of the
current world (dis)order and its prospects. Because, as Peter Evans puts it,

'Elites, no less than the rest of us, need to resolve the Polanyi problem' (Evans 2000: 239). But, can the dominant world power construct durable and robust hegemonic institutions and ideologies? For Polanyi, there was a point in the 1920s when the 'double movement' of economic liberalism and social protection led to such institutional strain that, with the onset of class conflict, 'turned crisis into catastrophe' and then 'the time was ripe for the fascist solution' (Polanyi 2001: 140, 244). If narrow sectional interests abuse the general political and economic functions of society, then this will be the result. There are, for Polanyi, 'critical phases of history, when a civilisation . . . is passing through a transformation' when 'no crudely class interest can maintain itself in the lead' if it does not become hegemonic 'unless the alternative to the social setup is a plunge into utter destruction' (Polanyi 2001: 163). So, in normal circumstances the disadvantaged will be protected by enlightened rulers, meaning today that 'global governance' would build its democratic institutions, and those marginalized by neo-liberal policies would be protected by the World Bank's 'safety nets'. World events over the last decade, however, suggest, as Silver and Arrighi put it, that such plunges into utter destruction 'are a sufficiently widespread phenomenon in the early twenty-first century that we might want to treat them as a more "normal" phenomenon, than Polanyi's concept of the double-movement seems to allow' (Silver and Arrighi 2003: 327).

The second issue that requires concretization, in my view, is the precise way in which 'society' might protect itself from the ravages of the self-regulated market. In an era when neoliberals and postmodernists alike query whether there is such a 'thing' as society, we cannot simply assume Polanyi's rather functional analysis of its response to the market mechanisms. Polanyi does tell us that: 'The "challenge" is to society as a whole; the "response" comes through groups, sections and classes' (Polanyi 2001: 160) but that is still quite under-specified in terms of a political sociology for a globalized complex era. Which 'groups' or 'sections' of society are likely to respond to the encroaching marketization and commodification of life? What is the role of social movements in this process, a set of actors rather absent in Polanyi's narrative? The problem is a broader one, namely, the tension between Polanyi's account of the double movement, and his belief that while such a counter-movement was vital for the protection of society, 'in the last analysis it was incompatible with the self-regulation of the market, and thus with the market system itself' (Polanyi 2001: 136). What thus emerges is a self-balancing system, where the social counter-movement is not allowed to go too far lest it undermine the system itself. The dual movement is thus more about embedding social relations within the market, rather than contesting its logic. The interests of society as a whole also remain fairly underspecified in Polanyi's account. This is where, following Bob Jessop, 'the role of specific economic, political and social projects, of hegemonic visions, and of associated capacities become crucial' (Jessop 2003: 7). If the fight-back by 'society' is to go beyond dispersed and possibly contradictory struggles, the basis on which social cohesion and political projects are forged needs to be examined in much more detail than that provided in the original Polanyi problematic.

Finally, we would need to explore further the political dilemmas posed by Polanyi's diagnosis that the counter-movement might equally take reactionary and progressive form. We simply cannot value equally all the disparate counter-movements that respond to the depredations of neoliberal globalization, through projects of social self-protection. On what basis do we decide which are 'good' and which are 'bad' counter-movements? Most claims based on the professed values of 'good governance' or 'transparency and accountability' do little to conceal an openly Eurocentric agenda. We can, maybe, move forward by 'spatializing' the Polanyi problematic and bringing to bear the recent 'politics of scale' debates. For many sections of the broad counter-globalization movement the 'local' is seen as a privileged site of resistance to globalization and it is valorized above all other forms.

Yet, there are countless examples of local parochial backwardness where a reactionary response to globalization leads to other forms of oppression, such as that of minorities and all things lacking 'authenticity'. We can only conclude that, from an analytical perspective, there can be no good or bad responses to globalization. Polanyi's problematic allows us to revisit creatively the local/global dichotomy or dialectic. For one, Polanyi was acutely aware of the very 'local' origins of the 'one big market' that globalization represents. It is not the 'hidden hand' of the market that creates actually existing globalization but concrete social and political forces and groups. However, and this is its limitation today, this analysis of the counter-movement focused almost exclusively on the scale of the nation-state. For Polanyi protectionism had produced 'the hard shell of the emerging unit of social life. The new entity was cast in the national mold' (Polanyi 2001: 211). Elsewhere, Polanyi refers to how: '*within the nations* we are witnessing a development, under which the economic system ceases to lay down the law to society' (Polanyi 2001: emphasis added). Clearly, Polanyi worked within the parameters of what we might call 'methodological nationalism' and that is not surprising of course. What we now need to do (see Adaman *et al.* 2003) is to bring both the local and the global back into the Polanyi problematic to explain how the counter-movement is generated and how market-driven globalization might be deconstructed. In developing this task, we are aided by Polanyi's rich anthropological studies of non-capitalist societies, and an understanding that capitalist commodification has never been complete and never can be, without destroying society.

1 Globalization

A new social, political and cultural matrix

Globalization, defined variously or not at all, is the obligatory point of reference for any discussion of contemporary social, political and cultural transformation. Globalization is, in short, the new matrix for our era, the framework for what is and what might be. The first section of this introductory chapter examines the contested and often contradictory meanings that globalization takes on as dominant paradigm for our time. This is followed by a summary of the socio-economic and cultural transformation it has generated in the world around us. How this new world order might be governed is the subject of the third section on *Global governance* which sets the parameters for many of the more radical contestations of globalization. Finally, I advance an integrated, holistic vision of globalization as a matrix for social and cultural transformation and the horizon of possibilities opening up for political contestation in the current era. Taking my cue from the classic work of Karl Polanyi, *The Great Transformation* (Polanyi 2001), I seek to develop a problematic capable of understanding the complexity of free market-driven globalization and the societal contestation of its effects.

Contested paradigms

Globalization is currently the dominant paradigm or 'way of seeing' the world around us, both for supporters of this phenomenon and for its detractors (for an overview see Scholte 2005). It is a 'grand narrative' as powerful, all-embracing and visionary as any that may have preceded it, including those of classical capitalism, colonialism or socialism. It is seen as an epoch-making moment in human history, a transition to a brave new world. Whereas the anti-globalization movement seemed to hold the discursive high ground at the turn of the century, it is now the defenders of globalization who are on the offensive. Recently, substantive seriously researched books have been published arguing for 'the truth about globalization' (Legrain 2003), or 'in defence of globalization' (Bhagwati 2004) and 'why globalization works' (Wolf 2004). These works are as passionate and as important as those seeking to defend an earlier model of capitalism from the ideological challenge posed by the rise of the Soviet planned economy in the 1920s. So, what is the case the neoliberal prophets make for a global market economy?

For the liberal globalizers, the essence of the phenomenon in question is the free movement of goods, services, capital and labour 'so that, economically speaking, there are no foreigners' (Wolf 2004: 14). They believe, quite literally, in the 'magic of the market' which they see not only as the source of material wealth but 'also [as] the basis of freedom and democracy' (Wolf 2004: 57). Liberal globalization is seen as something that encourages moral virtues. While it indeed 'makes people richer' it also, according to Martin Wolf, makes people 'more concerned about environmental damage, pain and injustice' (Wolf 2004: 57). Be that as it may, it is clear that the liberal globalizer world-view goes beyond simple economics and offers an alternative to all collectivist or social views of the world. Corporations are seen as virtuous as well as dynamic agents of progressive change. Globalization will, according to this view, lead to a decline of inequality and poverty worldwide as the market works its magic. While it might have some downsides – it is accepted that no market is perfect – overall there is simply no alternative. Freedom itself – defined variously or not at all – depends on the continued expansion of the global free market.

The case against globalization is equally passionate and categorical. Globalization, from this perspective, is seen as an economic process leading to the commodification of life itself. There is nothing that is not for sale, from health to education, from knowledge to our genes. Behind the rhetoric of free trade lies a sinister move towards introducing barriers around privatized technology, resources and knowledge to keep them safe for capitalist exploitation. The result, as Naomi Klein puts it, is that 'Globalization is now on trial because on the other side of all these virtual fences are real people, shut out of schools, workplaces, their own farms, homes and communities' (Klein 2002: xxi). The 'silent takeover' (Hertz 2001) by the transnational corporations is seen by others to be an imminent threat to the very possibility of Western democracy as we have known it. Corporations are taking over social functions previously carried out by the state, pressuring governments to follow their neoliberal global agenda, and leaving the political system devoid of any real choices.

It is probably impossible to adjudicate between the pro- and antiglobalization cases when stated in such a polemical and absolutist manner. It might anyway be more productive to avoid this type of binary opposition and start from the complexity of the globalization processes. As John Urry puts it: 'global ordering is so immensely complicated that it cannot be "known" through a simple concept or set of processes' (Urry 2003: 15). The global era cannot be reduced to a simple logic of the market, or of 'network society' or of empire. The complexity approach allows us to move beyond counter-positions such as those between structural determinism and pure chance or, put another way, between frozen stability and everchangingness as dominant trends. Complexity refuses all static and reductionist readings of globalization that should, in preference, be seen as 'neither unified nor . . . act[ing] as a subject nor should it be conceived of in linear fashion' (Urry 2003: 40). It is understandable that first generation globalization studies should have conceived of this complex process as more powerful and unified than it actually was, but from now on an approach that foregrounds complexity will be more productive whatever political choices we ultimately make.

Another common opposition in the vast literature on globalization now available is between those who stress the novelty of the situation and those who stress continuity with earlier periods of capitalism's internationalization. Among the popularizers of the first position must be counted management consultant Kenichi Ohmae who, in a series of books with titles such as *The Borderless World* (Ohmae 1990) and *The End of the Nation State* (Ohmae 1995), articulated a vision of modernity's nation-state era coming to an end as the liberating forces of the global market became dominant in the 1990s. The traditional order of national economies, industrial production, welfare states and so on, would be swept away by the new wind of free market dynamism. Ohmae stresses the revolutionary break with the past and the short time span, say 25 years, in which these world revolutionary events took place.

Academic promoters of the globalist case are more nuanced but, nevertheless, emphasis is laid very much on the novelty of the phenomena described. Thus, Anthony Giddens finds himself essentially agreeing with those for whom 'the new communications technologies, the role of knowledge as a factor of production, and the new discoveries in the life sciences, signal a profound transition in human history' (Giddens 2001: 4). The whole mood or tone of this discourse is revolutionary in that it conceptualizes globalization as a fundamental shift in the human trajectory that is now in full flow. There are, of course, optimistic and pessimistic renderings of the globalizer scenario but the unifying strand is that the shifts involved in all areas of human life are irreversible and of global significance, whether we view them as benign or not.

Against the globalizers, who believe in globalization, and the anti-globalizers, who also believe it is real even if they do not like its effects, we can posit the sceptics for whom the death of the traditional order is at best over-stated. None are clearer or more evidence-based than the arguments of Hirst and Thompson in their aptly entitled *Globalization in Question* (Hirst and Thompson 1999) which challenges what they call the necessary myth that globalization represents a qualitatively new stage of capitalist development. For these authors the globalization of production has been exaggerated, as have the forecasts of the death of the nation-state. While accepting, of course, that there is a growing international economy, they reject as fanciful the idea that multi- or transnational corporations are footloose and fancy free. They even turn the tables on the 'decline of the nation-state' arguments by showing how in many ways the nation-state has gained in importance, managing or governing the processes of internationalization. While arguably marked by a tinge of nostalgia for a pre-globalization era when 'normal' national politics prevailed, this approach is a healthy sceptical antidote to out-and-out globalizers.

Globalization follows or joins 'modernization' and 'Americanization' as seemingly inevitable processes heading towards a pre-defined end. They are thus, essentially, 'teleological' concepts, insofar as they share teleology's belief that there is design, directive principle and finality in all natural and mechanical processes. Teleology asserts a purpose to all activity and a direction towards a pre-established end. The problem with all teleological concepts as Taylor puts it is that: 'by conflating becoming with being, alternative future possibilities are discarded; the outcome is literally defined as inevitable' (Taylor 2000: 50). Modernization was deployed in the 1950s and 1960s to signal an end-state of development (equated essentially with the US) and the process whereby all countries could achieve this happy state by following a pre-established template. Likewise, globalization since the 1990s has come to signify both a process of internationalization that is creating a more globally integrated world order, and also an actually existing globalized society that all should aspire to. Even in specialist academic circles there appears to be a conflation between 'global studies' (studies of the world from a global perspective?) and 'globalization studies' that would be a more critical and reflexive take on the complex unfolding processes of internationalization in all their uneven and combined facets.

Globalization, today, certainly shows many new traits but one can also discern continuities with previous expansionary phases of capitalism. One way of putting it, albeit allegorically, is that 'one-third of the globalization narrative is over-sold; one-third we do not understand; and one-third is radically new' (Drache 1999: 7). From a complexity theory standpoint we might challenge this separation between being and becoming but the drift of the argument is well taken. There is a big difference between globalization as mutually reinforcing and causally related transformations following a pre-established path, and a conception based on the notion of 'contingently related tendencies' (Dicken *et al.* 1997: 161). There are also very diverse economic, political, social and cultural tendencies that vary widely across regions and time. There is simply no unified coherent and unilinear globalization strategy waiting to be applied as 'made in USA' modernization theory was in the 1950s. There is a complex restructuring and recomposition of the world order occurring around us all the time: the concept of globalization might point towards it in different ways and, even, partially explain it, but it cannot serve as a master framework to understand and explain it totally.

Having briefly analysed what globalization is 'not', what can we say about what it 'is' over and beyond the obvious complexity and uneven development of the phenomenon? Clearly it is no one thing and has various inter-linked economic, political, ideological, social and cultural facets. But if there is one overarching theme it is that of connectivity or interconnectedness. Following Ash Amin we could argue that 'the most distinctive aspect of contemporary globalization' is the 'interconnectedness, multiplexity and hybridization of social life at every level' (Amin 1997: 129). This means we can no longer draw clear and firm boundaries between local and global spheres or between national and international spheres of social life. We cannot separate the 'in here' of the city, community or locality in which we live from the 'out there' of global flows of money, capital, people, power and dominance. Thus, globalization is not an entity but a set of relationships. Our daily activities are all influenced by this complex and inter-related set of relationships that are 'stretching' social relations to an unprecedented degree.

Another useful image to understand globalization is that of time–space compression. Spatial barriers – for example, in trade or communications – have fallen away to a considerable degree. Space does not even matter any more according to some pundits. Time has also changed from being a reflection of natural processes to become instantaneous. The world has been 'shrinking' for a long time but this process has taken a qualitative leap forward in the last quarter of the twentieth century. We may not yet have achieved the 'distanceless' world that Heidegger once foretold but as David Harvey puts it, we are now living through 'processes that so revolutionize the objective qualities of space and time that we are forced to alter, sometimes in quite radical ways, how we represent the world to ourselves' (Harvey 1989: 240). The elimination of spatial barriers and the compression of time do not, however, spell a homogeneous spatial development. The changing spatiality of global capitalism is, if anything, more heterogeneous, differentiated and fragmented.

Above all else we must stress that globalization signifies interconnectedness of social fates. As Held and McGrew put it: 'Globalization weaves together, in highly complex and abstract systems, the fates of households, communities and peoples in distant regions of the globe' (Held and McGrew 2003: 129). Our own daily lives are becoming increasingly globalized in terms of their reference points, our consumption patterns and our mental maps. We imagine the world in a different way than our ancestors did at the turn of the nineteenth century. Globalization is, today, the 'imagined horizon' (García Canclini 1999: 32) of individual and collective subjects, be they governments, companies, intellectuals, artists or citizens. The repercussions both positive and negative of the St Stephen's Day 2004 East Asian tsunami demonstrated most clearly how real the weaving together of fates across the world now is. Whichever view of globalization is taken it has clearly transformed the world around us, and the way in which we understand it and seek to change it.

In terms of competing paradigms it might be premature to choose one particular rendition of globalization theory to guide us. David Held and his colleagues usefully distinguish between the globalizers, the sceptics (who doubt there is much new in it) and the 'transformationalist' approaches. The latter stresses the changes that are taking place and how explaining this arena in an open-ended way may help us in getting to know the one-third of globalization that is as yet unknown. As against fixed ideal-type paradigms of a new 'global market', 'global democracy', or 'global civilization' David Held and his colleagues prefer the 'transformationalist accounts [that] emphasize globalization as a long-term historical process which is inscribed with contradictions and which is significantly shaped by conjunctural factors' (Held *et al.* 1999: 7). A good example of the latter are the events of 11 September 2001 in the US and their sequel of unfolding conflicts across the world that effectively put an end to prevailing optimistic views of globalization as a new peaceful era of harmonious global development.

Changing worlds

A transformationalist approach to globalization starts from the premise that the world is changing rapidly and in fundamental ways, even if the direction of change is not (yet?) fully discernible. An underlying question is whether a new sense of 'globality' means we should abandon 'methodological nationalism', that is to say, the nation-state as obvious and self-sufficient frame of reference for understanding the changing worlds we live in. A closely associated issue is the viability of 'methodological territorialism', that is to say, forms of social enquiry that precede the rise of *supraterritoriality* (e.g. the Internet and global financial markets). While accepting that a new global optic is necessary to comprehend the changing worlds around us, I would not argue, however, that the nation-state 'does not matter' or that territorial forms of consciousness might not have a continuing (or even increasing) relevance. The point is, simply, that we live in the era of globalization and that this has an impact on all levels of life in our changing worlds.

It is not a belief in economic determinism that leads us to start with the economic world but, rather, an understanding that how people produce is crucial to social development. Early debates revolved around the question of whether economic internationalization was, indeed, new at all and whether it was, in fact, even global in the true sense of the word. Certainly, there were earlier periods of capitalist development when trade and finances were truly international. Nor is there any doubt that globalization is primarily a phenomenon affecting the richer and more powerful nation-states of the West/North, even though its effects are as significant as any tsunami on what was once known as the developing world. The underlying political question is whether economic internationalization and the operation of freer markets is spreading development or concentrating it in ever fewer hands. The supporters of globalization and the anti-globalization movement are, predictably, at opposite ends of this debate. While economic growth in China and India has accelerated along with increased integration with the global economy, overall the global South as the 'developing world' is now called has suffered from neoliberal policies favouring the free market.

The traditional 'modern' world of production is now joined by the virtual or 'new' economy characteristic of the 'information age', greatly enhanced communications and transport. As Jan Aart Scholte puts it: 'globalization has played an important role in redistributing the relative weights of accumulation away from "merchandise" (commercial and industrial capital) towards "intangibles" (finance, information and communications capital)' (Scholte 2000: 123). This is not really a 'post'-capitalist era in any real sense of the word, but simply the latest manifestation of a very dynamic and plastic economic system. This 'new' economy is, however, less bound to territory and is a harbinger of a more transnational order. Multinational corporations become truly transnational corporations. The 'death of space' is not just a clever business logo. This major transformation in how capitalism works has led to huge changes in the world of work and has also generated considerable opposition from social movements concerned with commodification, consumerism, effects on the environment and, of course, exploitation of workers.

In the *political* domain the early globalization debates focused around the 'decline' (even 'death') of the nation-state. The nation–global relationship was interpreted as a zero-sum game where the gain of one was seen as loss for the other. By the mid-1990s, however, it was widely acknowledged that 'states have significantly more room to manoeuvre in the global political economy than globalization theory allows' (Weiss 2003: 26). This was the case not least because globalization was beginning to be understood by its critics (as much as its supporters) as a process that could be enabling or empowering to some. Clearly, globalization was not some form of nebula hanging over the world as benign or malignant presence depending on one's point of view. What was called 'globalization' in the 1990s could be traced back to specific economic policies developed by the rich and powerful nation-states of the West going back most immediately to the neoliberal (anti-statist, pro-privatization) policies so dominant in the 1980s.

It was a very powerful image that developed around the 'decline of the nation-state' thesis. It seemed logical that increased economic internationalization would lead to a decrease of political sovereignty. The new global market modality of capitalist development certainly weakened statist or nationalist development models. The levers of economic power were no longer, straightforwardly, in the hands of national governments. Nor does the government control the national territory in quite the same way as they did in the era of the nation-state. However, even at the purely economic policy side, states may still steer the economy through supply-side measures such as technological innovations and training/education. Nor does 'pooled

sovereignty' such as that of the European Union (EU) or NATO or the WTO
prove any less powerful a means to pursue the objectives of the rich nation-
states. Finally, we must reject economistic visions of nation-state decline,
insofar as different states may clearly use their power in different ways
and the different 'varieties' of capitalism have markedly different political
effects.

The *social* facets of globalization are myriad, from transnational migration to the rise of the 'global city', from new forms of community to the
flourishing of global crime. Clearly the social has become more interconnected, less constrained by boundaries or limits. The social world is more
interlinked, social relations (for many) are less limited than they once
were. Social identities are no longer space-bound and geographical distance
sets few limits on social interaction. For Ash Amin we are witness to a
'greater hybridization and perforation of social, economic and political life'
due to the increasing 'interdependence and intermingling of global, distant
and local logics' (Amin 1997: 133). There is no global without its myriad
locals, a principle as important as the constraining of local development by
globalization. But it is the mixity, the hybridity and the perforation of
all social domains that are crucial to an understanding of society in the era
of globalization.

Social relations, today, are constructed in space as much as in particular
places. The various discourses of globalization construct social subjectiv-
ities in a complex and contradictory fashion. We are no longer place-bound
and our social links can be transnational and they can be virtual. Globalization opens up to social groups diverse forms of social organization from
the local to the regional, the national to the transnational. There is an
increased differentiation and fragmentation of social subjectivity and social
consciousness formation. Globalization has brought to the fore 'the issue of
subjectivity, the positions, agencies and forms of consciousness in and
through which identities, decisions, choices and interventions are produced
and enacted' (Kayatekin and Ruccio 1998: 76). What globalization cannot
produce is a totalizing vision that explains all or even determines 'in the
last instance' social relations. It does, however, produce new horizons of
possibilities for all social groupings, be they the new global elite or the
subaltern classes.

As to the *cultural* domain it might well have been our starting point,
such is the importance of what is called 'global culture' in the making of
globalization. As David Held *et al.* put it:

> Few expressions of globalization are so visible, widespread and perva-
> sive as the worldwide proliferation of internationally traded consumer
> brands, the global ascendancy of popular cultural icons and artefacts,
> and the simultaneous communication of events by satellite broadcasts
> to hundreds of millions of people at a time on all continents.
>
> (Held *et al.* 1999: 327)

The simultaneity and ubiquity of global cultural products and processes is, indeed, a major feature of the era. The commodification of culture along with every other facet of human life, including life itself, is a key driver of the free market expansion lying at the core of globalization. If globalization is made at the cultural level, it is also contested at the discursive level where different understandings of, and meanings of, globalization clash.

Early debates in this area focused around whether a 'global culture' was indeed emerging and, if it was, whether it would 'flatten' national or regional cultures. It is now widely accepted that notwithstanding the rise of a global consumer culture and a 'global youth culture', cultural diversity and hybridization will prevail over any 'coca-cola-ization' or 'Americanization' of the world's cultures. For Mike Featherstone the era of postmodern globalization has 'pointed to the problem of cultural complexity and the increasing salience of culture in social life through the greater production, mixing and syncretism of cultures which were formerly held separate and firmly attached to social relationships' (Featherstone 1995: 12). Global differences have been acculturated and 'brought home' through increased travel and migration. New forms of cultural resistance are emerging and there is even a return to the concept of 'cultural imperialism' that had prevailed during the anti-colonial revolution and the cultural revolt of the 1960s.

I would argue that the economic, political, social and cultural transformations of the world around us have one common feature: reflexivity. When referring to 'reflexive modernization', Ulrich Beck sets it in terms of a 'subversive, unintended and unforeseen self-questioning of the bases of political life' (Beck 2001: 101) created by the perception of risk that now prevails after the age of innocence. Rather than living through the 'end of history' as Fukuyama optimistically predicted at the end of the cold war, we are moving into a new era of global civilization where we all have a common destiny, albeit threatened by old and new forms of global risk (from famine to AIDS, from 'global terrorism' to the perils of genetic engineering). The point is that the era of globalization is characterized by intense *reflexivity* as individuals and institutions reflect on transformation, risks and how to construct a better future. This does not spell an era of consensus necessarily but all bets are off and the rationality of modernity does not imprison our minds and lives as it once did.

There is no question of 'globalization' explaining everything, or even anything, on its own. The emergent global risk society (to use Beck's terminology) is neither unified all-powerful or uncontested (even at the level of meanings). John Urry quite correctly takes to task simplified and static conceptions neglected in statements that '"globalization" is x or alternatively that "globlization" does x' (Urry 2003: 40). There is, in reality, nothing linear about the development of globalization as if it were some re-run of the teleological 1950s' 'modernization' theories based on an unproblematic expansion of a US-modelled and US-directed conception of modernity. While globalization cannot, thus, be treated as the subject of history, it can, I would argue, be conceived as a new matrix for global development. Thus, 'globalization' can be taken as a shorthand label for the complex economic, socio-political and cultural parameters that set the terms of reference and establish a matrix for the development of human societies.

A recent text on Latin America understands the concept of 'socio-political matrix' as 'the relationships among the state, the political system of representation, the socio-economic base of social actors, and cultural relations' (Garretón *et al.* 2003: 93) that are thus placed in the context of a comprehensive analytical framework. In this sense a 'globalization matrix' would refer not to globalization as this or that facet of the contemporary era but, rather, the overall or overarching parameter within which contemporary economic, socio-political and cultural relationships are forged. These relationships must be conceived as being mediated by nation-states, regions and locality and globalization as matrix does not 'determine' anything. The globalization matrix is not necessarily an agreed one and different parties may well have a different understanding of it. The point is simply that we now are faced with a world quite different from that where nation-states provided the broadest horizon of possibilities throughout their lives, and where internationalism still meant simply the interaction between nations.

Global governance

Of course, the changing worlds described above need to be governed. Until quite recently, the main parameters of governance were set by the regimes of national sovereignty. Today, global governance is required and it sets the terms of regional, national and, even, city-level governance. Nation-states had national governments ruling over the sovereign national territory through executive, legislative and judicial branches. Political parties expressed or represented the views of the citizens. In the era of globalization, government, in this traditional sense of the word, is being superseded by what we call 'governance'. This refers to the way in which states 'steer' rather than command society, and where the market is allowed to play a full role in allocating resources. Contemporary governance is seen to be less hierarchical or bureaucratic than traditional governments. Governance is, rather, achieved through coordination, consultation and community involvement, with its favoured form of organization being the network. This paradigm shift from government to governance had been completed in most countries by the end of the twentieth century.

The underlying reason why the traditional state and government were challenged as effective modalities for the new capitalism, was that as *territorial* based bodies they were ill-equipped to deal with *supraterritorial* phenomena such as the Internet or offshore banking, for example. The proliferation of supraterritorial issues has led to connections being formed 'above' national government level (such as the WTO) but also 'below' national government level as transnational connections flourish between cities and regions in pursuit of diverse interests that may or may not coincide with those of national governments. As Scholte explains: 'As a result of this multi-plication of substate and suprastate arrangements alongside regulation through states, contemporary governance has become considerably more decentralized and fragmented' (Scholte 2000: 143). As with other issues or facets of globalization explored above, there is a growing hybridity of organ-izational forms in keeping with the complexity of challenges faced by contemporary capitalist development.

'The world is now more than ever enmeshed in a process of complex globalization' as Cerny puts it, and 'the most urgent research agenda . . . is to identify the myriad dimensions of this complex process and evaluate the structure of the intersections and interactions among them' (Cerny 1999: 209). There is no neat hierarchy of spatial levels from the local to the global, through the national and regional. Rather, all issues are multilayered as are the strategies and structures to deal with them. In social policy we have the term 'wicked issues' to describe social problems such as youth crime that cannot be assigned to any one government department because the issue is multidimensional. Likewise, the issue of 'global warming' can be seen as a 'wicked issue' that requires a multilayered response. Since at least the end of the cold war, economic, political and social issues and ideologies have become more complex and less easily amenable to simple solutions. It is this move to a world 'beyond slogans' that explains the recent paradigm shift away from the once dominant Washington Consensus.

During the 'first wave' of neoliberal-led globalization in the 1980s and 1990s a quite fundamentalist economic doctrine and political philosophy prevailed. This was codified around 1990 in the so-called Washington Consensus centred upon the key tenets of trade liberalization, deregulation, privatization and financial liberalization. It was applied with particular rigour and fervour in Latin America where it became known widely as neolib-eralism. This was a form of free market economics pledged to the removal of the state from any areas where it might interfere with the free workings of the market. Against all forms of national protectionism – which had been essential for the industrialization in the 'developing' world – it called for removal of all tariff and other barriers so that international trade could be 'free'. It was seen as a way of overcoming the 'debt crisis' of the 1980s in Latin America and the Washington Consensus policies were imposed on debtor nations as forms of macro-economic conditionality for further loans.

The free market 'silent revolution' as its supporters called it was, however, to meet internal contradictions and external limits. The Asian financial crisis of the late 1990s began in Thailand in 1997 but rapidly spread to the Philippines and Indonesia, and later Russia and Brazil among others. Financial deregulation created the volatile 'hot money' markets where a collapse of confidence could spread like wildfire. Henceforth, even fervent supporters of free market economics such as Jagdish Bhagwati (Bhagwati 2004) would also call for renewed financial controls and regulation. Then, in Latin America there was another financial crisis in Mexico in 1994–95 and most dramatically of all, the economy of Argentina virtually collapsed at the end of 2001: and Argentina had been the country where the Washington Consensus was so faithfully implemented that the peso was even tied to the US dollar. Finally, around the same time, a number of corporate scandals in the US – the most notably newsworthy being Enron – showed that free market neoliberalism had to be 'saved from itself'.

Towards the turn of the century the contradictions of the Washington Consensus as the political economy paradigm of the era became apparent. According to Robin Broad, 'while some tenets of the old Consensus have been transformed more than others, we are unquestionably in the midst of a paradigm shift and a period of continued debate' (Broad 2004: 148). The rejection of full capital-market liberalization opened the door for further questioning of key tenets of the Washington Consensus. Far from rejecting the role of the state in economic affairs the new economic wisdom sought to restructure the state and created the 'new public management' approach. The global governance agenda as a whole can be seen as a response to the failings of free market liberalism as well as a response to the counter-globalization movements of the late 1990s and beyond. Over and beyond the economic debates, there seemed to be a recognition that the moral acceptance of capitalism mattered. The new Consensus was a pragmatic adaptation to new conditions but it had a distinct moral undertone.

We could say, following Richard Higgott, that 'the global market place of the 1980s and the first 6–7 years of the 1990s was an "ethics free zone"' (Higgott 2000: 138). Poverty was an unfortunate side-effect of globalization but these 'adjustment' pains did not cause any moral dilemmas. But by the late 1990s there was 'in some quarters a genuine recognition of the importance of tackling ethical questions of justice, fairness and inequality' (Higgott 2000: 139). A small, but probably not insignificant, sign of this mood swing was the conversion of George Soros from financial speculator par excellence to caring far-sighted articulator of 'Third Way' politics to save global capitalism from itself (see Soros 1998). More broadly this was an era when the corporate social responsibility agenda took off. Perhaps it was only due to Nike shares plummeting when conditions in their overseas plants were exposed, or because Starbucks was targeted by protestors in Seattle 1999, but even so the swing towards a more 'socially responsible' capitalism had begun.

None of the above means to imply that 'global governance' is simply benign compared to the Washington Consensus. Indeed, following Ian Douglas, perhaps we should be 'rethinking globalization as governance' (Douglas 1999: 151). The contemporary transformations in the modalities of political rule 'beyond' traditional government models can be seen as simply more effective ways to control global society. While the state may well have been 'hollowed out' as an effect of economic internationalization, and traditional models of political sovereignty have been rendered void, the replacement is by no means 'progressive'. Rather than be taken in by the concerned, humanitarian message of the Commission on Global Governance (1995), Douglas asks to first confront the question: 'to what problem is global governance the solution?' (Douglas 1999: 154). The move towards networks of governance that are largely self-reliant and the emergence of the self-organizing individual may be positive in a general sense but they may also reflect a Foucaldian drive for order and may well create new inequalities and hierarchies.

Global governance as reform and repression at the same time simply poses a more general dilemma. It goes back to early 1900s' debates on 'reform versus revolution' and the 1960s' notion of 'repressive tolerance'. For Foucault, for example, governance can be seen as a more effective, because it is a more totalizing, form of control in terms of bio-power. However, while it is easy to see how a non-governmental organization (NGO) or social movement might be 'co-opted' through engagement with the global economic agencies, their interaction is, nonetheless, real. Foucault might respond that this engagement, and even protest, against globalization is beneficial to the established order because it creates reform (the better to govern) but inaction is totally a more progressive option. Many critical thinkers now accept that globalization might open some doors (for progressive social transformation) as well as close others. Global governance may well be a reform of 'repressive tolerance' type and a simple modernization or rationalization of control mechanisms, but it is still different from government as previously understood.

A fundamental point about the global governance paradigm or problematic from the point of view of this text is that it allows the social movements back in. The NGOs, the global social movements and assorted advocacy or protest networks all play a role in the governance of the global economy. These 'non-state' or 'non-traditional' sectors have at least since the 1999 Seattle WTO debacle been at the forefront of debate on how global governance can be ensured. At its most 'official' level this shift can be seen in the attempt by the United Nations (UN) to develop a 'Global Compact' bringing together the corporate sector and issues such as human rights as well as labour and environmental standards. For Richard Higgott, 'while it sits firmly within a neoliberal discourse for developing an interaction between the international institutions and the corporate world, it is an important recognition of the need to globalize some important common values' (Higgott 2000: 140). Effectively this initiative is seeking to 'globalize' the socially embedded liberalism of the post-war era that served to create capitalist growth and social cohesion at the same time.

As the protests against globalization grew in the late 1990s so did the role of the NGOs or what others call 'civil society organizations' (CSOs). Yet, they faced the dilemma of either joining protestors in the streets or taking their critique into the conference halls and boardrooms of 'global governance' and the corporate sector. Of course, in practice they could do both but many more 'mainstream' NGOs chose to seek to influence policy from within, as it were. There are signs that they were often welcomed into the capitalist tent even if their influence was not always significant. There was also a strong move towards organizing parallel or 'unofficial' summits alongside those of the WTO and so on. While evidence is scanty (because it is hard to assess influence) one well-researched study concludes that while in the early 1990s only 20 per cent of unofficial summits had an impact on the official event, by the year 2000 this proportion had risen to 40 per cent (Pianta 2001: 186–7). Civil society was at least having some impact on the leading bodies of global capitalism.

The move towards global governance also allowed for more space to be created where social movements could intervene. To differing degrees the likes of the World Bank and other economic institutions became more 'porous' to the demands of some social movements. The international women's movement and the environmental movement had some significant successes but the labour movement, in a less public way, was also able to at least place its perspective on the negotiating table of the global corporate sector. One of the more systematic studies that have been carried out concludes that: 'there is a transformation in the nature of global economic governance as a result of the MEI [multilateral economic institutions]–GSM [global social movements] encounter' (O'Brien *et al.* 2000: 3). Whatever the particular verdict on each case of engagement (and there is always a sceptical view to match any optimism) there is undoubtedly a transformation in terms of the range of economic and political institutions engaged with social movements and their demands.

Polanyi's problematic

As Louis Althusser once put it: 'A word or concept cannot be considered in isolation; it only exists in the theoretical or ideological framework in which it is used: its problematic' (Althusser 1969: 253). At its most basic the Polanyi problematic was based on the notion of a 'great transformation' at the start of the nineteenth century leading to the dominance of free market principles. But this social transformation led to a counter-movement through which society protected itself from the effects of untrammelled free market expansion. History thus advances in a series of 'double movements' according to Polanyi whereby market expansions create societal reactions. We can posit that the emergence of 'globalization' in the last quarter of the twentieth century represents the belated fulfilment of the nineteenth-century phase of human history characterized by 'an attempt to set up one big self-regulating market' (Polanyi 2001: 70).

According to Polanyi, who was writing during the cataclysm of the Second World War, 'the fount and matrix of the [capitalist] system was the self-regulating market' (Polanyi 2001: 3). Polanyi traces the birth of market society as we know it to Britain's Industrial Revolution of the nineteenth century. Previous societies had been organized on principles of reciprocity or redistribution or householding: now, exchange would be the sole basis of social and economic integration. Markets were previously an accessory feature in a system controlled and regulated by social authority. Henceforth, the market ruled unchallenged and changed society in its image: 'A market economy can exist only in a market society' (Polanyi 2001: 74). Economic liberalism was the organizing principle of the new market society where economics and politics were, for the first time, split up. What is remarkable about this economic discourse is that: 'The road to the free market was opened and kept open by an enormous increase in continuous centrally organised and controlled interventionism' (Polanyi 2001: 146). As with neoliberalism in the 1980s 'laissez-faire' economics was nothing if not planned.

Polanyi's self-regulating market was to be based on the 'fictitious commodities' of land, labour and money. That labour should become a commodity that could be bought and sold was essential to the logic of the market economy. But, as Polanyi argues:

> labor, land, and money are obviously *not* commodities . . . Labor is only another name for a human activity which goes with life itself . . . land is only another name for nature, which is not produced by man; actually money, finally, is merely a token of purchasing power . . .
>
> (2001: 75)

Polanyi goes further than Marx to argue that 'labour power' is but an 'alleged commodity' precisely because it 'cannot be shoved about, used indiscriminately, or even left unused without affecting also the human individual who happens to be the bearer of this peculiar commodity' (Polanyi 2001: 76). This is more than a moral critique of capitalism, however, because Polanyi goes on to argue that trade unions, for example, should be quite clear that their purpose is precisely 'that of interfering with the laws of supply and demand in respect of human labour, and removing it from the orbit of the market' (Polanyi 2001: 186). Any move from within society to remove any element from the market ('decommodification') thus challenges the market economy in its fundamentals.

When Polanyi distinguishes between real and fictitious commodities he is going beyond the moral principle that people or nature should not be treated as though they could be bought and sold. The project of creating a fully self-regulating market economy required this fiction but, if fully implemented, then society and the environment would both be destroyed. In practice, against the basic tenets of liberalism (and in our era's neoliberalism), the state plays a continuous, intensive role in regulating the flow of labour across frontiers; educating and training workers, dealing with unemployment and so on. The use of land in rural and urban areas is tightly controlled by the state. In actually existing market societies the state plays a guiding economic role and is never 'outside' of the market in any real sense. As Polanyi puts it:

> Undoubtedly, labor, land and money *are* essential to a market economy. But no society could stand the effects of such a system of crude fiction for the shortest stretch of time unless its human and natural substance as well as its business organisation was protected against the ravages of this satanic mill.
>
> (Polanyi 2001: 76–7)

The self-regulating or self-adjusting market was, for Polanyi, a 'stark-utopia' in the sense that it could not be achieved: 'Such an institution could not exist for any length of time without annihilating the human and natural substance of society; it would have physically destroyed man and transformed his surroundings into a wilderness' (Polanyi 2001: 3). In modern terminology the self-regulating market was neither socially nor environmentally sustainable. Neoliberals, today, have developed a similarly fundamentalist discourse based on the 'magic of the market'. Central to this identity is the notion that government interference in economic affairs must be reversed and that the individual market agent or 'entrepreneur' should be given a free hand. In this grand schema society does not exist and nature is seen simply as a factor of production. This market system and the associated laissez-faire ideology, 'created the delusion of economic determinism' (Polanyi 1957: 70) against which Polanyi calls for 'the reabsorption of the economic system in society, for the creative adaptation of our ways of life to an industrial environment' (Polanyi 1957: 143).

For Polanyi, in his day, but probably even more so today: 'The true implications of economic liberalism can now be taken in at a glance. Nothing less than a self-regulating market on a world scale could ensure the functioning of this stupendous mechanism' (Polanyi 2001: 145). Globalization, in the broadest sense of the word, can thus be seen as inherent in the free-market project. The world, naturally enough from this perspective, becomes just one giant marketplace where everything and everybody can be bought and sold. Social relations are reduced to market relations. The 'opening up' of the world market becomes the *raison d'être* of development, with only some token gestures paid to social and human development. What Polanyi analysed for the national level – in terms of a separation of the economy from the social and political domains of human life – is now becoming realized and empowered on the global terrain. Even the proponents of 'globalization with a human face' in the UN and elsewhere simply take this free market project and ideology for granted.

Central to Polanyi's non-economistic understanding of the contemporary economy was the notion of 'embeddedness' that has since led to a copious literature in economic sociology. For Polanyi the economy is normally embedded in *social* relations; it is not autonomous. Prior to the emergence of the modern market society, 'The economic system was submerged in general social relations. Markets were merely an accessory feature of an institutional setting controlled and regulated more than ever by social authority' (Polanyi 2001: 70). The self-sufficient, pre-capitalist peasant household was not regulated by the market but, rather, by a moral order. Even when mercantilism began to free trade from localism, it was very much regulated. In fact, according to Polanyi, 'regulation and markets, in effect, grew up together' (Polanyi 2001: 71). Economic relations had always been subordinated or submerged within social relations that were at the core of human existence. Even today, at the height of globalization as dominant development matrix, we find many spheres of social life, such as the household, not subordinated to the logic of the market.

Much of Polanyi's analysis of 'embeddedness' depends on an analysis of pre-capitalist societies (see Dalton (1971) for Polanyi's 'anthropological' work). While it serves as a useful paradigm comparison with contemporary society, it is certainly dubious to assume that pre-market societies are necessarily more socially cohesive than market ones. Occasionally we might see Polanyi romanticizing 'primitive' and 'archaic' societies, perhaps reflecting his early commitments to Guild Socialism with its own particular version of a pre-market utopia. This nostalgia for a long-lost cohesive and secure past is common to most utopian discourses. On the other hand, contemporary analysis of 'embeddedness' shows there is no clear-cut and decisive break between embedded pre-market and disembedded market societies. Indeed, there is now a flourishing pro-capitalist literature, such as that by Fukuyama, on 'trust' (Fukuyama 1996) that builds precisely on the social and moral ties that bind the ostensibly purely rational agents of the market today.

The rise of the liberal order does require, however, the systematic 'disembedding' of the economy from society. This is an order in which 'instead of economy being embedded in social relations, social relations are embedded in the economic system' (Polanyi 2001: 135). There are long-term tendencies under capitalism towards marketization, commodification and what we could call 'economization'. They all entail a 'disembedding' of the economy and economic relations from social, community, cultural or religious forms of regulation. What Polanyi analysed in terms of the 'great transformation' wrought by the Industrial Revolution of the nineteenth century we can see, in magnified and more intense form, for the Globalization Revolution of the late twentieth century. As Altvater and Mahnkopf put it: 'The intensity of the process of disembedding is . . . increased due to . . . the money form taking on a life of its own *vis-à-vis* the "disembedded market" and . . . the economy becoming globalised' (Altvater and Mahnkopf 1997: 451). The dynamic of disembedding has now taken on a global character for the first time, with momentous consequences.

A final, and politically highly relevant, conundrum is whether it is possible to achieve 'disembedding'. In Polanyi's writings there is a contradiction between the arguments for disembedding and the recognition that this would be impossible to sustain. Polanyi is most often read as arguing that the liberals had successfully 'disembedded' the economy and that we now need to 're-embed' it. But Polanyi also appeared to be saying that the market liberals wanted to embed society in the economy, a project that was 'utopian' in the sense of unrealizable, not least because of the counter-movement from society that it engenders as society seeks to protect itself from the market. This protective counter-movement, however, weakens the ability of the self-regulatory market to function effectively. Fred Block gets round this ambiguity by arguing that 'Polanyi discovers the idea of the always embedded market economy, but he is not able to name his discovery' (Block 2001: xviii). This argument would imply that today's neoliberal globalizers will inevitably fail in their bid to create a global marketplace where society is embedded in the economy and thus, effectively, ceases to exist.

In his Foreword to the first edition of *The Great Transformation*, R.M. McIver wrote in 1944 that 'of primary importance today is the lesson it carries for the makers of the coming international organisation' (McIver 1957: iii). The post-war boom was dominated by multilateral economic organizations that only incompletely understood Polanyi's message. In the 2001 edition of *The Great Transformation* the Foreword, Joseph Stiglitz argues that 'Polanyi exposes the *myth* of the free market: there never was a truly free self-regulating market system' (Stiglitz 2001: xiii). As Stiglitz himself understands, as a critical insider in the making of globalization, the market is part of an economy and the economy is part of society. Neither the old laissez-faire nor the new Washington Consensus, which Stiglitz criticizes fiercely, recognize or understand that behind the 'freedom' of the market lies the very real lack of freedom from hunger, insecurity and risk for the majority of the world's population. Polanyi can thus become an inspiration for those seeking to reform globalization from within on behalf of the broader interests of society.

Polanyi's problematic in the era of globalization needs to be 'scaled up' to meet the challenges posed by the new matrix of social development. In the period following the Second World War, as Evans observes, 'the Polanyi problem of reconciling free markets with stable social and political life was taken up again through the construction of international norms and institutions' (Evans 2000: 238). For the core capitalist countries this led to a degree of social stability to the extent that liberalism was 'embedded' in a social compromise. For the majority or 'developing' world this was not the case as rule by the market was joined by political and military imposition of Western interests. As the long post-war boom waned from the 1970s onwards, social dissent broke out both in the core countries and through the anti-colonial revolution. Economic internationalization from the 1980s onwards was also undermining the nation-state. As Evans puts it: 'The "re-scaling" of the global economy brought the Polanyi problem back to life' (Evans 2000: 238) as the managers of the newly globalized capitalism sought to create a degree of sustainability for the machine they had created.

2   Contestation

Societal reactions to the free market

According to Karl Polanyi 'the one comprehensive feature in the history of the age' was the way in which 'society protected itself against the perils inherent in a self-regulating market system' (Polanyi 2001: 80). If that is, indeed, the case, then there is nothing unexpected in globalization generating what has been called, accurately or not, an anti-globalization movement. As a preliminary step this chapter reviews the various theoretical perspectives developed to account for the emergence of social movements, especially the so-called 'new' social movements that have emerged since the 1960s. What is it that is 'new' about the new social movements? Are these movements now finally flourishing and uniting as in an 'anti-globalization' movement? We also consider the complex relationship between these 'progressive' forms of contestation and those movements many observers would deem to be reactionary. Finally, I continue the task set in Chapter 1 of developing what I call the Polanyi problematic on social movements and the broader phenomenon of contestation in the era of globalization.

Social movement theories

Prior to the 1960s, the dominant approach to social movements stressed their anomalous, practically irrational character. In what was seen as a well-integrated and affluent society (at least in the West), only a 'demagogue' or 'charismatic leader' could possibly wish to disturb the peace by whipping up irrational fears or petty jealousies. The 'crowd' that formed would then become a 'mob' and, finally, chaos would ensue. The rise of the Nazis was the archetypal nightmare of this particular world-view. The revolt in the colonial world, the building of nationalist movements and the armed struggle against imperialism were given a different explanation. Here, the stress was placed on the 'civilized' nature of the imperial power and its promise of modernization and democracy. It was only an irrational or 'fanatical' terrorist who could revolt against this order. Ordinary people would be, or could be, hoodwinked into supporting the terrorist cause. The 'cultural revolution' in the West after May 1968 and the successful conclusion to the anti-colonial revolution were to bury these conservative delusions (for a while).

These attitudes were to change in the 1960s, particularly in North America, 'when for the first time in history large numbers of privileged people . . . had considerable sympathy for the efforts of those at the bottom of society to demand freedoms and material improvements' (Goodwin and Jasper 2003: 5). It was the Black civil rights movement in the US in particular that put to test the conception of social movements as a sign of immaturity or irrationality. Starting with Mancur Olson's 1965 text *The Logic of Collective Action* (Olson 1965), emphasis shifted to the ration-ality of collective action in which the individual basically conducts a cost-benefit analysis of whether it is advisable or not for them. Extending this analysis from the individual to the social movement organization (SMO) John McCarthy and Mayer Zald later developed an economistic vision of these SMOs in an analogy with the capitalist firm, selling their brand, recruiting staff and competing with others in the 'social movement industry' (see McCarthy and Zald 1973). This led to the emergence of the 'resource mobilization' approach focused on how social movements mobilized time and money in pursuit of their objectives.

The critique of the resource mobilization approach to social movements was quite excoriating. For one thing, as Alberto Melucci pointed out, 'collec-tive action is never based solely on cost-benefit analysis' (Melucci 1988: 343). Its focus on the individual – the rational actor – made it quite diffi-cult for this approach to fully grasp social and collective processes. A focus on the instrumental rationality of the individual simply precludes an under-standing of the collective identity at the heart of all social movements. If individuals were solely motivated by self-interest we would never see exam-ples of solidarity. Nor can we explain the emergence of social movements that never get to the stage where they might actually deliver benefits to their members. In a reaction to previous approaches to social movements as irrational they stress the rational and organized nature of contestation too much. Resource mobilization theorists stress the social integration effects of social mobilization. As Piven and Cloward put it, these analysts 'in recasting collective protest as politics have . . . normalized the organizational forms typically associated with protest' (Piven and Cloward 1978: 153). In fact, contestation, in practice, usually seeks precisely to disrupt, and not normalize conditions.

The shortcomings of the resource mobilization approach were addressed in part by the political opportunity structure theorists on both sides of the Atlantic. In the US, Sydney Tarrow began an ambitious research pro-gramme seeking to establish the connections between collective action and the political process (see, for example, Tarrow 1988). The 'normality' of placing demands on the state – as earlier social movements had done – was stressed, notwithstanding the extra-institutional modes of action deployed. In Western Europe a parallel focus saw the development of political exchange theories (for example, see Pizzorno 1978) focused on how collective actors sought inclusion into the political market. Social mobilization and conflict was thus reduced to a drive to be incorporated into the political system. But no more than 'economic rationality' can this serve as an adequate framework for the understanding of contemporary social movements insofar as, in general, 'they also seek goods which are not measurable and cannot be calculated' (Melucci 1989: 23). Neither economics nor politics alone, could thus serve as adequate theoretical frameworks for the analysis of social movements.

In Western Europe, the post-1968 interpretations of the 'new' social movements were developed more in relation to traditional Marxist accounts rather than conservative views. A range of social theorists such as Alain Touraine (France), Alberto Melucci (Italy) and Claus Offe (Germany) articulated different versions of a post-Marxist theory of society and social movements. The 'cultural' revolts across the West in 1968 but particularly in France, Italy and Germany, showed for them the exhaustion of the old capitalism and the emergence of a new 'post-industrial', 'programmed' or simply 'complex' society. This marked a qualitative shift in the nature of capitalist society and its crisis of governability (see Chapter 1 above). The affluent society was seen as a shallow society where consumerism took the place of community. People no longer wanted more material goods but were seeking self-realization, and other forms of post-material values became more central. From this ferment emerged the students' movement, the women's movement, the environmental movement, but also the anti-imperialist movement in the West.

At this stage, following Melucci, 'the era of industrial conflict is over' and social conflicts can no longer be reduced to political protest. Rather, 'contemporary social movements . . . have shifted towards a non-political terrain: the need for self-realization in everyday life' (Melucci 1998: 13). In brief, the new social movements of the 1970s were seen as challenging the logic of complex systems on mainly cultural grounds. The 'European' approach to social movements began to focus thus on the formation of new identities. Touraine referred to the need for 'bringing the social actor back in' (Touraine 1985) against what he saw as the actor-less structuralism of traditional Marxist accounts of capitalism and contestation. The processes of identity formation are crucial to an understanding of the new social movements. For many of the individuals who formed their own identity in building these movements, they were reclaiming this identity and rejecting the growing intrusion of the state and the market in social life. These movements were reaffirming the 'lifeworld' (Habermas 1987) against the dead hand of the market.

In recent years, social movement theory has sought to integrate the North American and European traditions. Jean Cohen, in particular, has argued that the two logics of collective action implicit in the two approaches actually represent a 'dual logic' of contemporary collective action (see Cohen 1987).

Thus, social movements can, at one and the same time, be involved in personal and collective identity formation, while also articulating instrumental strategic activities. The women's movement could thus be seeking economic and political transformation and the subversion of patriarchy in daily life. In general terms we can conclude that social movements are at once culturally and politically concerned with identity and strategy. The contemporary social movements are occupying the terrain both of civil society and of political society. It is, in fact, impossible to separate analytically the process of identity formation and political mobilization through what the contemporary social movements came to be.

In a general way we can now envisage how social identity theory shows us why social movements emerge, and resource mobilization theory shows us how they organize for their objectives. The problem is that these theories both emerged from and reflected the rather narrow world of the North Atlantic. Even the 'Polanyi problematic' we introduced in Chapter 1 mainly reflects the experience of the North Atlantic countries and not the rest of the world. Polanyi's prediction of a social counter-reaction to the spread of the self-regulating market required a national society to actually exist. In the post-war colonial world, nations remained to be constructed and modern society was yet to be achieved. The notion of a welfare state that could temper the social effects of the market was, and remained for many decades, a particularly Western social and political form. In terms of developing a global social movement theory we need to reconceptualize global society in a less homogeneous way than mainstream and radical approaches alike seem to do. Colonialism now takes the form of post-colonialism but it remains an overarching political condition affecting the uneven development of social movements worldwide.

The post-1968 identity-focused approach to social movements was also shaped by its particular historical and geographical setting. As Joe Foweraker puts it: 'both European and North American [social movement] theories tend to assume the presence of a dense, articulate and communicative civil society . . . just as they tend to assume liberal democratic regimes' (Foweraker 1995: 6). Yet many of the social movements that emerged across the global South during the 1970s and 1980s did so largely under authoritarian regimes. As to civil society, that was, itself, something that had to be constructed, a project of the pro-democracy movements and not a pre-existing social reality. The state was strong, it was 'everything', and social movements needed to struggle against it and create a space for civil association. The most basic forms of citizenship, as taken for granted in Western democracies, had to be established through struggle, as did also the concept of inalienable universal rights. Identities were also forged in the process of political struggle as people became aware of citizens' rights, workers' rights, women's rights and human rights.

Not only civil society but the very way in which social identities were constructed was different for those not living on the shores of the North

Atlantic. What a trade union means is different in an affluent Western democracy compared to a struggling, possibly authoritarian 'developing' country. There are no 'universal' social categories that can be used globally in an a-historical fashion. Social boundaries, political institutions and forms of consciousness are varied across the world and we should not take Western modalities as the norm. Thus, for example, in relation to the gendered construction of roles and the so-called 'cult of domesticity', French and James suggest that:

> one can rightly ask whether a concept designed to capture certain themes in the ideology of middle-class Victorian life can be meaningfully applied to working-class life, much less to the popular classes in other national and cultural contexts in other time periods.
>
> (French and James 1997: 16)

As against all forms of essentialism – 'a belief in the real, true essence of things, the invariable and fixed properties which define the "whatness" of a given entity' (Fuss 1989: xi) – we need to start from the inherently shifting, complex and constructed nature of all social life.

Clearly then, an international approach to social movements cannot be derived solely from the experience in advanced capitalist countries of the West. This applies equally to the task set in this text, namely to examine the complex interaction between globalization and contestation today. In this regard Sydney Tarrow correctly argues that 'terms like globalization and resistance open up topics for investigation . . . but they do not help us to grasp the mechanisms and processes involved in contentious interaction and how one episode of transnational contention may differ from another' (Tarrow 2002: 23). Thus, globalization and contestation may provide the broad overarching parameters within which diverse global social movements organize and mobilize but they do not provide an explanation. It is quite common for radical analysts to assume a direct correspondence between globalization and a given act or process of resistance. Globalization, also, far too often acts as a 'homogenizer' of quite distinct struggles and movements that may be responding to diverse issues and at different social scales, and may be only indirectly related to 'globalization'.

For our purposes in this text we may accept as a general definition that: 'Social movements may be said to be transnational when they involve conscious efforts to build transnational co-operation around shared goals that include social change' (Smith *et al.* 1997: 59). We are at the very beginning of a new field of study and of social action. Increasingly the processes of internationalization described in Chapter 1 will create the conditions in which global or transnational social movements will arise. Some of the lessons derived from the post-1968 'new' social movements (see next section) will, of course, be relevant to a study of the women's, environmental and peace movements that operate transnationally. Yet other forms of reaction to globalization will require a different lens. For instance, international Islam as a social movement, the struggle for land, or various 'reactionary' social movements (see the section after next) call for a less 'Western' view of the world moving always forwards to modernity and democracy.

New and old social movements

The 'European' identity-focused theoretical approach to social movements is inseparable from the 'new' social movements of the 1970s. In the cultural and political ferment following the 'events of May' in 1968 the whole of past history was reassessed. It was as if it was Year Zero of a new revolutionary movement. One of the main targets of the new generation was the 'old' trade union movement and its Communist Party political articulation. It was seen as bureaucratic, integrated into bourgeois society and basically senile. What revolutionary potential it might once have had was long since lost to the discrete charm of the bourgeois order. Workers in the West were seen as a 'labour aristocracy' living off the exploitation of the Third World, where a vigorous anti-colonial revolution was under way. These workers had been seduced and 'bought off' by Western consumerism, whereas the new generation rejected consumerism and conformity alike. The new social movements would start anew and create a new society that rejected both consumer capitalism and bureaucratic socialism.

The new social movements were seen as an expression of the new capitalism that became consolidated in the long post-war boom in the West. Advanced capitalist societies had been subject to a process of 'commodification' as social life became dominated by the market, and by 'bureaucratization' as the state intervened more and more at all levels of society. The 'new' mass media had also led to a cultural 'massification' creating conformity and repression of creativity. The new social movements thus reflected the new social antagonisms: the youth rebellion, the ecological movement and the rising of women against patriarchy. These movements were anti-institutional, anti-hierarchical and reaffirmations of individuality against collectivism. They are all based on social antagonisms other than those of social class, and the conflict between the worker and the capitalist in the factory, in particular. All forms of subordination were rejected, the imagination was in power and the future would be nothing like the past.

The new social movements rejected the 'totalizing' vision of the old movements such as the labour and nationalist movements. There was no single conflict to be resolved to reach the Promised Land insofar as there was a multiplicity of conflicts. The main thrust of these movements was the quest for autonomous identity against the 'totalizing' or tutelary aspirations of the traditional social movements. Tilman Evers offers four main theses that account for what was specific about these new social movements:

1   the transformatory potential within new social movements is not political, but socio-cultural;
2   the direction of this counter-cultural remodelling of social patterns is open;
3   central to this counter-cultural distinction is the dichotomy of alienation versus identity;
4   in creating an alternative cultural project the new social movements also create the germs of a new subject.

(Evers 1985: 49–59)

This framework seems a utopian project in the true sense of the word, based on the classic Marxist libertarian and egalitarian call for 'an association in which the free development of each one is the condition for the free development for all' as *The Communist Manifesto* declared boldly.

It is relatively easy to show, in hindsight, that there was, in fact, no hard and fast dividing line between the 'old' and the 'new' social movements. The labour movement in its origins was very much like the 'new' social movements today and only gradually and unevenly became institutionalized. It has also had to re-invent itself periodically and today it is rediscovering its vocation as a social movement to deal with the decline of traditional trade unionism. Labour movements were also a key component in the democratic challenge to authoritarian regimes in the 'developing' world in the 1970s and 1980s. It would be quite premature to accept the verdict of Manuel Castells (1998), for example, that the workers' movement is no longer an agent of progressive social change. Movements, by definition, can change and adapt to new circumstances through renewal and regeneration. Ultimately, as Dan Clawson argues from a perspective that is extremely open to the new social movements, 'no force in our society has more democratic potential (or radical possibility) than the labor movement' (Clawson 2005: 196). This would be especially true insofar as it adopts a social movement unionism.

Nationalist movements are also somewhat indiscriminately seen as the opposite of the 'new internationalism' of the 1970s and beyond. Yet the history of anti-colonialism since the Second World War shows it to be an integral element of global democracy. Resistance to Western colonialism and imperialism has taken many forms, some of which have been reactionary and many of which have later led to the curtailment of democratic liberties. As Robert Young writes from a post-colonialism theoretical approach, this resistance has also included 'anti-colonial internationalism (e.g. pan-Africanism, pan-Arabism, pan-Islamism, the *Khalifat* movement, the *négritude* movement, African Socialism) . . . [and] Marxist internationalism and the armed national liberation movements (e.g. China, Vietnam, Cuba, Angola, Mozambique)' (Young 2001: 166). National oppression is also a form of social oppression and resistance to it is part of the global democratic revolution, today as much as historically. It is hard, perhaps, from a Western perspective to grasp that nationalist movements can also be internationalist but that has been one of their underlying features, the Balkans wars notwithstanding.

Religion is another of the old, even 'pre-modern' social movements that has also come to the fore in the era of globalization. Most anti-globalization activists would resist any notion that any of these religious 'fundamentalisms' have anything in common with their movements. Yet religion is a key component of the cultural construction of identity and not for nothing did *The Communist Manifesto* refer to religion as 'the sigh of the oppressed, the heart of a heartless world, the soul of a soulless condition'. To posit al-Qaeda (or the IRA for that matter) as a new social movement seems absurd only from a Western rationalist perspective that is ultimately colonialist in its logic and world-view. As a micro-narrative we can note the life history of Mohammed Atta born in Egypt in 1968, who went on to study urban planning in Germany. In the mid-1990s he carried out fieldwork for his doctoral dissertation in both Syria and Egypt. In Cairo he was incensed over the 'restoration' of the old Islamic city, 'blaming Westernization and the Egyptian government's closeness to America for the plan to create an "Islamic Disneyland" in the heart of one of the Muslim world's most celebrated cities' (Burke 2004: 241). Atta's religion was offended but also his culture and society. He went on to organize the attack on the symbols of American power on 11 September 2001. Was Atta's motivation that different from that of the activists who came into political life in 1968?

While the problematic of the 'new social movements' may be limited if focused on the question of novelty, it might, however, direct our attention to an alternative vision of social movements. Alberto Melucci, while strenuously rejecting the 'new social movements' label, nevertheless starts from the premise that 'in complex societies fundamental aspects of human experience are presently undergoing profound changes, and that new needs, together with new powers and new risks, are being born' (Melucci 1998: 13). Whether we call the new order 'post-industrial', 'post-modern', a 'knowledge society' or 'network society' it is clear that some fairly fundamental social transformations are afoot. So we can expect social reactions to this order to become more network-based, more pluralist, less focused on institutions, more daring and innovative. In the era of 'disorganized capitalism' as a new dominant order is forged, social movements might well be more focused on identity questions, less confident in their meta-narrative and more sensitive to the contingency of structures and events.

The collapse of communism as alternative social order and of the national development state as agent of modernization does not ensure the sustainability of the dominant order. Indeed, global capitalism can be seen to carry many 'new' contradictions as well as those inherent in any exploitative and divisive social order. The new global capitalism has successfully co-opted much of the spirit of 1968. Mass consumption is out and individual choice is in, bureaucratic organizations and methods are out with flexibility the new watchword. Above all, democracy is sacrosanct across the world; no one today defends authoritarian regimes openly as was the case in the 1970s. This means that the democratic discourse that runs throughout most social movements today is not necessarily a challenge to legitimate authority as was the case in 1968. Grassroots democracy, bottom-up development, popular empowerment, gender-proofing, anti-racism – all these are largely accepted (although arguably co-opted) terms and concepts in the dominant order. It was the 'new' social movements that put them there maybe, but that is another story.

Perhaps the most enduring legacy of the new social movement analytical and political tradition is its emphasis on cultural politics. As Alvarez, Dagnino and Escobar note in relation to Latin America, the cultural politics enacted by these new social movements 'in challenging and re-signifying what counts as political . . . can be crucial . . . to fostering alternative political cultures and, potentially, to extending and deepening democracy' (Alvarez *et al.* 1998: 12). The rules of the political game and even what now counts as politics are openly in question. Social movements have subverted the traditional nostrums of the dominant political order. The legitimacy of what was once considered normal and natural is now in question. The women's movement has probably been the most successful in turning traditional politics inside out. Also the human rights movements of Latin America and Eastern Europe in the 1980s played a fundamental role in exposing the shallowness of established liberal human rights discourses and placed on the agenda current concerns with a substantive global human rights order.

In the era of the global social movement the lessons of 'new' versus 'old' social movements may also be apposite. The 'old' labour movement was, in its origins and in its very essence, global. Its slogan was 'Workers of all countries unite'. The early women's movement addressed women everywhere and not just in particular countries: 'sisterhood is global' as the slogan goes. Even the much maligned nationalist movements most often saw themselves as part of the 'fraternity of nations': their values were global even though their territorial expression was bounded. The universal claims of religions such as Catholicism or Islam have always transcended national boundaries and have, indeed, pre-dated the modern nation-state. Faiths recognize only their universal transcendental gods and not the man-made paraphernalia of politics and narrow self-interest. Thus religious, social and national movements all have a universal or global significance, as does, of course, the human rights movement with its origins in the European Enlightenment period.

The post-1968 social movements are also global and transnational but, perhaps, in a more direct manner. For instance, as Melucci puts it, 'the peace mobilizations have fundamental *transnational effects*: for the first time action, which is also located in a specific national context, has effects on the planetary level' (Melucci 1989: 88). Ever since Hiroshima and Nagasaki and the ever-present threat of 'mutually assured destruction' (MAD) the issue of peace has been a global one. As to the environment and the environmental movement, as least since the Rio Summit, they have become the paradigmatic example of a global issue calling forth a global solution. Modernization of human society is also, of course, a global issue insofar as development and underdevelopment are but two sides of the same coin. The biggest feature of the post-war boom was its uneven development and its failure in terms of what the modernization theories had promised the 'underdeveloped' world. Today, the promises of globalization in terms of overcoming poverty and inequality across the world have again put this issue on the table, causing expectations and creating the key challenge to the development of global democracy.

The 'new' social movements were already a quarter of a century old when the anti-globalization movement began to germinate in the mid-1990s. Was this the newest of the 'new' social movements, was it in other words the spirit of 1968 'gone global'? The language and discourse of social movements often needs to 'catch up' with changing social realities. Thus, the post-1968 movements borrowed much of their language and organizational forms from the traditional socialist and Marxist movements even as they were criticizing them. It is only much more recently that they found new terminology to express the new identities, led by the sexual liberation movements. Capitalism also needed the 'neoliberal revolution' of the 1980s to find its true vocation in what we now call globalization. So when the Seattle 1999 events occurred, we had two players 'coming out': capitalism with its WTO hegemonic vanguard party, and the new social movements now 'gone global' in a complex process that will be the subject of subsequent chapters. But the 'spirit of 1968' was not too far beneath the surface of events.

The good and the bad

Most definitions of social movements assume some kind of progressive or transformational impetus or motivation. This is not surprising given the close association between new social movement theories and the spirit of 1968. However, we need to consider whether the implicit distinction between good and bad social movements is actually tenable. Is it really just a question of reserving the label 'social movements' for those political associations the analyst feels comfortable with? When does a terrorist become a freedom fighter? When does a worthy social movement become a criminal gang? Can we really distinguish between social movements on the basis of the type of goal they aspire to? To answer these dilemmas we can start with Manuel Castells for whom:

> *Social movements* must be understood in their own terms: namely *they are*
> *what they say they are* ... social movements may be socially conserva-
> tive, socially revolutionary or both, or none ... from an analytical
> perspective, there are no 'bad' and 'good' social movements.
>
> (Castells 2004: 73)

There was a time when 'grand narratives' prevailed and dominated human
history and the thinking about it. This would include the discourses and
narratives of democracy, modernization, nationalism and socialism. History
was moving towards a pre-defined end, it was 'progressive' in every sense.
Then with the collapse of the Berlin Wall and the socialist project in 1989
we were told that 'the end of history' had been achieved and liberal capitalism
was the 'only game in town'. The spectacular attack by Islamic militants
on New York's Twin Towers and the Pentagon in 2001 changed all that.
It now seemed that Huntingdon's 'war between civilizations' was becoming
reality. Be that as it may, we certainly cannot foresee history in the first
quarter of the twenty-first century. Globalization and anti-globalization
forces of various types seem to operate as the major socio-political forces in
contention. But regardless of whether the latter are 'good' or 'bad' depending
on our particular political perspective, they are all, equally, symptoms of
the era we live in and deserving of the most careful analysis.

On the whole, as Amory Starr puts it: 'Religious nationalist movements
are portrayed as authoritarian movements unallied with democratic
humanism that reassert traditional social formations, including patriarchy'
(Starr 2002: 137). For most analysts religious 'fundamentalist' movements
are the very antithesis of a progressive social movement. They are seen as
obscurantist deniers of enlightenment, violent and irrational believers
in their own essential social or cultural identity. There can, supposedly,
be no reasonable democratic dialogue with those who have turned their
backs on universal values of reason and rationality. The Western or, more
precisely, the US backlash against the attacks of September 2001 very rapidly
took on this mantle and sought to portray those responsible (a very broad
and flexible category) as part of a new 'axis of evil'. The spirit of the medieval
Crusades when Christianity took on the world of Islam was alive and well
in the very late twentieth century. Even Hardt and Negri in their mood-
setting book *Empire* (Hardt and Negri 2000) had little to say about Islamism
and how its political manifestations are also part of the counter-movement
generated by globalization.

The reality is that 'Political Islamism, and Islamic fundamentalist identity ... always related to the dynamics of social exclusion and/or the crisis
of the nation-state' (Castells 2004: 21). There is no essentially different logic
of formation or dynamic operating in relation to these particular social movements. They are anti-systemic movements of a specific kind that have
displaced the previously dominant, more nationalist and traditionally leftist
movements such as Nasserism, for example. This shift from a more secular

to a more religious discourse can be related to neoliberal globalization. The nation-state in the developing world was weakened in this era and thus the benefits of taking over the state waned. The most often authoritarian governments that implemented the neoliberal agenda locally usually repressed political Islamism, thus further radicalizing these movements. Finally, growing levels of social exclusion, characteristic of the era of globalization, both within and between nations (see Munck 2005) provided a steady stream of recruits to Islamic political movements and generated causes to rally around.

Religious and ethno-nationalisms, of various types in different regions of the world, are all concerned with the 'search for fundamentals' (fundamentalism) in particular ways. They are as much about identity as any of the 'new social movements' focused explicitly around 'identity politics'. Politico-religious fundamentalism is about a quest for social identity in an era of 'cultural imperialism' and the apparent decline of secular nationalism. In Iraq, of course, these secular forms of nationalism can be reinforced and expressed by the new political Islam. The search for fundamentals, that is how we construct our identity, is central to Roland Robertson's analysis of globalization and religion (Robertson 1992). This analysis begins with 'an emphasis on time-space compression leading to the felt necessity for societies . . . to declare their identities for both internal and external purposes', but then goes on to lay more definite stress on the idea that the 'expectation of identity formation is built into the general process of globalization' (Robertson 1992: 175). That is to say, fundamentalism is not only a reaction to globalization but also an integral element of how it is constructed in relation to identities.

For the American 'Patriot' movement:

> the New World Order is a utopian system in which the US economy . . . will be 'globalized'; the wage levels of US and European workers will be brought down to those of workers in the Third World; national boundaries will for all practical purposes cease to exist; an increased flow of Third World immigrants into the United States and Europe will have produced a non-white majority in the formerly White areas of the world . . .
>
> (William Pierce, cited in Castells 2004: 87)

Except for the White supremacist element of this statement it contains much that would be shared territory with the anti-globalization movement. The US Patriots (or false patriots as their mainstream detractors call them) believe fervently that the New World Order is destroying American sovereignty and that it represents a conspiracy of global financial interests. The enemies are the same as those of the left such as the International Monetary Fund (IMF) and the WTO although the Patriots also include the UN that the left internationalists would view as ineffective but basically moving in the same direction as themselves. Where the Patriots differ from the left is that they find the answer to the threats posed in the Bible and the US Constitution (see Chapter 7).

What is particularly relevant to our purposes is the extent to which the US far-right or fundamentalist forces are actually part of the new 'common sense' for American workers in the era of globalization. During negotiations for the formation of the North American Free Trade Agreement (NAFTA) in the early 1990s, we found the labour unions (for a while) following the right wing populist leader Ross Perot for whom NAFTA was a form of capitalist internationalism that US patriots should oppose. There is a populist counter-ideology to globalization that can take right wing and left wing forms but both share a nationalist framework. The left nationalist position would be more cosmopolitan and democratic and it is not incompatible with internationalism. And, as Mark Rupert puts it:

> The antiglobalist position of the far-right, on the other hand, envisions a world in which Americans are uniquely privileged inheritors of a divinely inspired socio-political order which must at all costs be defended against internal intrusions and internal subversion.
>
> (Rupert 2000: 184)

The US Patriots espouse a racist anti-democratic and anti-state ideology of the extreme right. Their opposition to globalization as manifestation of some bizarre 'Jewish-Communist' conspiracy has nothing in common with the anti-globalization movement in terms of the social project they articulate. However, the socialist tradition is also having to re-negotiate the relationship with the national domain in the era of globalization. For Donald Sassoon, concluding his long-view retrospective of the European socialist movement, states that 'The pressures on all parties, especially those of the left, to remain enclosed in national shells are compelling' (Sassoon 1996: 776). The rapidly globalizing world we are living in creates profound dilemmas for all political traditions. Both right wing and left wing variants of nationalism (and European socialism since the First World War has been mainly a patriotic left) have to grapple with the effects of globalization. There is a sense in which, while capitalism has made the paradigm shift to thinking globally, the left, in its party political incarnation at any rate, is reaffirming its commitment to the nation-state as main parameter of its action.

From within the ranks of those social movements generally seen as benign by academic observers there is also a particular rendering of the 'good' versus 'bad' dichotomy. Essentially what we see is an instinctive, if not always explicit, equation of local = good and global = bad. This is part of a 'bottom-up' or 'people-centred' critique of globalization, though possibly not a necessary element. One collection of essays subtitled 'People Challenging Globalization' claims to tell 'an untold story – what ordinary people are doing in life-affirming response to the juggernaut of globalization. Small farmers in Honduras, migrant workers in the Andes, urban poor in Bosnia, Cambodian wood cutters, Mexican textile workers, Korean community activists' (Feffer 2002: cover). The editor of this collection, John Feffer, argues in his introduction that:

> Rather than be at the mercy of economic decisions made in faraway places, producers and consumers take greater control over their lives. If civil society requires active civic *participation*, then this empowerment at the local level is a precondition for true democracy.
>
> (Feffer 2002: 19)

At one level there is little to quarrel with this as a philosophy of *praxis*. The problem lies in the distance and separation between the local and the global that this world-view is based on.

Globalization is seen to be run by anonymous forces 'in faraway places', the local level is inhabited by real people going about their daily business. It is as though globalization is some sort of nebula 'out there' doing things or casting its shadow 'down here' in the real world. There is a double problem here. On the one hand, this view demonizes globalization in the sense that its concrete origins and contradictory dynamic (as seen in Chapter 1) is somewhat elided. On the other hand, the local level is falsely seen as somewhere calm and virtuous where the evil storms of neoliberalism can be kept at bay. But, in essence, the global and the local depend on each other to exist, there is no global other than in its local manifestations. Furthermore, localism is far from being an unambiguously progressive space. The local level and the sense of 'community' it so assiduously fosters is also a place of exploitation and class/gender/race divisions and conflicts.

We can start by applying Doreen Massey's logic when she argues that: 'setting up the question as local versus global is to accede to spatial fetishism'. That is: 'imagining that "space" or "spatial scale" has a political meaning, to assume for instance, that the local is always better simply because it is local' (Massey 2000: 2). The geography of power is far too complex to accommodate or be amenable to this type of conceit. Power is embedded socially and spatially in ways that can never result in one level of human activity, such as the local, being seen as more virtuous than others. The left has grown up historically as a national left and, for this reason among others, it is suspicious of the global or transnational level. The right has always been more comfortable with the philosophy of 'blood and belonging' and thus the sanctity of local parish or community. It is ironic that the right and left, or certain sections of them, have come together in a defence of the local as against the 'impersonal' global world of finance capitalism.

This section has opened up our analysis beyond those movements usually covered in the social movement or anti-globalization literature. It is not meant to be seen as a Nietzschean call to go 'beyond good and evil'. The argument is simply that market-led globalization will inevitably be challenged by a wide range of social and political forces: not all, or even most, progressive in the normal European Enlightenment sense of the word. Certainly, writers such as David Held are perfectly entitled to argue that the reconstruction of the world order should take us towards 'global social democracy' (Held and McGrew 2003, Chapter 9). Likewise, Mary Kaldor may choose to define 'global civil society' (Kaldor 2003) in such a way that it excludes social forces she deems to be uncivil. But these are normative positions and should not be confused or conflated with the complexity of the world around us and the choices we face today. What the next section of this chapter considers is whether Karl Polanyi's theory of a 'double movement', whereby society reacts against rule by the market, might provide some purchase in understanding it better.

Polanyian perspectives

Polanyi's problematic poses the possibility that history advances through a series of 'double movements'. So market expansion, on the one hand, leads to the 'one big market' we call globalization today. Yet, as Polanyi argued in his day and we could argue today, 'simultaneously a countermovement was afoot' (Polanyi 2001: 136) that reacted against the dislocation of society and the attack on the very fabric of society that the self-regulating market led to. The 'double movement' consisted of economic liberalism driving the extension of the self-regulating market on the one hand and the principle of 'social protection' on the other defending social interests from the deleterious action of the market. For Polanyi, this can be through protective legislation or various collective associations such as trade unions. As a new way of life spread over the planet – 'with a claim to universality unparalleled since the age when Christianity started out on its career' (Polanyi 2001: 136) – so a diverse counter-movement began to check its expansion. This involved specific social classes – directly involved in the process – but was also a generalized societal reaction. It was largely a defensive movement; it was, for Polanyi, 'spontaneous' and there was no agreed societal or political alternative involved.

Taken in its broadest sense, Polanyi's notion of a social counter-movement could be seen as an incipient theory of counter-hegemony. That is certainly the argument of Michael Burawoy (2003) for whom Polanyi provides a necessary counterpart to Antonio Gramsci's influential theory of capitalist hegemony. For Gramsci, modern 'Western' class orders are able to impose 'hegemony' over society as a whole, with consent being as important as direct control or repression. It is through the organs of civil society – such as the churches, schools, trade unions and the media – that capitalist hegemony is constructed and maintained. Gramsci, in practice an orthodox communist, saw the proletarian party as the agent of counter-hegemony. For Polanyi, on the other hand, who had broken with communism and was more influenced by the socialist Guild and Christian socialist traditions, it was a social reaction to the market that would spur a counter-hegemonic movement. Not only the subaltern classes but also powerful capitalist interests would be threatened by the anarchy of the market and would thus react. For Polanyi:

> This was more than the usual defensive behaviour of a society faced with change; it was a reaction against a dislocation which attacked the fabric of society, and which would have destroyed the very organisation of production that the market had called into being.
>
> (Polanyi 2001: 136)

Today, as Stephen Gill puts it:

> we can relate the metaphor of the 'double movement' to those socio-political forces which wish to assert more democratic control over political life, and to harness the productive aspects of world society to achieve broad social purposes on an inclusionary basis, across and within different types of civilisation.
>
> (Gill 2003: 8)

Movements struggling for national or regional sovereignty, those seeking to protect the environment and the plethora of movements advancing claims for social justice or recognition, are all part of this broad counter-movement. In different, but inter-related ways they are bids to re-embed the economy in social relations. Challenging the movement towards commodification they seek to 'decommodify' society and reassert moral and cultural values. Against materialism and market-determined values, the social counter-movement generated by neoliberal globalization brings to the fore the democracy of civil society and the social value of all we do. As Polanyi put it for his era: 'The great variety of forms in which the "collectivist" counter-movement appeared [was due to] the broad range of the vital social interests affected by the expanding market mechanism' (Polanyi 2001: 151).

There are many ways in which the self-protection of society can operate. For example, the Western welfare states that emerged following the Great Depression of the 1930s and the social dislocation it produced was one such self-defence mechanism. Likewise in the post-colonial or 'developing' world, the post-Second World War years saw the emergence of the development state, also a mechanism of defence against the self-regulating market. The development state of the 1950s and 1960s was a conscious bid to temper the free market to create national development based on state-led industrialization behind protectionist barriers. While not to the same extent as the 'developed' Western states with their strong social protection mechanisms, the development state also introduced a degree of social security, the concept of a minimum wage and respect for trade union rights. Since the neoliberal offensive (or counter-counter-movement in Polanyi's terms) of the 1980s and 1990s both the above elements have been severely curtailed or reversed. The development state has been forced to 'open up' the developing economy to powerful transnational capitalist interests. And even the advanced industrial societies that can, of course, afford it, see their welfare states and welfare rights cut back on the basis that the marketized individual should provide for their own future.

In a little-known article written immediately after the Second World War, Polanyi raised the possibility of 'regional planning' as a counter-movement to the 'universal capitalism' as he called it (see Polanyi 1945). This debate prefigures the development of the EU and current discussions on regionalism as a counter to or expression of globalization. While recognizing explicitly that 'regionalism is not a panacea' (Polanyi 1945: 89), Polanyi did see the potential of new forms of capitalism and socialism after the cataclysm, and the collapse of totalitarian ideologies would inevitably take on a *regional* form. Eastern Europe, for Polanyi, would overcome 'intolerant nationalism' and 'petty sovereignties', those 'inevitable by-products of a market-economy in a region of racially mixed settlements' (1945: 88). Britain, in the post-war period, was 'breaking the taboo on non-interference with industry' as the country 'left the atmosphere of liberal capitalism, free competition, the Gold Standard, and all of the other names under which a market society are hallowed' (Polanyi 1945: 90). Only the US, in post-war hegemonic mode, remained committed to the Utopian strategy of 'universal capitalism'. These thoughts resonate today as a European alternative to the US model of free market capitalism is debated and different forms of regionalism are articulated in the West, the East and across the South.

After drafting *The Great Transformation* in 1939–40, as the cold war began and his ideas fell on deaf ears, Polanyi turned to the study of pre-capitalist societies. He articulates a three-fold model of economic integration which, over and above its merits as anthropology, serves to show there is more to human life than the market. In non-market economics the two main forms of economic integration are, for Polanyi, reciprocity and redistribution, usually in combination. Reciprocity mainly operates within family and kinship networks and is crucial to family production and subsistence. Redistribution 'obtains within a group to the extent to which the allocation of goods . . . takes place by virtue of custom, law, or *active* central decision' (Polanyi 1957: 153). Land and labour are integrated into the economy through the norms of reciprocity and redistribution. Sometimes one or other model may prevail and exchange through barter may also play a role. It is only at a specific point in history though that 'exchange becomes *the* economic relationship, with the market as the economic institution' (Polanyi 1957: 169). Market and exchange become co-extensive, with the market the sole *locus* of exchange and, in Polanyi's words, where 'economic life is reducible to acts of exchange all embodied in markets' (Polanyi 1957: 169).

However, that it was not always so means, in terms of contestation, that 'another world is possible'. It is only Western ethnocentrism that could imagine other human worlds were not possible. Other world-views and cosmologies exist that are opposed or quite independent of what Polanyi called 'our obsolete market mentality' (Polanyi 1957). Market sovereignty is daily contested by social action based on reciprocity. Even 'actually existing capitalism' recognizes that the market could not exist without trust and shared norms of reciprocity. Those expelled from the market society through the various forms of social exclusion characteristic of global capitalism (see Munck 2002) also revert to reciprocity and redistribution in order to survive. These norms are imbued with moral-ethical principles at odds with those of the 'market mentality'. Sustainable economic cultures are being built today seeking ecological sustainability and based on social solidarity. The pre-capitalist and today's non-capitalist worlds show to what extent the society as market is a recent and quite limited human innovation.

Against all forms of economic determinism and the 'class reductionism' of classical socialism, Polanyi stresses that social class is not always determinant. This critique resonates with the contemporary transition towards 'new' social movements mobilized around non-class issues. For Polanyi, 'class interests offer only a limited explanation of long-run movements in society. The fate of classes is more frequently determined by the needs of society than the fate of society is determined by the needs of classes' (Polanyi 2001: 159). Certainly, Polanyi recognized the essential role played by class interests in social change but he refuses a narrow class logic: 'There is no magic in class interest which would secure to members of one class the support of members of other classes' (Polanyi 2001: 160). This is particularly the case in times of social crisis – 'those critical phases of history, when a civilisation has broken down or is passing through a transformation' (Polanyi 2001: 163) – when new options for society are being debated, sometimes in extremely short periods of time. In this dramatic situation no narrow class interest can well defend one's own class interest: 'Unless the alternative to the social setup is a plunge into utter destruction, no crudely selfish class interest can maintain itself in the lead' (Polanyi 2001: 163). These are precisely the types of consideration lying behind current concerns with 'global governance' from above and they should inform any articulation of 'good globalization' from below.

The critique of economism implicit in Polanyi's work also has a contemporary ring, as when he stresses the 'cultural' element in social dislocation and resistance. A cataclysmic event such as the Industrial Revolution in the nineteenth century and the 'Globalization Revolution' today are, in Polanyi's words, 'economic earthquakes' that transform the lives of vast multitudes of peoples. But, 'Actually, of course [argues Polanyi], a social calamity is primarily a cultural phenomenon that can be measured by income figures of population statistics' (Polanyi 2001: 164). When peoples are dispossessed of their traditional means of livelihood, when customs and ways of life are disrupted and 'alien' cultural values are imposed, this affects the very way in which people ascribe meaning to their condition. So, argues Polanyi, 'not economic exploitations, as often assumed, but the disintegration of the *cultural* environment of the victim is then the cause of the degradation' (Polanyi 2001: 164, emphasis added). While fully cognizant of the role of social classes in 'the great transformation' and with an acute interest in the working class and its forms of organization, Polanyi articulated a quasi-Gramscian notion of the need to provide societal leadership, or what Gramsci called 'hegemony'.

Does, then, a classical Marxist understanding of how the working class develops and struggles for socialism have no relevance under the 'new capitalism' and globalization? A response could start from the distinction drawn by Beverley Silver (2003) between 'Marx-type' and 'Polanyi-type' forms of labour unrest. The 'new international division of labour' in the 1960s and 1970s had led to the forging of an industrial working class in many parts of the 'developing' world. They were much like Marx's proletariat created by the Industrial Revolution. Today, new working classes are being created by the 'new capitalism' and they will form trade unions or similar associations and probably develop class interests. But, there are also Polanyi-type forms of unrest emerging across the globalized world, these being defined by Silver as:

> backlash resistances to the spread of a global self-regulating market, particularly by working classes that are being unmade by global economic transformations as well as by those workers who had benefited from established social compacts that are being abandoned from above.
>
> (Silver 2003: 20)

So, for example, the blue-collar workers in the West displaced by the shift of investment to cheaper labour locations, or those affected by the collapse of manufacturing and other sectors typical of the 'old' capitalism would engage in defensive and even reactionary labour struggles.

More broadly, this distinction between different types of reactions to globalization confirms the point made by Gill, that 'some of today's counter-movements involve attempts to reassert democratisation, whereas others are highly reactionary: the neoliberal globalization tendency is being challenged in complex ways' (Gill 2003: 10). It is precisely the Polanyi problematic that allows us to grasp the complexity and tensions between the different reactions to globalization. An example would be the various forms taken by the 'new localisms' that can be extremely reactionary (backward-looking) or progressive, sometimes at the same time. Whether it is anti-immigrant ideologies in post-colonial France, or the so-called Patriot movement in the US, the struggle against the impact of the self-regulating market and the onward march of globalization can easily take a reactionary form that seeks a reversion to exclusionary social patterns identified as the source of stability and social cohesion. Whether reactionary or progressive, it is important to recognize the growing contemporary importance of struggles against dispossession by the expansion of the 'free market'. David Harvey argues coherently, that 'struggles against accumulation by dispossession were considered irrelevant' (Harvey 2003: 171) by most Marxists, and that the anti-globalization movement today 'must acknowledge accumulation by dispossession as the primary contradiction to be confronted' (Harvey 2003: 177). A modernist Eurocentric Marxism finds it difficult to acknowledge the effectiveness, or even legitimacy, of struggles against globalization that are not recognizably socialist. The Polanyi problematic, on the other hand, is well equipped to understand the way in which the counter-movement against economic liberalism is 'a spontaneous reaction' against 'a threat to the human and natural components of the social fabric', expressing 'an urge on the part of a great variety of people, to press for some sort of protection' (Polanyi 2001: 186).

3 Transnational social movements

From the First International to the World Social Forum

The concept of transnationalism, according to Michael Clarke, 'is difficult to place with any precision in international theory. In itself, it certainly does not constitute a theory; it is rather a term which recognizes a phenomenon or perhaps a trend in world politics' (Clarke 1985: 146). This imprecision I take to be an advantage for the purpose of this chapter so we do not read backwards into history from the perspective of globalism as a social theory, nor do we take the internationalism of the First International as our guiding light. Instead, we simply examine transnational social movements which, in their own organization and aims, transcended national boundaries. The first section of this chapter deals with the origins of internationalism in the European labour movement. Why did this emerge? What were its limitations? And, above all, why did the spirit of internationalism die so abruptly as the European powers lined up for the Great War? The second section takes up the story of the communist internationalists who came to the fore after 1917. What did this 'proletarian internationalism' actually represent in practice? Was there a less Eurocentric orientation towards the colonial revolution? The third section takes up the colonial and post-colonial situations from the perspective of transnationalism. Could nationalist movements also be internationalist? How did anti-imperialism influence the new social movements of the late 1960s? Finally, we turn to what I call the 'contemporary cosmopolitans'. What exactly is this 'global civil society' they take as a foundation for cosmopolitan transnationalism? In terms of global contestation is this movement not essentially Eurocentric?

European internationalists

While the nineteenth century is generally read as the century of nationalism, there is another tendency, namely internationalism, making its presence felt from 1875 onwards. From that date until the close of the century, 130 international non-governmental organizations (INGOs) were formed, with the numbers formed between 1900 and the outbreak of the First World War in 1914 rising to a staggering 304 (Lyons 1963: 14). So while this period may end with the outbreak of national chauvinism and an inter-imperialist war, there was also a developing sense of international coop-eration, not least in labour and socialist circles. As Eric Hobsbawm puts it: 'Internationalism is an integral part of bourgeois liberalism and progress in the nineteenth century' (Hobsbawm 1988: 3). The question then arises as to whether internationalism is a discourse linked to a general theory of social evolution as part of international development, or whether there is a specific-ally labour or working-class variant of it.

The creation of the working class and of the early labour movement was, in essence, internationalist for the simple reason that the era of the nation-state had not yet dawned. The mid-nineteenth century was a period of extensive and intensive labour movements (some 40 million workers migrated from Europe alone) both overseas and between neighbouring European countries. The trade union form of organization was quite expli-citly internationalist not only because many of its leaders were formed through internationalism, but also because any form of nationalism would be as divisive as gender, religious or racial divides. Michael Forman puts it most simply: 'As a class, the proletariat had to be internationalist to achieve its political and social goals, because the basis of its very existence *as a class* was an international system' (Forman 1998: 47). Even labour support for the democratic republic was based on an internationalist rather than a narrow nationalist logic.

The first wave of labour internationalism in the mid-nineteenth century had various facets. At one level this early trade union internationalism was a simple response to the use by employers of overseas workers to undermine strikes and thwart trade union organization. To this defensive motivation we can add the socialist ideal of the emancipation of global labour and the democratic ideal of national self-determination. Pragmatism and idealism could often go hand in hand in the development of labour organization and ideologies. But another contradiction lay in the fact that this early inter-nationalism required, if it was to be successful, the formation of strong *national* trade union movements. To some extent, then, the very success of the early internationalism would lead to alternative national poles of attrac-tion for the incipient working-class movements and its members.

An underlying trend in the 1875–1914 period we have been concerned with is precisely the 'nationalization' or national integration of the working class across Western Europe. Capitalist development of a national infrastruc-ture and national-state formation led to a progressive, if uneven, incorp-oration of the working class. As Linden puts it: 'in the transitional phase between 1870 and 1900 we thus see a decline of the possibilities for an effective old style working class internationalism' (Linden 2003: 19). Thus, the very success in creating strong and viable national labour movements removed some of the urgency from the internationalism of the previous era. Working-class integration in the key European nation-states such as France, Germany and Britain may have strengthened the respective labour and socialist movements but at the same time it undermined the internationalism that had played such a crucial role in the making of the European labour movements.

To refer to this first wave of internationalism as European is at one level a truism given Europe was a geographic reality, but it also leads us to the question of Eurocentrism, which has a very direct and contemporary relevance. First of all we should recognize with Samir Amin that Eurocentrism is not 'simply the sum of the prejudices, errors and blunders of Westerners with respect to other peoples. If that were the case, it would only be one of the banal forms of ethnocentrism shared by all peoples of all times' (Amin 1989: 104). Rather, we need to conceive of Eurocentrism as the totalizing and enduring dominant paradigm of Western social science. It is a worldview that dominates through the creation of its Others (such as the 'Orient') and even when it is challenged, as in most national liberation movements that took a 'Western' model for granted. It is inextricably bound up with imperialism, colonialism and racism which it has often helped underpin with pseudo-scientific notions of modernization and progress.

The recent post-colonial theory bid to 'provincialize Europe' (Chakrabarty 2000) is much more than a narrow form of intellectual nationalism and nor is it a simple cultural relativism. It certainly does not seek to substitute Enlightenment rationalism with some form of irrationalism or mysticism. It involves a properly decentred historical contextualizing of Europe in its full and contradictory history of modernity and imperialism, unravelling the narratives and highlighting contestation. As Kenyan novelist Ngugiwa Thiong'o puts it by 'moving the centre' we can move towards an effective and liberating 'decolonization of the mind' (Thiong'o 1981). The critique of Eurocentrism thus plays a key role in building any global movement for contestation and liberation. The displacement of Western knowledge claims and creates the conditions for new forms of knowledge and action that are not subsumed by the myth of the West.

Where Eurocentrism is most apparent, in the socialist and labour movement, is in relation to the colonial question. This is the field where internationalism is weakest and whatever the contradictions of Marx's period of influence, under the Second International a frankly colonialist policy was pursued. As Fritjof Tichelman, historian of the colonial policies of European social democracy, concludes, 'The general idea was that after the socialist revolution in Europe, the backward peoples would be liberated from capitalist exploitation' (Tichelman 1988: 91). Behind the pacifist and humanitarian banners lay an openly racist attitude towards the colonialized peoples. While Europe's social democrats sought to prevent war at home over international disputes in relation to colonial expansion, their concern with the peoples of the colonies was mainly to 'civilize' them. The language of 'backwardness' and 'barbarism' tripped easily off the tongue of the European socialist of the era who saw it as their mission to 'educate and civilize'.

Already in 1896 Eduard Bernstein, the leading intellectual of German social democracy, had declared in relation to an anti-colonial revolt in Turkey that 'we will oppose certain methods through which the savages are subdued, we will not question their being subdued and the rights of civilization upheld' (Bernstein 1978: 49). Bernstein quite consistently argued that the Marx and Engels slogan of workers having no fatherland would have to be modified. As the European workers became fully enfranchised citizens and began to participate in the civil life of 'their' nations, so they could share in the nation's destiny. Henceforth, declared Bernstein, 'internationalism [would] not prevent the safeguarding of national interests' (Bernstein 1978: 21). Where this would be done most assiduously would be in relation to colonial expansion where the 'social-imperialist' policy adopted even envisaged the possession of colonies by European countries after the achievement of socialism.

In organizational terms Europe's internationalists came together in the First International formed in 1864 and then the Second International that was formed in 1889. The International Working Men's Association or First International was conceptualized in a London pub between English trade unionists and French visiting delegates to the Great Exhibition, with the rationale being more 'economic' than political. It was essentially an instrument to build strike solidarity across national frontiers and in this task it soon established its effectiveness. It was also successful in overcoming national or cultural differences such as those between the Walloons and Flemish in the Belgian section. In 1866 the International launched a coordinated campaign in Europe and in North America in pursuit of the eight-hour day, which demonstrated transnationalism in practice. Stevis argues that the First International was quite like today's ecological organizations: 'within limited means it engaged in cross-border activism, promoted the formation of labor organizations, had significant ideological prestige and impact, and put the idea of labor internationalism on labor's agenda' (Stevis 1998: 56).

A new chapter in labour transnationalism opens with the formation of mass-based socialist parties in Western Europe in the 1880s. The Second International was formed in 1889 with internationalism as a key theme, demonstrated not least in the International May Day and International Women's Day demonstrations. Trade unionism began to grow rapidly in the 1900s and by 1910 there were 28 different international trade union secretariats organizing specific trades (e.g. builders, engineers, miners, transport workers, etc.) across national boundaries (Lyons 1963: 157). While the Second International had a much more solid social base than the First, its objectives were, in some ways, more limited, at least in terms of its commitment to internationalism. It organized national socialist political parties and not the more ecumenical support the First sought. Its internationalism was geared specifically to achieving some political harmonization across national frontiers around socialist principles. It sought the reform of capitalism within national boundaries and not the world revolution that the First International preached and practised.

In his broad history of the West European left in the twentieth century, Donald Sassoon concludes that for the leaders of the Second International in 1914:

> Internationalism was just a word, not a key component of a coherent strategic line ... Their understanding of international affairs was minimal. Their internationalism was a façade, not in the sense that they were opportunists as the Leninists believed, but in the sense that they did not imbue it with any strategic content.
>
> (Sassoon 1996: 29)

Nevertheless, the first wave of internationalism in Western Europe did have a lasting effect and created an historic memory of considerable importance. The machinery of international cooperation would be rebuilt and the European labour movement eventually came out of the world wars more unified and coherent in its outlook than ever.

Internationalism arose in the mid-nineteenth century at least partly in response to the broad socio-economic and political transformations of the era. Capitalism was spreading across the globe and the nation-states of the centre were consolidating. The 'universal interdependence of nations' this process generated needed to be matched by what *The Communist Manifesto* of 1848 called the 'universal interdependence of peoples'. The theory and practice of internationalism had real roots and universal political goals such as place, equality and democracy were widely shared across national boundaries. As Alejandro Colás puts it: 'internationalism becomes both cause and consequence of the expansion of civil society' (Colás 2002: 57) during this era. International solidarity between peoples had material roots but the *principles* of internationalism also had real material effects, such as in undermining employers' efforts to divide the working class along national lines.

Communist internationalists

In the wake of European social democracy's succumbing to nationalism in the 'Great' or inter-imperialist war, a new radical, combative international-ist communist movement was born. From its inception the beleaguered Soviet state understood that it had to extend its revolution or perish. As Fred Halliday puts it: 'At the moment of coming to power in October 1917 the Bolshevik leadership was convinced that it was both possible and oblig-atory for the revolutionary regime to do all it could to promote revolution on a world scale' (Halliday 1999: 103). In 1919 the Bolsheviks established the Third (or Communist) International which saw itself as the general headquarters of a global revolution. From 1919 to 1921 this policy was pursued aggressively but afterwards a period of 'capitalist co-existence' with the capitalist countries began to prevail. Until its dramatic dissolution in 1943 the Communist International was to dominate the ebbs and flows of global revolution.

The First Congress of the Comintern (as it became known) held in 1919 was quite classically Eurocentric in terms of how it viewed world revolution. In terms reminiscent of the Second International with its frankly pro-colonialist views, the First Congress declared that:

> The emancipation of the colonies is possible only in conjunction with the emancipation of the metropolitan working class. The workers and peasants [of the colonial world] will gain the opportunity of independent existence only when the workers of England and France have overthrown Lloyd-George and Clemenceau and take state power into their own hands.
>
> (cited in Claudin 1975: 246)

This may well have been a strategic calculation rather than a reflection of Eurocentric bias but it nonetheless postponed the spread of revolution in the East. This strongly European orientation would only be partly redressed by the Second Congress of the Comintern in 1920.

As the revolutionary wave in the West subsided, Lenin and the other Bolshevik leaders realized that they must tap into the anti-imperialist potential of the East. The First Congress of the Peoples of the East held in Baku in 1920 signalled the start of a more global Bolshevik orientation. However, the Third Congress of the Comintern in 1921 was decidedly 'European' in its flavour. While the Fourth Congress in 1922 declared that 'the Communist International supports every national revolutionary movement against imperialism', at the Fifth Congress of 1924 delegate Nguyen Ai Quoc (later known as Ho Chi Minh) could declare that 'Comrades have not thoroughly grasped the idea that the destiny of the world proletariat . . . is closely bound up with the destiny of the oppressed classes in the colonies' (cited Munck 1986: 93). The tension between a lingering Eurocentrism and a more radical understanding of internationalism was always present in the Third International.

The 1930s saw the biggest test for internationalism since the First World War break out as Spain's Civil War became internationalized as part of the build-up to the Second World War. In 1936 General Franco led a section of the Spanish army in a *coup d'état* against the Republican government. An international democratic and anti-fascist movement began to mobilize to defend the Republic, backed politically and materially by the Soviet Union. This was to be a small encounter building up to the next 'great war', this time between imperialist powers but also between democracy and fascism. It also showed the limits as well as the very real significance and impact of official and unofficial forms of 'proletarian internationalism'. Inspired by the discourse of communist internationalism, but drawing also on earlier democratic and even religious modalities of solidarity, internationalist consciousness penetrated deeply into the working classes of Western Europe and further afield.

One such group of workers who participated actively in defence of democracy and in pursuit of communism in Spain were the miners of Wales. As Hywell Francis writes, 'There is a long and enduring, if sometimes tenuous and disjointed, internationalist tradition in Wales, closely associated with religious and political dissent, with its roots reaching back to the Enlightenment of eighteenth century Europe' (Francis 1984: 28). There were pacifist, idealist and religious dissenter incarnations but after 1917 the proletarian pro-Soviet variant became dominant. In the early part of the century racism and jingoism were as prevalent in Wales as elsewhere in the British Empire and pro-war sentiment in 1914–18 was high. However, communism and a certain type of cosmopolitanism (through Cardiff being an international port) gained ground and became a hegemonic force in parts of the labour movement, especially among the South Wales miners. Proletarian internationalism was sometimes more than a ritual incantation at party congresses.

In Ireland a more complex and contradictory form of internationalism was mobilizing in relation to the conflict in Spain. On the one hand socialists, communists and republicans (IRA) were quick to gather their forces to play a part in the International Brigades fighting to defend the Spanish Republic. But, on the other hand, conservatives and the Catholic Church organized equally fervently to create the Irish Brigade under General O'Duffy to come to the aid of General Franco and the forces of Catholicism which they saw to be under threat by atheistic communism. This case is particularly interesting, not only because internationalism is not seen as the sole preserve of the left, but also because of the complexities it revealed within Irish nationalism. Some Catholic Republicans went to fight for Franco, others joined Frank Ryan in the International Brigades, but yet others stayed at home on the basis that true internationalism meant fighting against British imperialism in the traditional manner.

Russia's Stalin at the time described Spain as 'the common cause of all advanced and progressive humankind' but many progressive individuals and organizations around the world believed that the Soviet Union betrayed the Spanish Revolution. Most researchers agree that Soviet aid to the Spanish Republic was measured rather than unconditional and was ultimately dictated by the state interests of the Soviet Union. However, it is also recognized that without the military aid supplied by the Soviet Union no amount of International Brigades would have been able to defend democracy in Spain. Whatever ambiguities the international solidarity of the first 'worker's state' displayed, the events in Spain from 1936 to 1939 were to prove a trial run for a great global conflagration between the forces of democracy and the growing fascist tide.

With the Chinese Revolution achieving victory in 1949, the 'turn to the East' announced in Lenin's era came to fruition. Part of the great wave created by communist internationalism, the Chinese revolution also led, however, to a resurgence of nationalism within communist discourse. For the Chinese communists, the true internationalists were necessarily nationalist in the developing world. For Fernando Claudin, coming from an orthodox pro-Soviet communist tradition:

> The Chinese revolution was the second great act of the world revolutionary process which began in 1917. It was the first major defeat of imperialism – and, importantly, of American imperialism – after the Second World War. It gave the struggle of the colonial and semi-colonial peoples for national and social liberation their present impetus.
>
> (Claudin 1975: 574)

The Eurocentric conception of internationalism had been replaced by a conception of 'world revolution' in which the 'world of the Country' (the developing world) would encircle the 'city' (the West).

During the 1950s the Chinese regime's vision of internationalism was muted by its subordination to the Soviet Union as the senior communist power. However, by the early 1960s China was articulating a new form of 'internationalism' based on independence from the Soviet Union on a basically nationalist platform. While a handful of states and parties around the world took up a 'Chinese' line, the Chinese communists rejected classic notions of the 'export' of revolution. The virtual annihilation of its main ally in Asia, the Communist Party of Indonesia (see Törnquist 1984), in the mid-1960s effectively tempered its hegemonic ambitions. Halliday refers to China's subsequent 'rhetorical and often self-defeating militancy abroad' (Halliday 1999: 115) that led to a real crisis of internationalism and a conservative turn both at home and abroad.

For independent communist states such as Yugoslavia, 'internationalism' was simply a mask for Soviet domination. The Comintern's successor, the weak Cominform set up in 1947, was to epitomize the new internationalism as code word for the foreign policy of the Soviet Union. This perverse form of internationalism was used to justify the Soviet military interventions in Hungary (1956) and in Czechoslovakia (1968). It was not until the late 1970s, with the emergence of 'Eurocommunism', that major Western communist parties broke with 'proletarian internationalism'. What had begun with Marx and Engels as a symbol of global workers' solidarity had become a shabby and authoritarian remnant of the Stalinist era that effectively buried the dream of democratic socialism.

The 1980s were to see the final decline of a by now impoverished and traditional Soviet-style internationalism. Already the war between Vietnam and Cambodia, which began in 1979, had caused a serious credibility gap for the official doctrine of proletarian internationalism. The subsequent

Soviet military intervention in Afghanistan undermined even further any notion that 'internationalism' was a progressive foreign policy. By 1987 Mikhail Gorbachev was effectively burying official Soviet doctrine on the matter and replacing it with a bland argument around the common interests of humanity. When communism fell across Eastern Europe in 1989 following the collapse of the Berlin Wall, according to Fred Halliday:

> one of the concepts most openly rejected and reviled, along with central planning, the emancipation of women and the abolition of religion, was 'internationalism': it had become a term associated both with the legitimation of Soviet domination and with the expenditure of large sums of money on politically motivated solidarity with other, mainly Third World, communist states.
>
> (Halliday 2000: 87)

Communist internationalism from the perspective of today's 'global justice movement' may seem a quaint, if rather authoritarian, relic of a bygone era. But the October Revolution of 1917 did transform the world and inaugurated an era of global transformation only closed or reversed in the 1990s. From an anti-communist perspective – and that can take a left wing as well as a right wing connotation – proletarian internationalism meant simply a servile adherence to the twists and turns of Soviet foreign policy. Yet, in the 1920s and 1930s in every corner of the world a new internationalist consciousness arose, that took its highest expression in the solidarity movement in support of the Spanish Republic. The Chinese Revolution for its part – notwithstanding all its terrible costs and later evolution – did overcome the Eurocentrism of an earlier social-democratic version of internationalism. It was the anti-colonial revolution and post-colonialism that would generate the next active phase of internationalism in the 1960s.

Colonialism and contestation

When the Western capitalist countries subjected wide swathes of Africa, Asia and Latin America to colonial rule (of various types) one could have expected some internationalist reaction in solidarity and protest. As we have seen that was often muted in the socialist (or social democratic) tradition and fairly instrumental in the communist movement, being tied as it was to the state interests of the Soviet Union. There was an older liberal tradition that motivated the anti-slavery movement and which did express solidarity with the democratic advances of the colonized peoples. What I want to address here is what Wallerstein refers to as 'those rarer but very important moments when nationalism mobilizes significant anti-systemic sentiment, and thereby affects the politics of the entire world economy'

(Wallerstein 1984: 130). To what extent is this nationalist anti-colonial revolt then part of internationalism and a precursor of the 'global justice' movement?

The success of the Chinese revolutionary nationalist/communist revolt in 1949 had an impact in the majority world every bit as powerful as the effect Russia's October 1917 revolution had in Europe. As already mentioned above, China did not seek to build an international communist movement to compete with the Soviet aligned bloc, but its impact was nonetheless considerable. The Chinese Revolution, and its image overseas in particular, centred the rural over the urban dimension, an approach later codified in a conception of the world revolution in which the 'countryside' (the Third World) encircled the 'city' (the advanced capitalist countries). After the Chinese split with Russia in 1956 Robert Young notes that, 'much of the Third World allied itself ideologically with China' (Young 2001: 188). The watchwords were 'struggle from below' as against bureaucratism, agrarian revolution instead of corrupted trade unions and, above all, an emphasis on the armed struggle against imperialism and against all forms of compromise and 'sell outs'.

The Bandung Conference of 1955 brought together many of the leaders of the national liberation struggles of the post-war era: Nehru from India, Sukarno from Indonesia, Nkrumah from Ghana, Nasser from Egypt and Tito from Yugoslavia. Abdel-Malek called it 'the first blueprint for solidarity between the colonized countries' (Abdel-Malek 1981: 108). Bandung was the first post-colonial international(ist) gathering and it marked a move towards self-determination on a global scale through greater economic and cultural ties between, principally, the countries of Africa and Asia. As Robert Young notes, Bandung thus represented a first move towards 'an independent transcontinental political consciousness in Africa and Asia' (Young 2001: 191). Some one hundred years after the first stirrings of internationalism in the narrow confines of Western Europe, a new internationalism was being felt across vast continental reaches of the majority world.

Internationalism had long marked the national liberation movements of Africa. The concept of Pan-Africanism traced its roots back to the 1920s and 1930s, linked to the *négritude* movement, but by the 1940s it was espousing a broad socialist modernization project for an independent Africa. As a transnational ideology Pan-Africanism had some roots in the international communist tradition, but it was also heavily influenced by the North American, and especially Caribbean, early Black consciousness movements. While nowadays this movement is often criticized for its 'essentialism' (*négritude*) and its acceptance of a basically European idea of 'Africa', it was undoubtedly a grand transnationalist liberatory project in its era. Leaders of the first wave of national liberation movements such as Nkrumah were well aware of the limitations of nationalism and held to this transnational project as a means to create an 'African socialism' which was neither 'communist' nor 'tribalist'.

In the contemporary post-colonial theoretical tradition Frantz Fanon, the Martinique-born voice of the Algerian Revolution is still, and perhaps increasingly, influential. Influenced by both the communist and *négritude* movements, Fanon articulated a powerful and original analysis of the anti-colonial revolt. While probably best known for his seemingly positive attitude towards revolutionary violence, Fanon also took a very sceptical view towards nationalism, much as Guevara (another non-native revolutionary leader) did. For Fanon, 'if nationalism is not made explicit, if it is not enriched and deepened by a very rapid transformation . . . it leads up a blind alley' (Fanon 1969: 165). The victory of the national liberation movements was a necessary step in the global struggle against oppression but Fanon was conscious of, and warned about, how: 'From nationalism we have passed to ultra-nationalism, to chauvinism, and finally to racism' (Fanon 1969: 125). Algeria's subsequent tragic history certainly does not belie Fanon.

Vietnam's success against US imperialism in 1975 was to have a marked regional impact. The war in Vietnam had radicalized a whole layer of youth in the West, but it also created strong guerrilla movements in neighbouring Laos and Cambodia. But when in late 1978 the socialist Republic of Vietnam invaded neighbouring Democratic Kampuchea and then the People's Republic of China invaded Vietnam, the whole concept of 'proletarian internationalism' was brought into question. Of course, this was on top of the Soviet invasions of Hungary in 1956 and Czechoslovakia in 1967, also conducted in the name of 'proletarian internationalism'. The influential German newspaper *Der Spiegel* (26 February 1979) declared with some satisfaction that: 'Karl Marx wanted to make his supporters into cosmopolitans. "The workers have no fatherland". But when they get into power, the Reds very soon become flaming patriots, mostly at the expense of neighbouring countries' (cited in Munck 1986: 140).

Undoubtedly these events sounded the death knell of 'proletarian internationalism' but also of the ideology of Thirdworldism as a progressive option. It was a largely futile exercise that some Western Marxists engaged in during 1979 seeking a progressive side in the fraternal Indo-China wars. In fact, Vietnam had quite astutely managed to combine its drive to 'internationalize' the Indo-Chinese revolution it espoused, while at the same time seeking to defend the national frontiers of the Vietnamese nation-state. Kampucheans, not surprisingly, saw 'proletarian internationalism' as a cover for Vietnamese imperialist claims over their revolution. In their perversion of internationalism this series of events showed the very real limits of anti-colonial contestation, even when this was dressed in the language of classic communism.

The undoubted voice of the post-colonial revolt on behalf of the exploited peoples of the world (as against the 'working class') was Ernesto 'Che' Guevara who was killed in Bolivia in 1967. The previous year, in 1966, Havana had hosted the Tricontinental Conference of Solidarity of the People of Africa, Asia and Latin America that brought the spirit of Bandung up

to date and generalized it. Post-colonialism had come of age and internationalism was at the heart of the new movement and its whole discourse.
Guevara's message to the Tricontinental famously called for the creation of
'Two, Three, Many Vietnams' with that ongoing struggle playing a pivotal
role. This, according to Young:

> constitutes the first moment where a general internationalist counter-
> hegemonic position was elaborated by a dispossessed subject of imperial-
> ism, powerfully and persuasively invoking others throughout the three
> continents to open up new fronts of resistance, in a global strategy of
> guerrilla warfare conceived from an internationalist perspective.
>
> (Young 2001: 213)

The Tricontinental and OSPAAL (Afro-Asian Latin American People's
Solidarity Organization), the organization it spawned, did not last long but
organizations represented there were to take power in the ex-Portuguese
colonies in Africa and Indo-China in the mid-1970s, and, later, in Nicaragua
(1979) and Zimbabwe (1980). In Cuba, itself a lever for revolutionary struggles abroad, it marked a phase of practical internationalism not seen since
the early days of the Russian Revolution. Guevara's own early expeditions
to the Congo and later Bolivia were followed by more organic interventions
organized by the Cuban state directly. Support for the Nicaraguan upsurge
against the dictator Somoza was crucial. The prolonged intervention in
Angola on behalf of the MPLA government against Chinese/US-backed rebel
Jonas Savimbi was important in its own right but also because of the effect
it had on South Africa's apartheid regime within whose sphere of influence
it fell. When democratic majority rule was established in South Africa in
1991, Cuba had played a key role.

The struggle against colonialism and for national emancipation played
a critical role in the Western revolt of 1968 and the emergence of the
'new' social movements. The Paris May worker/student revolt, the Prague
Spring against bureaucratic socialism and the Vietnamese Tet offensive
against US imperialism all occurred in 1968. This conjunction made it a
truly world revolution – albeit a failed one – and internationalism was at
its very core. Marcel van der Linden refers to the wave of protest that swept
across the world from 1966 to 1976 as a set of interconnected movements
that represented 'one great transnational cycle of contention' (Linden 2003:
117). Much coverage of '1968' has been Eurocentric, focusing on Western
students and workers, but the true significance of these events in world
historical terms can only be grasped in relation to a very active phase of the
anti-colonial revolution and its internationalist repercussions.

Five years after the Tet offensive of 1968 the most powerful military
machine ever invented was forced to withdraw from a small, peripheral
and poor nation of the South. North–South relations would never be the
same again. This despite the fact that the end of the cycle in the mid-1970s

was marked by the demise of the Cultural Revolution in China, the inter-socialist wars in Indo-China, and the failure of guerrilla opposition movements in Latin America and elsewhere. While the anti-colonial revolt was very much part of an 'old' nation-building social movement, it took on a world-historic significance in this phase and imparted many key characteristics to the 'new' social movements in the West. Contemporary concerns with the South, with the depredations of globalism and with cultural autonomy, all have their roots in the mid- to late 1960s with '1968' very much a dress rehearsal for events such as Seattle 1999 and the whole anti-globalization wave.

In the era of the global justice movement from 1999 onwards the relevance of anti-colonialist contestation seems less important. Iraqi resistance following the US-led invasion of that country in 2003 is less obviously attractive to the young anti-globalization protestors than the image of Che was in 1968 to their student counterparts of that year. For Hardt and Negri in their influential and passionate *Empire* (Hardt and Negri 2000) 'subaltern nationalism' may have once been progressive, serving as a defence against an aggressive world order and an instrument for revolution, but that is no longer the case today. For Hardt and Negri, post-colonial theorists fail to recognize adequately the real enemy today, and 'national liberation and national sovereignty are not just powerless against this [new] global capitalist hierarchy but themselves contribute to its organization and functioning' (Hardt and Negri 2000: 133). We shall return to this key issue but for now we take this position as a given.

Contemporary cosmopolitanism

Contemporary cosmopolitanism has something in common, I would argue, with that upsurge of European internationalism in the period leading up to the First World War (see section on European internationalists, above). While the number of INGOs grew steadily in the post-Second World War era, there was a remarkable acceleration in the 1990s coinciding with the end of the cold war and the rise of globalization. It is estimated that around one quarter of the INGOs in existence at the turn of the century had been formed in the 1990s, and over one third of the members of these associations had joined during the 1990s (Anheier *et al.* 2001: 4). These international organizations were to provide much of the structural backbone to what became known in the 1990s as 'global civil society', a concept we shall now seek to define.

The authoritative *Global Civil Society Yearbook* sought to define its key concept thus in the first issue: 'global civil society is the sphere of ideas, values, institutions, organizations, networks, and individuals located *between* the family, the state and the market and operating *beyond* the confines of national societies, politics and economics' (Anheier *et al.* 2001: 17). While recognizing that 'global civil society' (GCS) is an essentially *normative* concept its politics are seen as too contested to allow for an agreed more specified definition. Thus, GCS came into being in a rather fuzzy or open definition, eminently contestable and contested. At the very least we must distinguish between a liberal rendering of GCS that sees it as part of the drive to push back the state, and a more radical (in a traditional sense) version where GCS operates as a vehicle for popular empowerment and for the reform of political institutions.

During the 1990s a range of academic observers and then international institutions began to develop the discourse of 'global civil society' as a common human good (see, for example, Commission of Global Governance 1995). As Jan Aart Scholte describes the process of civil society, it can be 'global' in at least four different ways. It may be on the basis of:

1   addressing transworld issues such as 'global climate change';
2   civic networks created through supraterritorial electronic means of communication;
3   civic activity based on transnational organization (the NGOs);
4   Supraterritorial solidarity between social groups such as workers or women.

(Scholte 2000: 217–18)

In practice many of these 'modalities' of GCS may overlap but that is not necessarily the case and not all 'criteria' need to be met conjointly for us to witness GCS at work.

Then, of course, there are more or less radical inflections of the GCS discourse. For radical observers such as Peter Waterman, global civil society 'means a non-capitalist/non-state, or anti-competitive/anti-hierarchical, sphere for democratic efforts, within and without the multiple existing global terrains' (Waterman 1998: 227). As an aspiration or as a project this may well be laudable but it is not a practical policy perspective, nor is it designed to be. So GCS as something to strive for, as Ghandi once referred to democracy, is one thing but as an actually existing policy, it is another thing. From a quite different perspective we have the 1995 report of the Commission on Global Governance by the 'good and the great' of globalization with a human face for whom: 'To be an effective instrument of global governance in the modern world, the United Nations must . . . take greater account of the emergence of global civil society' (Commission on Global Governance 1995: 253). Here we see a quite openly instrumental attitude towards GCS as something to be 'taken account of' by the globalizers of the new capitalist order.

One particular way in which the GCS discourse has impacted the anti-globalization movement has been as an underpinning for the notion of 'globalization from below'. For Ronnie Lipschitz, one of the promoters of GCS, 'the growth of global civil society represents an on-going project of civil society to reconstruct, re-imagine or re-map world politics' (Lipschitz 1992: 391). The nation-state is being challenged 'from below' from this perspective. GCS is seen, more or less, as a unified, coherent and purposeful project with an unambiguously positive content. In challenging the 'globalization from above' project that currently prevails, GCS will bring, according to this view, more and better democracy. Of course, in practice, it is clear that the divisions of gender, ethnicity, culture and religion, among others, not to mention differences of political orientation, make the notion of a unified GCS look distinctly utopian and unrealistic.

However, the fact that the concept of GCS has acquired such prominence in both academic and policy circles in so short a time would indicate that it must have some theoretical and/or political purchase in our rapidly changing times. It has undoubtedly brought to the fore the question of the 'democratic deficit' in actually existing globalization. It has also acted as a favourable terrain, albeit conflictual, for the development of non-state organization and social movement organizations in particular. In spite of its undoubted conceptual slipperiness and 'conceptual inflation' by some, GCS has captured some novel social and political transformations currently under way. It is part of an internationalist grand vision to build a new global order based on democracy, participation and the struggle for equality. As such GCS is largely an enabling discourse.

From the prevailing liberal perspective GCS is 'seen as a domain of consultation and co-operative participation' according to Alejandro Colás (Colás 2002: 155). Social and political transformation, from this optic, is necessarily constrained by existing international social and political structures and power relations. The political limitations of this perspective, from the standpoint of radical social transformation, are thus clear. GCS works within clearly delineated parameters, and it can be seen as the social or 'unofficial' wing of the 'official' capitalist globalization structures. It could thus be seen as equally 'top-down' in spite of all the 'bottom-up' rhetoric within the more radical reaches of GCS. To continue to promote GCS and urge social movements to see themselves as part of GCS might appear as a co-optive manoeuvre to tame rebellious movements of contestation.

For André Drainville global civil society is like a 'cosmopolitan ghost' created 'by simultaneously pulverizing humanity into functional bits and reassembling it into an abstract bearer of rights, responsibilities and moralities' (Drainville 2004: 22). The people, the multitude, the toiling masses, all become reassembled and reconstructed as heat boxes in the construction of 'global civil society'. This GCS becomes an abstract – as in not grounded or concrete – bearer of classic democratic rights and the ethics of liberal internationalism. It may, of course, be 'progressive' in a generic or academic sense, but what if GCS is simply a creation of neoliberal governance strategy: 'a strategic site of decontextualization, occupied by a politically neutered humanity' (Drainville 2004: 22)?

A more specific problem with GCS as a concept is its 'presentism', that is, an assumption that present-day observable phenomena are essentially novel. Fred Halliday, for example, has challenged the notion that the 'non-state actors' that create GCS are that new insofar as 'the erosion of the Westphalian system rests upon a contemporary optic and illusion' (Halliday 2000: 27). In reality the new GCS actors can trace their heritage to long before the Westphalian nation-state became dominant. Furthermore, the history of internationalism, as we have seen, goes back far beyond the 1990s when GCS came to operate as a seemingly novel paradigm of transnational social links. This presentism is, of course, not particular to the GCS literature and we saw towards the end of the twentieth century a whole range of theoretical/political perspectives declaring in millenarian fashion the 'end' of democracy, the nation-state and even history.

A further problem that needs to be addressed is the irredeemably Eurocentric bias of much of the GCS literature. Thus, for John Keane, a central writer in this tradition, 'global civil society' names 'an old tendency of local and regional civil societies to link up and to penetrate regions of the Earth that had previously not known the ethics of civil society in the modern European sense' (Keane 2001: 28). It is an explicitly European Enlightenment version of democracy, civility, ethics and rationality that underpins the notion of GCS. This cultural universalism is at odds with the contemporary understanding of 'cultural hybridity' and the post-colonial approach. It simply does not allow for diversity nor can it grasp the distinctive paths to modernity across the globe. Eurocentrism is presented as universalism and 'Enlightenment man' is the essential central actor in the GCS project to 'civilize' globalization.

David Held and Anthony McGrew subtitle the concluding chapter of their *Globalization/Anti-Globalization* 'Towards Cosmopolitan Social Democracy' (2002). I think that more or less captures the ambition and the limitations of the 'global civil society' project. It is clearly, as I have argued above, Eurocentric (or North Atlanticist) not only in its geographical remit but also in its overall political orientation. It simply assumes a political world where 'rationality' prevails or should prevail, and where cosmopolitanism is a more virtuous political philosophy than nationalism. Of course, there are many far worse political futures on the horizon than a globalized European-style social democracy. Yet, if the 'global civil society' project is to become truly global it will need to broaden out its scope to a horizon of possibilities beyond the confines of social democracy, which remains essentially a European political project.

The parallel with the historical period leading up to the First World War goes beyond a parallel upsurge in the numbers and influence of INGOs. Nineteenth-century internationalism (1815–1914) was also based on a liberal cosmopolitanism and a remarkable communications revolution (post and telegraph). F.S. Lyons, though, in his remarkable history of this first wave internationalism, concludes that:

The internationalism of the few was no match for the nationalism of the multitude, and the essential sanity and tolerance of the tiny minority consciously working towards the creation of a civilized world community was inevitably drowned by the passionate hatreds which each succeeding crisis called forth in greater measure as Europe reeled towards the precipice.

(Lyons 1963: 309)

Today's cosmopolitans sound very like these early enlightened and civilized minorities fighting against the passions of the barbaric multitudes.

4 The anti-globalization movement

From Seattle (1999) to the future

While many participants reject the label 'anti-globalization' movement, I will retain it simply for presentational purposes insofar as that was how it emerged in Seattle in 1999. Certainly, most of its supporters would probably now feel that they were presenting an alternative globalization project and that they were not opposed to globalization per se. I will also use the term restrictively to cover only the major street protests since Seattle aimed against symbolic agents of globalization such as the WTO and older organizations such as the IMF and the World Bank. It thus excludes more formal events such as the World Social Forum (see Chapter 5) and the myriad forms of local social contestation (see Chapter 6).

This chapter begins with the protest events known as the 'Battle of Seattle' in late 1999 that effectively prevented the WTO from concluding its business on that particular occasion. For many observers, analysts or participants this was the 'coming out' party of the anti-globalization movement. But what happened after the party? Did the unifying momentum of Seattle build up or did divisions within and between the various interest groups prevail? We follow the events at Genoa, Prague and Quebec City to explore the prospects and meaning of this post-Seattle movement. We then turn to a quite different movement, the Zapatistas, part indigenous peasant revolt in a remote part of Mexico, part star and inspiration of the Western anti-globalization movement. Who are the Zapatistas? What is the significance of this movement in terms of the broader anti-globalization movement? Finally, I turn to the main interpretations of the Seattle/Zapatista transnational contestation movements. Are they simply a resurgence of traditional anti-capitalism as one tendency argues? Or is there something new and complex in the way in which the anti-globalization movement has captured the discursive terrain and generated a social counter-movement against neoliberal globalization?

Coming out

Clearly the contestation of neoliberal globalization did not begin in the US city of Seattle in 1999: only a narrow North Atlanticism (today's

Eurocentrism) could lead us to that conclusion. The first wave of global protest began in the mid-1970s and focused on the austerity measures adopted as part of the 'structural adjustment' programme of the IMF. This was the 'pre-globalization' global re-structuring of international capitalism. The so-called 'debt crisis' in the developing countries was its most visible symptom. Reacting against it in, often spontaneous, strikes and protest demonstrations, a social counter-movement began to take shape across the Third and Second (socialist) worlds. Walton and Seddon in their history of this phase of transnational popular protest recall that 'between 1976 and late 1992, some 146 incidents of protest occurred, reaching a peak from 1983 to 1985 and continuing to the present [1994] without alleviation' (Walton and Seddon 1994: 42). While these protests were not, on the whole, coordinated across national frontiers and nor was the opposition entirely clear and consistent, they were clearly part of the direct pre-history to the anti-globalization struggles of the 1990s.

The second wave of global popular protest that began in the 1990s was increasingly more coordinated and organized, with much clearer political targets now emerging. This was also a period of democratization across the majority world and the post-authoritarian governments then emerging allowed for greater space for the social counter-movements to organize. The development of a transnational militant Islamic movement was one particular facet of this period's mobilization. In other developments the human rights, environmental and women's movements began to develop a much more transnational agenda. The annual World Bank and IMF meetings began to act as a focus for an emerging anti-globalization movement. In 1995, the 50th anniversary of the Bretton Woods agreement, which set up the World Bank/IMF system, was marked by an active 'Fifty Years Is Enough' campaign. As Jackie Smith recounts: 'Many of the older activists in Seattle . . . traced their opposition back to the 1980s mobilization around Third World debt and its relationship to conflict and economic justice in Central America and other developing regions' (Smith 2002: 210). The background to Seattle was thus a global one and a rather 'traditional' anti-imperialism was certainly a powerful motivating factor.

So there is a broad historical context that needs to be provided to make sense of the Battle of Seattle in 1999 but there is also a very local labour history that plays a key context-setting role. Contrary to the media images of the incongruity of anarchists smashing windows in the genteel home city of Boeing, Amazon.com and Starbucks: 'Seattle is a city with a long past of militant labor and anarchist actions' (Levi and Olson 2000: 309). This stretches back to the militant Seattle General Strike of 1919 and the 1934 West Coast dockers' strikes. This region was a strong organizing base for the Wobblies (Industrial Workers of the World), the anarcho-syndicalist and internationalist 'one big union' of the early twentieth century. When the US labour federation, the American Federation of Labor-Congress of Industrial Organizations (AFL-CIO), organized a big unionization drive in the mid-1990s Seattle was to become one of the first 'union cities'. There have been major strikes at Seattle's Boeing plants and the unions have managed to break in to unionize at Microsoft and other software companies.

One of the apparent ironies of the Battle of Seattle, write Levi and Olson, 'was the presence of the longshore workers who thrive on international trade, at the forefront of actions directed at regulating international trade' (Levi and Olson 2000: 316). Yet if we take a long view of Seattle's labour history it is not odd at all to see a group of workers struggling in a militantly particularistic manner over their own conditions, while also seeking to forward a broad social and environmental progressive agenda. Dockers have often been seen as a traditional male/manual/militant occupational group but they have often, even naturally, taken up internationalism. There is no need to romanticize the labour struggles of the longshore to understand that they were well able to move from local to national to transnational forms of labour solidarity. The threats they faced in the mid-1990s could lead to a protectionist response but also to an internationalist strategy. That they became part of the mass labour contingent which formed the backbone of the mass events of Seattle shows that political agency still counts and can alter the course of political events.

The Battle of Seattle did not, of course, simply happen, it was *organized* by clearly identifiable social and political organizations. One of the key organizations was the People for Fair Trade (PFT) network of labour, trade and environmental groups that had previously mobilized around NAFTA. Symptomatic of the fluid globalization politics emerging, the PFT mobilized in tandem with the 'Network Opposed to the WTO' (NO! WTO) even though the latter aimed to 'shut down' the WTO, while the PFT was seeking, rather, the incorporation of labour and environmental standards into the WTO agreements. As Gillian Murphy puts it:

> By framing the issue as a critique of neoliberal trade policies rather than an opposition to globalization per se, and by celebrating the diversity of participants rather than pressing for conformity, the group advocated creating an environment in Seattle that would enable it to attract the maximum number of participants.
>
> (Murphy 2004: 32)

Organized labour was also to the fore in the mainstream political arena and as Ron Judd, one of the organizers, recounts: 'What happened in Seattle was not an accident. For months labor led an effort to educate and inform the community about the devastating impact of the WTO and its policies' (cited Murphy 2004: 33).

Alongside the big battalions of labour and the mainstream environmental groups such as the Sierra Club, a very different alternative mobilizing model was being implemented by fringe groups such as Direct Action Network

(DAN). This was a young movement, influenced by anarchism (of which more later) and committed to direct action. Their aim was not to find 'a seat at the WTO table' as the labour federation AFL-CIO wished to achieve, but, rather, to mount a festival of resistance to the forces of global capitalism. DAN invested in massive non-violent resistance training and the creation of self-reliant 'affinity groups' of around a dozen members, not unlike the old Communist traditional cells but without the secrecy. From this milieu came the 'shock troops' who were committed to 'Shut Down Seattle'. Though shunned by the majority of trade unionists and mainstream environmentalists it was the innovative and energetic direct action tactics of these sectors that in the streets of Seattle made the difference between symbolic protest and actually influencing the management of globalization.

Finally, Seattle 1999, like all key episodes of contestation, was also a 'happening' to use a 1968 term. One of the most famous retrospective images was the alliance between labour and environmentalists around the symbolic issue or image of the sea turtle. The latter was the subject of a WTO ruling that a US endangered species regulation that shrimps should be caught with a device that excludes sea turtles was, in fact, an unfair trade barrier. Jeffrey St Clair recalls how at Seattle he:

> walked next to Brad Spann, a burly longshoreman from Tacoma, who held up one of my favourite signs of the entire week: Teamsters and Turtles – Together at Last! Brad winked at me and said 'What the hell do you think old Hoffa thinks of that?'
>
> (St Clair 2000: 84)

But perhaps even more significant, the marchers dressed as sea turtles and the union members took up an old Chilean Popular Unity era chant: 'The people united will never be defeated'. There was much at Seattle that was part of the new battle against globalization with 'new' social movements involved, but much that was part of a much older struggle for social justice.

In a sense the Battle of Seattle can be read as a conglomeration of images and symbols. From the teamster/turtle allegory we can turn to French rural leader José Bové handing out rounds of Roquefort cheese outside McDonald's to protest against US protectionist laws. But after a rousing speech against Monsanto and GM foods, the crowds stormed McDonald's and the battle was on. As the police reacted and used vastly disproportionate force and armour, some small groups of 'direct action' activists attacked symbolic targets such as Starbucks. Another symbolic moment was when they were met outside Nike and the Gap by members of Global Exchange, one of the more mainstream counter-globalization groups, keen to protect the corporations and anxious for the police to arrive. But neither this nor the massed ranks of 'robocops' and the National Guard could dampen the spirits of an event that saw longshoremen and radical environmentalists engaging the state to the sound of the Civil Rights anthem 'We Shall Overcome!'

When the dust had settled in Seattle after the great refusal of 'globalization as we knew it' what had changed? For one observer the achievements
included:

> shutting down the opening ceremony, preventing President Clinton
> from addressing the WTO delegates, turning the corporate press around
> to focus on police brutality, and forcing the WTO to cancel its closing
> ceremonies and adjourn without an agenda for the next international
> meetings.
>
> (St Clair 2000: 91)

This was not, of course, the end of the WTO but its hegemonic role was
seriously and very publicly contested. According to Nederveen Pieterse:

> Seattle showed the lack of coherence among OECD governments and
> the steep differences between them and governments in the South. It
> showed the lack of preparation in the WTO organization and the govern-
> ments backing it in the face of governmental and non-governmental
> dissent. Perhaps most of all Seattle signalled the lack of democratic
> process in issues of worldwide importance.
>
> (Pieterse 2000: 465)

In brief, the events of Seattle had brought the issue of 'global governance'
to the fore; there would henceforth be 'No Globalization without Representation!' as demanded at Seattle.

All moments of contestation also have an impact on their participants and in this sense the Battle of Seattle was truly a watershed. The anti-
globalization movement had made its mark, brought together disparate
social movements and created a myth-making event in Seattle. At the level
of social relationships and networks its impact was enduring. While mainstream US labour returned to its protectionist ways (on China's entry to the
WTO, for example) many activists and local unions had been impacted.
Boundaries had been broken and new modalities of struggle shaped up and
tested. Above all, the events of Seattle culminated in a long process – going
back to the anti-IMF protests of the 1980s – through which 'globalization'
emerged as the unifying focus for a whole series of struggles around the
environment, indigenous people's rights, jobs and people's livelihoods, and
a general feeling of cultural alienation.

While Seattle 1999 was, indeed, a turning point in the struggle between
the architects of globalization and the great counter-movement against it,
we should also be clear about its limitations. The first one surrounds the
popular image of Seattle 1999 in terms of the 'Teamsters and Turtles unite'
slogan signifying a new labour-environmentalist alliance. The reality was
more prosaic, as Gould *et al.* recount, insofar as: 'At no time in Seattle did
a unified rhetoric connecting labor and environment emerge from either

camp. That unifying rhetoric was provided by the organizations focused specifically on corporate globalization such as Public Interest Trade Watch and Global Exchange' (Gould *et al.* 2004: 94). The social movements representing labour and the environment did not naturally coalesce and, in fact, the ideological or discursive bonding element was provided by third parties that were seeking to build a common platform against neoliberal globalization. The 'blue-green' alliance has, in brief, still to be built.

The other main structural issue arising out of Seattle 1999 was the gap it exposed between the anti-globalization and the anti-racist movements in the US. As Betita Martínez asks:

> In the vast acreage of published analysis about the splendid victory over the WTO last November 29–December 3, it is almost impossible to find anyone wondering why the forty to fifty thousand demonstrators were overwhelmingly Anglo. How can that be, when the WTO's main victims around the world are people of color?
>
> (Martínez 2000: 141)

The Colors of Resistance Network gathered together much of the critical discourse around 'race'/ethnicity within what was billed a 'movement of movements'. Anti-racist activists in North America were keen to take globalization up as a key issue but also to 'bring it back home' and show there were always the included and the excluded also within the imperialist heartlands. A broader-based critique but not unrelated to this one is that the anti-globalization movement 'as we know it' reflected mainly Northern or affluent country concerns and not those of the majority world in terms of the issues they took up and where they focused their energies.

Zapatistas

While the street festival and subsequent 'carnival of repression' at Seattle in 1999 captured the imagination of the Western media, another revolt against globalization was well under way in the *México profundo* (hidden Mexico). On the first day of 1994 as NAFTA came into effect consolidating globalizing regionalism, an obscure group called *Ejército Zapatista de Liberación Nacional* (Zapatista National Liberation Army) took over some small towns on the edge of the Lacandón rainforest in the southern Mexican state of Chiapas. Was this a belated manifestation of the 1970s' wave of guerrilla movements in Latin America? Was it the start of a new wave of indigenous revolts that would spread to other countries? Many on the international left were encouraged to see the global retreat since the collapse of the Berlin Wall in 1989 had at least halted in one particular corner of the world. But at first, generally speaking, no one put too great an importance on this revolt which seemed more a gasp from the past than a harbinger of a new storm of popular revolt.

The Zapatistas (as they became known) were, at least in part, derived from a small Marxist group that 'went to the hills' in the 1980s and coalesced in the one hundred strong EZLN in 1983. In the early 1990s, however, it began to take serious roots among the indigenous peoples – Tzeltal, Tzotzil and Chil communities of Chiapas. As Subcomandante Marcos himself recounts, from 1990 onwards the Zapatista rebel army 'made itself bigger, made itself more Indian, and definitively contaminated itself with communitarian forms, including indigenous cultural forms' (cited in Gilly 1998: 300). Government repression, electoral fraud and failure to deal with a pressing land question created the conditions for rebellion. Despite the unfavourable international conditions the will to revolt spread and the Zapatistas initiated a wide-ranging *consulta* (consultation) that resulted in legitimacy across the population when the revolt was eventually launched as the year 1994 began.

In the mid-1990s – as neoliberal globalization was getting into its stride – the Zapatista revolt achieved a certain 're-enchanting of the world' (Lowy 1998). Another world seemed possible, history had not come to an end. What this led to was a remarkable flourishing of a transnational Zapatista solidarity network that is our main interest in this chapter. What was most remarkable – and most interesting to the theme of globalization and contestation – was the speed at which this solidarity movement spread and consolidated its activities. Harry Cleaver, a radical US economist at the heart of this movement, described how 'it took six years to build the anti-war in the 60s, it took 6 months to build the anti-war movement in the Gulf War, and it took six days to build an anti-Mexican government movement in 1994' (cited Olesen 2005: 184). The transnational Zapatista support network went through various phases.

During 1994 the transnational Zapatista solidarity network began to take shape around the activity of international activists who arrived in Mexico to protest against the state repression of the Zapatista revolt. In 1995, according to Thomas Olesen's meticulous history:

> the transnational Zapatista solidarity network starts to develop an infrastructure of its own. The very intense activities in this phase are mainly aimed at monitoring the human rights situation in Chiapas following the Mexican army's invasion of EZLN territory in February 1995.
> (Olesen 2005: 3)

In subsequent years the network becomes intensely politicized as Zapatismo becomes, to some extent, a transnational (albeit mainly virtual) social movement. There were also intense phases of more traditional 'solidarity' work as, for example, subsequent to the Acteal massacre in December 1997. There have also been fairly quiescent periods and, more recently, a move by the Zapatistas to regain some control over their rather disparate international support networks.

Taking a broad overview of the Zapatista transnational solidarity network Olesen is undoubtedly correct to conclude that 'the interest and attraction generated by the EZLN beyond its national borders is matched by no other movement in the post-Cold War period' (Olesen 2005: 2). It certainly appears to vindicate, in many ways, the more positive reading of globalization as a process that has made the world more interconnected physically, socially, politically and culturally. The very 'local' indigenous world of Chiapas became a 'global' issue and had an impact, directly and through its 'demonstration effect' across many other places. There was no 'centre' to this transnational solidarity network as there was with the 'old' inter-nationalism and the network mode of capitalist development was truly reflected in the mode its contestation took. Its impact in creating and providing a beacon of hope for the anti-globalization movement has been considerable.

This remarkable Internet movement or network of transnational solidarity was not without its critics on the left. Judith Hellman advanced a coherent critique in the Socialist Register 2000 where she argued that: 'virtual Chiapas holds a seductive attraction for disenchanted and discouraged people on the left that is fundamentally different than the appeal of the struggles underway in the real Chiapas' (Hellman 1999: 175). There, on the ground, not everyone is a 'Zapatista', there are divisions and weaknesses, and *realpolitik* does not always reflect the seductive political rhetoric of Subcomandante Marcos online. Nor is 'civil society' such a homogeneous and progressive milieu as the international supporters of Zapatismo might believe. There are roman-ticized, essentialized views of indigenous peoples permeating the virtual Zapatismo, and vicarious participation through transnational solidarity may well act as a roadblock to grassroots activism according to this critical perspective.

In the Socialist Register of 2001 Justin Paulson, an active member of the Zapatista solidarity movement, responded to Hellman. While accepting that the second-hand and third-hand transmission of events on the ground on the Internet can lead to a certain 'flattening' and loss of complexity, overall: 'It may well be that the ability of Zapatismo to stir up support around the world has less to do with oversimplification of the message, and much more to do with the vitality and resonance of the message itself' (Paulson 2000: 286). To take up Zapatismo outside of Chiapas is not to avoid struggle but to internationalize it. The struggle for *dignidad* (much more than 'dignity') by the Zapatistas is a universal one and its generalizing across the world is thus positive. While some may well be seeking to 'revolt vicariously' by taking up Zapatismo many more visit Chiapas or learn about it in detail and become informed participants in *World War IV* (a Zapatista term) between neoliberalism and a dignified existence.

This exchange was extremely interesting – over and beyond the specifics raised – because it problematized the new global solidarity modalities.

My own view is that 'international Zapatismo' is no more homogeneous than civil society 'on the ground' in Chiapas. There are undoubtedly tendencies imbued with Eurocentrism who see the revolt in Chiapas in terms of the 'noble savage' (Rousseau) who will redeem comfortable corrupt Westerners. There is more than a whiff in this milieu of Jean Paul Sartre's Foreword to Frantz Fanon's classic *The Wretched of the Earth* where he argued that 'to shoot down a European is to kill two birds with one stone, to destroy an oppressor and the man he oppresses at the same time: there remains a dead man and a free man' (Sartre 1969: 19). Nevertheless, the Zapatista revolt has had an overwhelmingly positive resonance across the world, teaching and energizing a whole generation of young activists that another world is, indeed, possible. The dangers of 'armchair activism' seemed more than out-weighed by the exemplary courage and originality of the Zapatistas.

This is not the place to analyse the full political significance of the Zapatista movement as case study of contestation in the era of globalization but we can draw some general conclusions to strengthen the arguments of this chapter. A dominant interpretation of Zapatismo is that it is 'the *first informational guerrilla movement*' (Castells 2004: 82) or as the security appa-ratus would put it, a precursor of 'social netwar . . . likely to involve battles for public opinion and for media access and coverage, at local through global levels' (Ronfeldt and Arquilla 1998: 22). There is a popular image lying behind these interpretations – from a left and a conservative position alike – that Subcomandante Marcos sat with a laptop in the middle of a jungle consciously reaching out through the Internet to construct international soli-darity. In practice, the Zapatista Internet presence was mediated through support structures as we saw above.

In reality very little of what became the international phenomenon of Zapatismo, especially after Seattle, was part and parcel of how the revolt occurred in practice. Marcos and his colleagues went into the revolt expecting either that the masses would hear their call to war or ignore them. In the event, civil society, across Mexico and then further afield, did not support armed revolt but did support the Zapatistas' aims and sought to shelter them from repression. The new way of 'making revolution' without seizing power was forced on them and was not a far-sighted aim there from the very start. Nor was the motivation of the indigenous *campesinos* that new and, rather, resounded with the fervour of 'primitive rebels' (Hobsbawm 1959) across time. Thus, Comandante David when asked in 1996 about the motives for the uprising said that:

> Indians have never lived like human beings . . . but the moment came when those very same indigenous *pueblos* started to make themselves aware of their reality by means of reflection and analysis, and also by studying the Word of God, thus they began to wake up.
>
> (cited in Gilly 1998: 306)

The Zapatistas have been variously called the 'first post-communist rebellion' (Fuentes 1994), the 'first informational guerrilla movement' (Castells 2004: 82) or, more prosaically, 'armed democrats' (Touraine 2001). They are, in a sense, all of these and none of these. The Zapatista rebellion is, for a start, simply incomprehensible outside of the context of the history of the Mexican Revolution. When an indigenous army marched in to take over San Cristóbal a las Casas in 1994 it immediately and automatically triggered an historical folk memory of Villa and Zapata's peasant armies marching into Mexico City in 1914. This points to the crucial role of discourse in constructing and understanding Zapatismo. As Adolfo Gilly puts it: 'The EZLN has inaugurated a debate about discourse, within discourse and through discourse' (Gilly 1998: 312). The mobilization of the Zapatistas and their construction as an international pole of attraction is, fundamentally, a discursive construction. Gilly refers to the Zapatistas as a 'singular combination of ancient myths, mobilized communities, clandestine army, *golpes de escena*, literary resources, and political initiatives' (Gilly 1998: 312). It is a unique and complex concatenation of social forces, ideas and political circumstances that produced Zapatismo. It is not a new transnational model for revolution in the era of globalization. The international communication of the Zapatista revolt is, however, the most significant single episode of global solidarity since the Spanish Civil War in the 1930s. For that to have occurred Zapatismo must have touched certain chords, in particular creating a general 'democratic equivalent' that served to create common ground for various diverse struggles against globalization. In this sense, Zapatismo is seeking neither to reconstruct a mythical past nor pursue a totally utopian future. Rather, Zapatismo has clearly articulated *Ya Basta!* (enough) to neoliberal globalization and its failure to create a modernization process characterized by social inclusion and basic human dignity.

After the party

If Seattle 1999 was the culmination of the first wave of anti-globalization protest what happened after the 'coming out party' as it has been called? In its immediate aftermath many observers spoke of the 'Seattle effect' whether hoping or fearing that the example set by the protestors at Seattle would spread far and wide. The *Financial Times* of London, not usually given to hyperbole, declared that:

> Protests now threaten to halt the global momentum of open markets and free capital, stopping the World Trade Organization's effort to launch a new trade round for a second time in Doha, Qatar, in November [2001]. The world's most powerful politicians are in retreat, withdrawing to remote spots such as Kananaskis in the Canadian Rockies for the next Group of Eight meeting.
>
> (Harding 2001: 2)

For the two years after the Battle of Seattle similar coalitions and similar protests were built and mounted in several Western countries. The first big 'anti-capitalist' event to follow Seattle was the April 2000 anti-IMF/World Bank meeting in Washington DC. While it was smaller than Seattle it was some ten times bigger than the 1998 demonstration against the same international economic institutions. In Millau (France) a gathering in June focused on the trial of local farmers for destroying a McDonald's outlet but it also served to generalize the anti-globalization Seattle wave across Western Europe. Another event in Prague in September 2000 targeting the IMF and World Bank in joint session brought the once-communist Eastern Europe into the sphere of influence of the 'Seattle effect'. After Seattle, as Jeffrey Ayres puts it: 'the contest over what "globalization meant" – between the struggle to convince a wider set of domestic and international audiences of the supposed benefits or downsides of neoliberalism – grew intense' (Ayres 2004: 22).

The protests in Québec City in April 2001 were not directed against the WTO or IMF/World Bank but, rather, the proposed Free Trade Area of the Americas (FTAA). Some 60,000 activists, including many trade unionists, were involved in what turned out to be the most significant protests since Seattle. The summit of heads of states was called to promote what was billed as the world's biggest free trade area running from Anchorage, Alaska to Tierra del Fuego. It was a lynchpin in the project to 'regionalize' global neoliberalism across the Americas and neutralize nationalist or regionalist tendencies in Latin America. Organized by the Réseau Québecois d'Intégration Contintentale and by Common Frontiers (Canada), a People's Summit of the Americas was to provide a blend of teach-ins, festivities and serious protest action. The state responded with a hitherto unprecedented security operation to insulate the heads of states from the people's carnival. Inevitably there were confrontations between security forces and protestors committed to 'direct action' which, as happened in Seattle, could actually halt proceedings. What is probably most significant about Québec 2001 was the extent to which it was 'made' internationally by the anti-globalization network. As André Drainville notes: 'For three days in April, Québec City was part of what Saskia Sassen calls the "world-wide grid of strategic places". Like other places in that grid, it was a contested terrain' (Drainville 2001: 33).

The next link in the anti-globalization chain of events occurred in Genoa in July 2001 against the rich nations' G8 summit meeting. Genoa represented a quantitative and qualitative shift in the pattern of anti-globalization protests. For one thing, over 300,000 people took part in the main protest events marking a high-point in terms of mass participation. Also, the types of participants and motives were broader than hitherto. Essentially Genoa was as much a protest about the right wing Berlusconi government as it was about global issues. The bridging between international and national dimensions was also demonstrated by the opening salvo of the protest that

was led by Genoa's immigrant communities in pursuit of freedom of movement. The Genoa Social Forum represented a critical bridge between the
global and the local. It brought together representatives of ATTAC (*Association pour le Tex Tobin pour l'Aide aux Citoyen* (Association for the Taxation
of Financial Transactions for the Benefit of Citizens)) with a 'reformist'
project to control international financial markets and those such as the
Network for Global Rights committed to more 'local' issues such as employment, immigration and the environment. While before the Genoa events
mobilizations in Italy had occurred through fairly ad hoc coordination, the
Genoa G8 protests initiated a pattern of local social forums forming to create
stable and locally 'grounded' formal political structures.

After the Siege of Genoa there was a period of introspection within the
anti-globalization movement. The death of a protestor at Genoa and the
wider repressive reaction of the Italian state brought the question of violence
and non-violence to the fore. Some such as the Black Bloc (which traced its
discourse back to the Italian *Autonomía Operaia* of the 1970s) asked why
protestors should limit their responses to a violent state. Others argued that:

> The very notion of 'militancy' is problematic. To pretend that it is more
> militant to mask up and throw cobblestones at police than it is to main-
> tain a peaceful blockade despite beatings, horse charges, and persistent
> attacks with pepper spray is deluded.
>
> (Notes from Nowhere 2003: 323)

The anti-globalization movement became less visible, the biggest rebellion
since 1968 seemed to be running out of steam. A not unsympathetic newspaper report asked 'was its brief stretch in the spotlight – two years after
surfacing in Seattle and to its apotheosis at Genoa – simply a passing fad,
and its youthful mainly middle-class army of protestors yesterday's children?'
(Bygrave 2002: 1).

In the US a number of organizations, such as the Anti-Capitalist
Convergence (ACC), Mobilization for Social Justice and others, were planning and organizing since the start of 2001 for a Seattle II in September in
Washington DC. As one report put it: 'A perfect storm of dissent was
brewing that involved organized labor, the anti-globalization movement,
anarchists, NGOs, anti-capitalists and the Latin America solidarity movement' (Munson 2004: 3). Then the attacks on the Twin Towers of New
York and on the Pentagon occurred on 11 September and these plans were
derailed. Subsequent US wars of aggression against Afghanistan (2002) and
Iraq (2003) led to a resurgence of a broad peace movement. And no one,
particularly in the imperialist heartland itself, was keen to mobilize in ways
that could be identified as 'pro-terrorist'. Some fevered imaginations even
conflated '9/11' and the anti-globalization movement.

As the 'easy' phase of globalization gave way to a new era of imperialist
wars, the anti-globalization movement began to disintegrate for a while but

then it also was reconfigured. Not least, this period saw the emergence of the largest pro-peace (and partly anti-imperialist) mobilizations ever. In early 2003 massive and coordinated street demonstrations across Europe protested against the war being prepared by the US and Britain. Millions of concerned citizens came together across the world against war and for a better society. Other tendencies were also at work forcing a reorganization of the anti-globalization movement. In the North a certain exhaustion and wariness had set in but in the South a new wave of anti-globalization protest was beginning. This, in part, led to the mobilization of large developing countries to block the Cancún WTO negotiations in 2003. And, from above as it were, the international economic organizations began to co-opt the anti-globalization protestors.

What happened in the US, according to Chuck Munson (an analyst activist), is that: 'The 9/11 attacks and the rise in patriotism and jingoism afterwards scared some activists into withdrawing from visible activism. Many core movement organizers were burned out from two and three years of organizing summit protests' (Munson 2004: 5). The 'internal' reasons pointing towards a certain exhaustion of this phase were several. Like most social movements, once the first successful mobilizing phase was over, divisions came to the fore. The issue of violence was divisive as was the target of the movement (capitalism?, globalization?, imperialism?, something else?). Above all, the travelling activist model involving young people going from one big summit demonstration to another had natural limits. For many early activists the time was coming to 'ground' the movement more in local communities and actually build an alternative future.

The other side of the coin was a decisive move by the international economic organizations themselves to co-opt the anti-globalization protests, or at least divert their energies. The World Bank had, since the mid-1990s, involved feminist and environmentalist activists and intellectuals in its work. After Seattle the other international economic organizations saw the benefit of co-opting the NGOs in particular. As the *World Economic Forum* magazine put it in 2003: 'At present one wing of the movement – mainstream NGOs – seeks to change the shape of globalization through open dialogue with governments, multi-lateral organizations and companies' (Hay 2003: 2). Communication was seen as more effective than confrontation. Again, this is an inherent tendency in social movements – the problem of success, as it were – that when it is effective in pursuing its aims some of these, or sections of the movement, will be 'mainstreamed'.

Clearly, if we take a global rather than a Northern perspective a post-'9/11' picture of exhaustion/co-option is not valid at all. Even the Battle of Seattle was set in the context of highly significant protests in many parts of the majority world. In Latin America in particular the year 2000 was marked by a series of diverse but convergent social struggles all focusing ultimately on neoliberal globalization. These were qualitatively different from the wave of anti-IMF protests in the 1980s in that clear and viable alternatives were being posed. This wave of contestation culminated in the World Social Forum held in the southern Brazilian city of Porto Alegre in January 2001 (see Chapter Five). The Forum was only partly a culmination of the 'Seattle effect' and its internationalization, because it was also a result of social and political struggles across Latin America, often nationalist in character and with a strong, more traditional anti-imperialist motivation.

When the WTO held its ministerial conference in Cancún, Mexico, in September 2003 it was the large countries of the South that would block progress on a trade deal rather than the protestors outside. A deal had seemed possible with the rich countries reducing agricultural protectionism and the South agreeing more lax foreign investment and competition regulation as well as trade 'facilitation'. In the event, led by Brazil (where President Lula of the Worker's Party was in power), the so-called Group of 22 including Argentina, India and South Africa came together to reject US pressure to sign up to a deal. While the collapse of talks in Cancún did not translate into immediate failure for the Doha round of trade negotiations the original 1 January 2005 deadline for completion was no longer possible.

Anti-capitalism?

Critical theorizing of the anti-globalization movement from Seattle 1999 to Genoa 2001 was inevitably going to be a contested terrain. One decisive and influential move in the discursive terrain came from those who believed it was (or should be) an 'anti-capitalist' movement. Globalize Resistance in particular began to redefine the rather inchoate anti-globalization movement emerging out of Seattle 1999 as an anti-capitalist one. It was as if the fall of the Berlin Wall a decade earlier and the collapse of 'actually existing socialism' were now behind us. After a decade-long hiatus the old working-class struggle against capitalism was back on course. Looking at the agenda of the anti-globalization movement Chris Harman declares that: 'There is no other choice if you really want to understand these things than to return to Marx' (Harman 2000: 25). The movement needed to forge an alliance with the organized working class, the only social force capable of challenging capitalism and providing an alternative.

Certainly in Britain the anti-capitalist perspective has taken root not least through the efforts of the party-building politics of the Socialist Workers Party (SWP) reflected in Globalize Resistance. Many young anti-globalization activists do also look towards the organized Marxist currents in the movement for analysis. The Marxist critique of capitalism is at least coherent and can explain how the corporations, the environment and world debt are inter-related for example. However, in seeking to impose the anti-capitalist frame through definitional *fiat* as it were, this interpretation suffers from various drawbacks. It is rather economistic in its 'classical' focus on production and it is a form of 'class essentialism' to privilege the working class as sole global agent for social transformation. Politically it is also rather disabling insofar as it has a patronizing attitude towards the 'infantile leftism' of the more anarchist currents and it is opportunistic towards the liberal currents that it uses as cover but does not grant any long-term viability to.

Within the broad reaches of the anti-globalization movement itself there was also a diffuse, but nonetheless real, feeling that anarchism was in the air once again as a political philosophy and guide to action. For Barbara Epstein it is more of an anarchist 'sensibility' than a fully fledged anarchist programme we are talking about. For the young activists of the anti-globalization movement anarchism is about a decentralized organizational structure (the famous 'affinity groups') and 'it also means egalitarianism; opposition to all hierarchies; suspicion of authority, especially that of the state; and commitment to living according to one's values' (Epstein 2001: 1). Taken in this broad libertarian anti-authoritarian sense, today's anarchism is closely related to the 'spirit of 1968'. The new social movements, the discovery of 'identity' and the rejection of authority of that period is being revived and reinvented by today's activists who, to some extent, see themselves as anarchists. For Epstein, 'anarchism is the dominant perspective within the [anti-globalization] movement' (Epstein 2001: 1). But it is a particular neo-anarchism which, for example, could describe the practical politics of those such as Naomi Klein among others with their emphasis on the movement as a 'swarm of mosquitoes'. It is an anarchism that takes on board much of the Marxist analysis of the nature of global capitalism and the anti-corporate movement's emphasis on consumerism. These are not Bakuninists or Proudhonists with clear ideological and programmatic commitments. There is not, for example, an absolute commitment to a leaderless movement whatever the rhetoric. What the anarchist current contributes is a great spirit of activism and a moral critique of globalization. The limits of anarchism today would lie mainly in the limitations of a strategy based on telling the truth to power.

Among the 'organic intellectuals' of the 'network of networks' such as Naomi Klein, for example, the anti-corporatist dimension of the movement was perhaps stressed most, to the extent that she refers to the 'anti-corporate movement' on the whole. The emphasis here is not on capitalism as a mode of production or imperialism as worldwide capitalist domination but, rather, on the multinational corporations themselves. Klein fully accepts 'the limits of brand-based politics' but argues that:

> eliminating the inequalities at the heart of free-market globalization seems a daunting task for most of us mortals. On the other hand, focusing on a Nike or a Shell and possibly changing the behaviour of one multinational can open an important door into this complicated and challenging political arena.
>
> (Klein 2002: 421)

Certainly, in the lead up to Seattle 1999 a major section of the organizers were part of the anti-corporate movement in the US.

Anti-corporate discourses have a long tradition in the US going back to Vance Packard's 1950s' classic *The Hidden Persuaders* (Packard 1957) through to David Korten's best-selling *When Corporations Rule the World* (Korten 1995). While this represents a certain home-grown US radicalism and provides a set of popular themes for the anti-globalization movement it is by no means a dominant strand. Noreen Hertz, for example, writes of how 'across the world corporations manipulate and pressure governments . . . and how corporations in many parts of the world are taking over from the state responsibility for everything' (Hertz 2001: back cover). This is very much along the lines of Polanyi's critique of commodification as the free market encroaches on the social domain. However, few anti-globalization movement activists would agree with Hertz's political conclusion that: 'My argument is not intended to be anti-capitalist. Capitalism is clearly the best system for generating wealth, and free trade and open capital markets have brought unprecedented economic growth to most if not all of the world' (Hertz 2001: 13). Even if this is a quite extreme contradiction between anti-globalization and not being anti-capitalist it does signal the ambiguity at the heart of the broad range of counter-globalization movements.

One could also make a case that the anti-globalization movement was the 'second coming' or the real internationalization of the 'cultural' revolt of 1968. First of all we need to recognize with Buttel and Gould that 'the anti-corporate globalization movement has not been formed *de novo*, but has drawn many of its adherents from the groups and networks associated with previous social movements' (Buttel and Gould 2004: 39). What happened after 1968 was an unprecedented (since 1848) transnational wave of con-testation. The traditional labour unions were revitalized and took up the new politics of demanding something more than just a pay cheque. The women's movement flourished across the West as a second feminist wave that has had a massive impact on gender relations still being felt today. The revolt of students, and youth more generally, was also a direct product of 1968. The ecology and peace movements would also see a 'take-off' period subsequent to 1968.

It is interesting that one of the first books to deal with the phenomenon of *Global Social Movements* (Cohen and Rai 2000) chose to focus on the labour, women's, environmental and human rights/peace movements, all 'children of 1968' in a manner of speaking. Like the rapid spread of revolutionary ideas after 1968 today's anti-globalization movement is clearly transnational, if not global, in reach. While most of the activists were not, of course, even born in 1968 many of the 'organic intellectuals' of the movement (for example in the World Social Forum) are clearly from the '68 generation. The confluence of an old and a new 'new left' is helping to create consid-erable advances in political creativity and relevance. As Hilary Wainwright puts it: 'Many of us '68-ers of various hues for too long took for granted what we considered to be a new left politics' (Wainwright 2002: 1). While many of the '1968' themes have been co-opted by the ideologies of the 'Third Way' and those who sing the joys of the 'network/knowledge society', many of the subversive themes of 1968 are being reborn and revitalized in the street protests of the new century.

I take on board elements of all four above interpretations but prefer to situate the overarching interpretation in terms of Polanyi's 'double movement' (see Chapter 2). The steady encroachment of free-market mechanisms into social relations – which lies at the core of neoliberal globalization – is matched by a social counter-movement that may be defensive, reactive or even alternativist. Global transformation since the 1990s has created the conditions for a great counter-movement of which the post-Seattle 'anti-globalization' movement is a key component. Neoliberal globalization has taken the market deep into society to undercut any obstacles to free trade, be they environmental protection measures, state subsidies of any kind or labour codes. What brought together the various components of the Seattle protest – environmentalists, trade unionists, anti-corporate activists and others – was precisely a confluence of interests around opposition to the free market globalization.

While the double movement thesis may be effective at the structural level of analysis, we need to understand at a discursive political level why the anti-globalization movement made the impact it has. As Jeffrey Ayres puts it: 'Activists by the late 1990s successfully developed a contentious, increasingly transnationally accepted master collective action frame to challenge the prevailing neoliberal orthodoxy' (Ayres 2004: 14). Previously there had been campaigns around discrete elements or effects of neoliberal organization, be it trade, debt, labour, environmental or human rights. However, what happened towards the end of the 1990s was a crystallization of these various movements and campaigns around a shared diagnosis that neoliberal globalization (as promoted by the WTO/IMF/World Bank) was the common source of the particular issue they dealt with. That Seattle 1999 occurred in the US made it particularly visible and promoted the elevation of globalization to the position of master frame for many forms of contestation.

I have retained the 'anti-globalization' label in this chapter for a number of reasons. For one, it seems a more accurate label for the post-Seattle movement in the streets than anti-capitalist, anti-corporate or anarchist. Of course, many of the protestors would argue that they do not oppose globalization per se, they just want a better globalization. So we can think in terms of a counter- or alter-globalization movement. However, for many activists there is a strong direct action element that is simply anti-system without too many nuances. Most activists do probably want to see the end of the WTO/IMF/World Bank rather than to work within to reform them. But there is another reason to use this label for this particular section of the movement of movements we have been dealing with, namely to characterize the mainly young, urban, educated, Western activists who became travelling protestors from Seattle to Washington, Prague to Genoa, etc.

In conclusion we might agree with Jackie Smith that:

> The Battle of Seattle is one of the most significant recent episodes of collective action, and it points to a future of social movements that is increasingly global in both target and form and that finds itself in more direct confrontation with global institutions than its historical predecessors.
>
> (Smith 2002: 223)

The global had emerged as a real terrain for contestation, it was no longer virtual or confined to the carefully orchestrated realm of inter-state relations. Whether this movement has peaked or not is a matter for time to tell. Given the extraordinary difficulties faced by any incipient transnational social movements, its achievements have been considerable. Very few analysts or people in power still talk about globalization without referring to the anti-globalization movement as the other side of the coin. These two are probably mutually constitutive of each other from now on.

5   Transnational political fora

Actors, issues and prospects

Transnational political organization in pursuit of a progressive human goal is not particularly new even if the era of globalization has, arguably, witnessed a flourishing of such political fora. The notion of universal human rights was an integral element of the European Enlightenment tradition and it was, by definition, transnational. Women's rights and the contemporary international women's movement are inherently transnational too and, for many observers, a very successful example of a global social movement. Finally, we consider in this chapter the World Social Forum experience as the defining transnational political forum of the counter-globalization movement. But, in considering these three transnational political processes we need to reflect back on the notion of 'global civil society' (see Chapter 4). To what extent are we witnessing 'ghosts in the machine' of globalization that distract attention from more grounded and challenging movements of resistance from below?

The case studies in this chapter go to the core of the issue of global governance (see Chapter 1). INGOs and social movements have effectively engaged with the multilateral economic organizations that lead and co-ordinate the globalization project. Human rights in general, and women's rights in particular, are now an integral element of that project, at least rhetorically. So are they still elements of contestation of the dominant order? The World Social Forum is not yet in that position but it is also now becoming 'mainstreamed' and is no longer a merely 'alternative' presence. An underlying issue to also consider in this chapter is whether the humanist universalism implicit in all three movements is adequate to deal with diversity, multiculturalism and the rise of non-Western civilizational projects.

Universal human rights

The concept of 'human rights', whether based on religious or ethical principles, appeals to a transcendent principle that can, ultimately, only apply universally. Human beings are deemed to have universal rights regardless of where they live, their ethnicity, gender or any other particularizing factor. Universal human rights are also deemed to be inalienable, that is to say they cannot be granted or withdrawn, and they are non-derogable. Thus, we all have a right to life, to be free from slavery, to be free from torture and so on. While it has, traditionally, been part of the Western political tradition, 'universal human rights' has become much more internationalized since the rise of contemporary globalization towards the end of the twentieth century. Global social movements have, not surprisingly, emerged, promoting the concept of universal human rights in relation to women, workers and the politically persecuted, for example.

Historically, human rights were not only part of a Western political tradition but they were also based squarely on the nation-state for their protection and enforcement. Universal claims to human dignity needed an agency to ensure they were respected and that was the national government. These are 'positive' human rights in the European legal tradition such as the right to education and to equality before the law. The Anglo-American legal tradition, in contrast, dictated what the state should *not* do. The 'negative' human rights of the British and US Bill of Rights included, for example, freedom of speech and of assembly. In the post-war period a more globalizing approach emerged with the Universal Declaration of Human Rights (1948) approved by the UN (with 56 member states at the time), describing in 30 articles an extremely broad and comprehensive set of human rights deemed universal. With the collapse of the state socialist alternative in 1989 it appeared this Western tradition had become universal.

However, the UN, at the end of the twentieth century, had 191 member states, while the original 30 white Western states still numbered only 30. At the 1993 World Conference on Human Rights a number of Asian member states argued that human rights were not universal but rather a product of Western industrial cultures. The West has often been accused of using human rights as a rhetoric that allows them to impose their particular world-view and material interests over the majority, or so-called developing world. In the decade and a half since these views were articulated there has been ample evidence that human rights can serve as an ideological spearhead of a Western or US imperialist crusade against political systems in the East and the South which it would remove as competitors or subjugate. The violation of human rights in Iraq by the invasion forces of the US and UK is but the most visible example.

The question we need to ask then is why the concept of human rights has been such an integral element of the new global social movements when they appear to be part of a Western imperialist tradition. In spite of the post-modern critique of human rights as metanarrative and the inherent forms of essentialism that lie at its core, certain defining political moments do seem to capture the original Enlightenment idea of universality. It might be the campaign to free Nelson Mandela from his apartheid jail, stop the execution of Ken Saro-Wiwa in Nigeria or highlight the plight of Aung San So Kyi in Burma. For Baxi, a fierce critic of human rights essentialism and the false universality of its discourse, nevertheless the latter:

embodies human rights *essentialism*; so do the Afghan women under dire straits who protest the Taliban regime. So also do UNICEF and the Save the Children movements, which (thanks to the globalized media) seek at times to achieve the impossible.

(Baxi 2003: 86)

Human rights activism – mainly organized through NGOs – has success-fully put together transnational coalitions of considerable effectiveness. There are, of course, a plethora of human rights oriented NGOs and there are many internal conflicts in the human rights field. Nevertheless, many of these campaigns have practically *created* new human rights such as those around sexual orientation. The communications revolution has been instru-mental in facilitating transnational dialogue on human rights, and it has helped create the conditions for effective campaigns through the mass media. The 'connectedness' that is an integral element of globalization has allowed NGOs, in particular, to access and impact on the international human rights regime. While blatant flouting of basic human rights occurs constantly – with Abu Ghraib and Guantánamo just providing highlights – there is now a generalized transnational discourse transgressors must confront.

While globalization has, indeed, presented opportunities for social movements campaigning around human rights, it has also presented new challenges. As Alyson Brysk puts it, beyond the emergence of an inter-national regime for human rights and its positive aspects, '*new* human rights problems may result from the integration of markets, the shrinking of states, increased transnational flows such as migration, the spread of cultures of intolerance, and the decision-making processes of new or growing global institutions' (Brysk 2000: 2). So, while a weaker nation-state may seem an advantage in the short term to a contestatory movement it does, at the same time, remove the sovereign power that could be made accountable for human rights. The new transnational managers of globalization – such as the WTO – are, for their part, notoriously unaccountable for decisions they take that may impact fundamentally on human rights.

During the cold war the state socialist countries and those in what was then called the 'Third World' actively challenged the Western concep-tion of human rights. Against the liberal view of individual rights and the 'freedoms' bestowed by private property, they articulated the rights to devel-opment and self-determination. The right to control a country's natural resources versus the rights of a multinational corporation to exploit them were very different ways of viewing rights, for example. Since the end of the cold war and the rise of contemporary globalization in the 1990s the Western *idea* of human rights has ruled supreme, except in relation to cultural relativism. Thus, the radical universalism of hegemonic liberal human rights theory can be countered by a radical relativism that conceives of human rights as determined by their particular cultural setting. Even milder versions of relativism that simply take into account the cultural context may serve to undermine the cultural imperialism underlying the doctrine of universal human rights as presently articulated in the West.

So, as is true with the overall relationship between globalization and democracy, so also with human rights: while some doors are opened through the creation of a new global order, other doors are closed. Overall, we must note that human rights are no longer tied exclusively to national sovereignty. These rights can cross national borders and Chilean ex-dictator General Pinochet can be arrested and charged in London for human rights violations in Chile. We thus witness growing levels of transnational accountability on the terrain of human rights. This has given a considerable boost to transnational human rights activism which can gain real results when 'swimming with the current' of the dominant world order and, even, sometimes when they go against the tide.

Global social movements based on the concept of universal human rights – such as Amnesty International – tend not to problematize the notion. Thus Amnesty International argues that:

> One answer to growing 'anti-globalization' sentiment is to make respect of human rights, of the rule of law, of good governance and transparency, of freedom for the people, as essential an element of the new architecture of globalization, as the free movement of capital, currencies and commodities; to convince citizens . . . that *the agents of globalization can also be the agents of the globalization of human rights*.
> (Amnesty International 2004: 1, emphasis added)

For Amnesty International, the commitment to the realization of 'all human rights for all' must include 'reaffirming the universality and indivisibility of human rights' (ibid.). We could argue that Amnesty is taking liberal democratic rhetoric at its word and demanding that human rights are, in practice, applied to all peoples. Yet, is this move to make rhetoric into reality sufficient reason to accept the universality of human rights as a valid principle for democratization of a global order based on unregulated market expansion?

It may be useful to start answering this question in terms of Upendra Baxi's distinction between a politics *for* human rights and a politics *of* human rights (see Baxi 2003). The contemporary politics for human rights of organizations such as Amnesty and countless local, national and transnational movements seeks to make power accountable to the people and for governance to be just. By contrast, for Baxi:

> The politics *of* human rights deploys the symbolic or cultural capital of human rights to the ends of management of distribution of power in national and global arenas. 'Human rights' become the pursuit of politics, and even war by other means.
> (Baxi 2003: 41)

We could perhaps argue that if politics is the pursuit of war by other means as classically put by Clausewitz, so then, today, human rights form the terrain on which the battle for democracy in the era of globalization will be played out. From this perspective the rhetoric of liberal cosmopolitanism and the doctrine of 'humanitarian war' would not be seen as part of the democratic path of human development.

Human rights can thus be seen as a 'floating signifier' capable of very different, even opposed articulations in political practice. That does not mean at all that human rights are somehow neutral, standing above politics as some practitioners argue. Rather, it is a question of human rights being seen as a contested discursive terrain. On the one hand, the silent oppression and abuses committed against landless peasants, poor women or political activists across the world can be exposed through transnational advocacy groups. However, on the other hand, and just as frequently, an imperialist discourse of human rights can be deployed to de-legitimize governments of the South and even engage in 'regime change' when that suits the imperialist agenda.

Another fundamental problem in articulating a progressive politics of human rights in the era of globalization is the issue of prioritization. Contrary to the rhetoric of universal and indivisible human rights, in practice, between and within campaigns there is often a fierce struggle over the prioritization of rights to the extent that many perceive there to be a hierarchy of human rights. What is a 'fundamental' right and what is not? What happens if different human rights are at odds with each other, for example the 'rights' of private property versus the 'right' of life? We must recognize that human rights campaigns are socially, politically and discursively constructed and are not pre-given. The visibility of various human rights abuses does not, as Clifford Bob puts it, 'result from a rough meritocracy of suffering in which the worst abuses attract the greatest attention' (Bob 2002: 133) but, rather, from political processes and struggles.

Global sisterhood

In 1984 the radical US feminist Robin Morgan published *Sisterhood is Global: The International Women's Movement Anthology* (1984) which represented an early manifestation of the belief that women shared a common identity and had the same interests wherever they lived. However, Morgan's book came in for fierce criticism from Third World women and US 'women of color' alike. Essentially the argument centred around the Euro-US centricity of the collection and the homogenizing vision of women's oppression that it created. Even the notion of a unified category of 'Third World women' was seen as problematic (see Mohanty 1991) insofar as it assumed a unity of condition and consciousness that simply did not exist. The underlying issue today, the same as it was 20 years ago, is whether the diversity of women's lives across the world allows for the creation of a transnational movement for 'global sisterhood'.

The issue is whether globalization – in the sense of greater socio-economic integration and communication across nations – is recreating more fertile conditions for transnational feminist activism. For Angela Miles this process of convergence has, indeed, led to a new consensus:

> Global feminisms hold the seeds of the world they want to create. Their response to alienated and exploitative globalization is not simple withdrawal, refusal, or reaction but the creation of autonomous, democratic and empowering global relations in the struggle for alternative visions.
>
> (Miles 1996: 133)

A new transformative global understanding of the complex forms of gender oppression and resistance is emerging. To the equality agenda was added an understanding of diversity. Above all, the new wave of international feminisms in the 1990s began to articulate an alternative vision of society enriched by an understanding of women's diverse patterns of oppression and resistance across the world.

Western liberal feminists in the 1970s and 1980s had, as a major focus of their intervention, gaining influence on mainstream political decision-making bodies. The women's agenda would be advanced through assertion of women's equal rights in the formal political arena. While many gains were made in various Western parliamentary arenas, a drive towards influencing the UN was soon to become a major focus. The pressure of Western second-wave feminism had already made an impact when the UN declared 1975 to be the International Year of Women, followed by the UN Decade for Women from 1975–85. While national governments would still have an onus to address women's issues, the UN would provide an overarching international framework supported by an active network of women's NGOs. As globalization became the dominant development discourse in the 1990s, so inevitably the UN's Fourth World Conference on Women in 1995 became a major site for debate, and a landmark event.

The long preparatory work for the 1995 Beijing Conference on Women finally came to fruition and an NGO forum was also held in Huairou on the margins of the official event. For Sonia Alvarez, women of the forum:

> appeared to revel in an effusive celebration of post-Robin Morgan 'global sisterhood'. A festive climate of mutual recognition, exchange and solidarity . . . prevailed . . . among many forum participants, who not only had encountered a planetary venue in which to call attention to the needs of women in their own countries but also had discovered their commonalities and differences with women's struggles around the world.
>
> (Alvarez 1998: 293)

Meanwhile in the 'official' UN event another group of women academics, activists and legislators engaged in an ambitious and privileged agenda-setting exercise for the global women's movement in the twenty-first century. Feminism had 'gone global' with a vengeance.

With the UN now officially committed to a progressive agenda on women's rights, did this mean the feminist agenda could be developed 'from above' as it were? What the feminist international lobby has achieved is the legitimacy of an international women's regime, understood as a set of principles, rules and decision-making procedures agreed to by states in a given area of international relations (Evans 2000: 126). This regime, like the global human rights regime, is centred around the 'United Nations family', itself based on the principle of national sovereignty. National NGOs and social movements can thus appeal to the international gender norms to advocate for local policy reform in relation to gender. As one Chilean feminist activist put it: 'globalization requires that the State demonstrate sensitivity to gender . . . resources come tied to that' (cited Alvarez 2000: 14). While effective in its own terms this approach is not without its critics.

Can the NGOs who operate in terms of the international gender regime not be accused of becoming a gender technocracy or, even, as some autonomist feminists put it: 'handmaidens of neoliberalism'? Even without going that far, there are many feminist activists who believe that: 'the movement cannot think beyond the UN and its institutions' (Toro 2004: 2). It is not at all uncommon for feminist activists to ask whether the UN conferences since Beijing have actually benefited women at all. These UN fora are, after all, set up on the basis of national sovereignty, and right wing national governments, including, in the front line, the Vatican, can attend and roll back the gains made for the gender agenda at previous meetings. Yet, rather than become confrontational many women in the NGO/social movement (and the dividing line between the two is often hard to draw) milieu do not wish to lose the positions they have gained within the UN constellation.

Perhaps an underlying question in this tension between a new international regime and *realpolitik* is, in fact, the national question. Many feminists in the global arena would probably subscribe to the statement by the novelist Virginia Woolf in 1936 that: 'As a woman I have no country. As a woman I want no country. As a woman my country is the whole world' (Woolf 1936, cited in Kaplan 1994). This cosmopolitan world vision is certainly worthy but it may also elide certain obvious and overarching power differentials. Lacking a clear politics of location this type of essentialism will elide the differences that stand in the way of a unitary world of women. As Caren Kaplan puts it: 'In a trans-national world where cultural asymmetrics and linkages continue to be mystified by economic and political interests at multiple levels, feminists need detailed, historicized maps of the circuits of power' (Kaplan 1994: 148). Without that understanding of the complex power geometry of gender relations in the era of globalization, a cosmopolitan feminism will, necessarily, not be able to meet the needs of women worldwide.

But if the United Nations could at best deliver a 'false universalism' on the question of women's rights, would the rapidly developing NGO movement be better placed to develop that agenda? As the voice of 'global civil society' would they be able to articulate globalization from below in relation to women's empowerment? We need to consider what Alvarez called the 'NGO-ization' of Latin Americanism in the 1990s to be able to answer these questions. For Alvarez, 'the growing "developmentalization" of women as new "client groups" of states and international regimes ... contributed to NGO-ization by infusing the more professionalized sectors of the feminist movement filled with significant material resources' (Alvarez 1998: 306). So, while the more acceptable aspects of the feminist agenda were absorbed by powerful international political organizations, many of the more 'professionalized' sections of the women's movement were also, themselves, absorbed if not co-opted.

For the autonomous feminist currents the above process of co-option is a simple one-way street. They accuse the 'institutional current' (as they call the NGO sector that engages with the international gender regime) of becoming simply 'decorative and functional complements of patriarchal policies' (Mujeres Creando, cited by Alvarez 2000: 28). There is a clear divide posed between all 'autonomous' feminist social movements and the NGO-dominated, more institutionalized 'technocratic' sector. In practice, the dividing lines are not so clear cut and many activists intervene in the institutional arena without being compromised in some essentialist political sense. There is no 'iron law of oligarchy' as was posited for the early trade union and socialist movement implying an automatic conservatism and corrupting influence from participating in mainstream society.

In fact, the 'mainstreaming' of gender policies in the 1990s into organizations such as the World Bank can be viewed in a much more positive, even empowering sense for the advancement of women's rights. DAWN (Development Alternatives with Women for a New Era), a global South oriented women's network focused on gender equity and sustainable development, notes that 'Post Beijing [they] have been active in inter-linking with social movements and male-led NGOs in what we refer to as negotiating gender in the male-stream' (cited in Mayo 2004: 144). This process of negotiation might at times be very fraught and it may not always produce results. But, in practice, the autonomous space is extremely limited and most women's movements do engage with the main/male-stream in a continuous process of confrontation, compromise and concessions.

While much of the above analysis has a rather sceptical tone to it, we should not neglect the very real advances made in relation to global women's rights over the last decade. Manuel Castells, perhaps, overstates the gains with his thesis of 'the end of patriarchy' but he does at least draw attention to 'the inseparably related processes of the transformation of women's work and the transformation of women's consciousness' (Castells 2004: 193) in the era of globalization. The economic internationalization that is at the heart of globalization has led to a dramatic increase in the number of women entering the paid labour force to such an extent that the concept of the 'male breadwinner' is but a dim and distant memory. On the other hand, all the varieties of feminism from liberal to lesbian, from essentialist to 'practical' feminist, all agree that patriarchy must go, a politics reflected in widespread popular acceptance of women's equality in most countries.

Finally though, we might stress with Angela Miles that: 'Only a very small proportion of feminists are active globally. Increasingly widespread local feminist practice sustains the global feminist presence, however, and is enriched by it' (Miles 1996: 116). It is not thus a question of prioritizing the global or local level of intervention but of understanding the complex interaction between the two. Beijing 1995 represented a 'global' manifestation of many thousands of local, national and regional women's movements and NGOs. This is a grounded universal and not a spectral presence with no body behind it. Conversely, the international feminist networks have had a greatly empowering effect on local level organization, mobilization and 'conscientization'. Transnational feminist practices have thus involved a quite self-conscious politics of location.

World Social Forum

The World Economic Forum had become, in the 1990s, the leading 'think tank' for the leaders of the globalization process. However, in January 1999 its Davos meeting met a counter-demonstration involving, among others, a French organization ATTAC and the MST (*Movimiento Sêm Terra*), the landless people's movement in Brazil. This was the start of the movement to create a 'parallel summit' to the hidden, elitist and technocratic managers of globalization symbolized by Davos where they got together with their own 'organic intellectuals'. The Seattle events of 1999 showed that the power of the supranational decision-making bodies was not omnipotent. Parallel summits could confront directly and in a very visible manner the architects of the new globalization and articulate the programme or project of the emerging 'global civil society'.

The French political monthly *Le Monde Diplomatique* was the seemingly unlikely progenitor of ATTAC. Its driving force, Bernard Cassen, describes how the *Diplo* (as it was known) had published an editorial in 1997 entitled 'Disarming the Markets' that ended with a call for action to control the tyranny of the financial markets: 'The appeal was launched like a bottle into the sea, without any idea of what the reaction might be' (Cassen 2003: 41). In the event, ATTAC was formed and grew to 30,000 members as well as semi-autonomous branches in Scandinavia, Germany, Italy and elsewhere who all saw themselves as loosely part of a 'no-globo' movement. ATTAC is probably known best for its meticulously researched analysis of globalization and neoliberalism, shifting public opinion firmly away from '*la pensée unique*' (one way of thinking) on economic policy. In France it effectively 'mainstreamed' the critique of neoliberal globalization and in international terms it played an important role in generating the World Social Forum (WSF).

The other proximate cause of the WSF experience lay in Brazil as part of and following the re-democratization of that country in the second half of the 1980s. The social revolt against state authoritarianism was led by the workers' movement, but it also created the conditions for a flourishing of the NGOs, many influenced by the radical sections of the Catholic Church. In organizational terms this movement coalesced in the formation of the Workers' Party (*Partido dos Trabalhadores* – PT) in 1980 which soon began to make significant gains in elections, not least in the southern city of Porto Alegre. The Porto Alegre 'participative budget', developed under a PT governorship, became known worldwide (see Bruce 2004) and thus made the city a logical choice for hosting the WSF when the Brazilian NGOs – along with the MST, the landless peasants movement – met with Bernard Cassen and ATTAC and agreed to organize a counter-summit to that in Davos.

The First World Social Forum took place in Porto Alegre in 2001 as an explicit counter to the World Economic Forum taking place at the same time in Davos. While this event had vague precursors in Bandung 1955 and the 1968 counter-movement, it was new in many ways. The Workers' Party in Porto Alegre was understandably nervous that it might be outflanked on the left by this gathering. Many of the more traditional labour organizations were also reticent to support a movement with such a strong counter-cultural flavour. But the event was a huge success and symbolically put an end to the international retreat of the left already slowed down in Seattle in 1999. As Bernard Cassen described WSF 1, 'in purely geographical terms its range was limited. But in media terms, its impact was enormous, because it coincided with the meeting of global elites in Davos' (Cassen 2003: 49). In the new globalized media-dominated times of the new century, this media visibility of the counter-movement was crucial.

Following the largely unexpected success of the first World Social Forum, the Brazilian Organizing Committee sought to draw out the lessons and articulate a Charter of Principles. This foundational document was subsequently debated at some length across the world and is worth quoting in full:

1 The World Social Forum is an open meeting place for reflective thinking, democratic debate of ideas, formulation of proposals, free exchange of experiences and interlinking for effective action, by groups and movements of civil society that are opposed to neoliberalism and to domination of the world by capital and any form of imperialism, and are committed to building a planetary society directed towards fruitful relationships among Humankind and between it and the Earth.

2 The World Social Forum at Porto Alegre was an event localized in

time and place. From now on, in the certainty proclaimed at Porto Alegre that 'another world is possible', it becomes a permanent process of seeking and building alternatives, which cannot be reduced to the events supporting it.

3   The World Social Forum is a world process. All the meetings that are held as part of this process have an international dimension.

4   The alternatives proposed at the World Social Forum stand in opposition to a process of globalization commanded by the large multinational corporations and by the governments and international institutions at the service of those corporations' interests, with the complicity of national governments. They are designed to ensure that globalization in solidarity will prevail as a new stage in world history. This will respect universal human rights, and those of all citizens – men and women – of all nations and the environment and will rest on democratic international systems and institutions at the service of social justice, equality and the sovereignty of peoples.

5   The World Social Forum brings together and interlinks only organizations and movements of civil society from all the countries in the world, but intends neither to be a body representing civil society.

6   The meetings of the World Social Forum do not deliberate on behalf of the World Social Forum as a body. No-one, therefore, will be authorized, on behalf of any of the editions of the Forum, to express positions claiming to be those of all its participants. The participants in the Forum shall not be called on to take decisions as a body, whether by vote or acclamation, on declarations or proposals for action that would commit all, or the majority, of them and that propose to be taken as establishing positions of the Forum as a body. It thus does not constitute a locus of power to be disputed by the participants in its meetings, nor does it intend to constitute the only option for interrelation and action by the organizations and movements that participate in it.

7   Nonetheless, organizations or groups of organizations that participate in the Forum's meetings must be assured the right, during such meetings, to deliberate on declarations or actions they may decide on, whether singly or in coordination with other participants. The World Social Forum undertakes to circulate such decisions widely by the means at its disposal, without directing, hierarchizing, censuring or restricting them, but as deliberations of the organizations or groups of organizations that made the decisions.

8   The World Social Forum is a plural, diversified, non-confessional, non-governmental and non-party context that, in a decentralized fashion, interrelates organizations and movements engaged in concrete action at levels from the local to the international to build another world.

9 The World Social Forum will always be a forum open to pluralism and to the diversity of activities and ways of engaging of the organizations and movements that decide to participate in it, as well as the diversity of genders, ethnicities, cultures, generations and physical capacities, providing they abide by this Charter of Principles. Neither party representations nor military organizations shall participate in the Forum. Government leaders and members of legislatures who accept the commitments of this Charter may be invited to participate in a personal capacity.

10 The World Social Forum is opposed to all totalitarian and reductionist views of economy, development and history and to the use of violence as a means of social control by the State. It upholds respect for Human Rights, the practices of real democracy, participatory democracy, peaceful relations, in equality and solidarity, among people, ethnicities, genders and peoples and condemns all forms of domination and all subjection of one person by another.

11 As a forum for debate, the World Social Forum is a movement of ideas that prompts reflection, and the transparent circulation of the results of that reflection, on the mechanisms and instruments of domination by capital, on means and actions to resist and overcome that domination, and on the alternatives proposed to solve the problems of exclusion and social inequality that the process of capitalist globalization with its racist, sexist and environmentally destructive dimensions is creating internationally and within countries.

12 As a framework for the exchange of experiences, the World Social Forum encourages understanding and mutual recognition among its participant organizations and movements, and places special value on the exchange among them, particularly on all that society is building to centre economic activity and political action on meeting the needs of people and respecting nature, in the present and for future generations.

13 As a context for interrelations, the World Social Forum seeks to strengthen and create new national and international links among organizations and movements of society, that – in both public and private life – will increase the capacity for non-violent social resistance to the process of dehumanization the world is undergoing and to the violence used by the State, and reinforce the humanizing measures being taken by the action of these movements and organizations.

14 The World Social Forum is a process that encourages its participant organizations and movements to situate their actions, from the local level to the national level and seeking active participation in international contexts, as issues of planetary citizenship, and to introduce onto the global agenda the change-inducing practices that they are experimenting in building a new world in solidarity.

Approved and adopted in São Paulo, on 9 April 2001, by the organizations that make up the World Social Forum Organizing Committee, approved with modifications by the World Social Forum International Council on 10 June 2001.

The Second World Social Forum was held in 2002, again in Porto Alegre but now focused on giving meaning to the emergent slogan of 'Another World is Possible'. The WSF concept was beginning to 'internationalize', at least in part due to the initiatives of the large Italian contingent who attended WSF 1. The Genoa counter-summit to the G8 in 2001 was thus dubbed a 'social forum'. In Durban, in protest against the limits of the World Conference Against Racism also in 2001 another 'social forum' was created. In Latin America there were a series of regional 'social forums', most noticeably in Argentina, then in the midst of a cataclysmic crisis due to a mechanical application of neoliberal economics for over a decade. Some 60,000 people attended WSF 2 conference compared with the 20,000 who were attracted to the first event. But the social forum concept, principles and particular mode of organization began to spread to most parts of the world, with the exception of Asia.

The Third World Social Forum in 2003 took up the theme of how the WSF might itself actually embody the principles of 'another world'. The 100,000 or more participants who attended the forum this time included many 'mainstream' political and social leaders attracted by the WSF 'brand'. The US anti-globalization movement, quite insignificant at the previous events, was also now making its presence felt. Some of the more radical anti-globalization participants began to feel somewhat isolated. Was the WSF moving from the 'alternative' end of the political spectrum towards becoming the 'mainstream'? Certainly there was a noticeable re-emergence of the 'old' new left of 1968 in leadership positions and in the WSF general discourse. Peter Waterman, at the event from a critical pro-labour stance, argued that 'there is a danger that the Forum will be overwhelmed by the past of social movements and internationalism' (Waterman 2003: 7). Nationalist reactions to globalization were certainly much in evidence and many components of WSF were quite state-oriented. A new model of inter-nationalism was certainly not going to be born fully formed overnight.

Addressing the relative lack of the WSF phenomena in Africa (except for South Africa) and in the vast expanse of Asia, the fourth WSF was held in Mumbai (India) in 2004. According to one observer: 'Beyond the success of the Indian organizational process, Mumbai demonstrated the flexibility of the WSF's identity, which enables it to adapt to local social and polit-ical contexts without losing its energy' (Caruso 2005: 205). This might be a slightly self-congratulatory view insofar as Mumbai was often dominated by the large organizations whether of civil society or politics of an older, more traditional left. One of the organizers of the Mumbai event, Jai Sen, had already warned of the dangers of 'giganticism' or what might be called

the problems of success (Sen 2004: 3). The WSF as 'big event' was beginning to make it look like a 1960s' Woodstock Festival with most of the
audience being fairly passive 'hearers' or 'observers' of the 'big names' who
now felt compelled to attend the WSF.

Following the Mumbai WSF a decision was made to return to Porto
Alegre in 2005 but then to make the 2006 WSF a decentralized affair with
events in Africa, Asia and Latin America. The issue of 'giganticism' and the
dominance of 'big names' had already been tackled by reducing the number
of plenaries at Mumbai. After that event, as Hilary Wainwright explains,
'the International Committee of the WSF took the risky decision to elimi-
nate the official programme altogether' (Wainwright 2005: 3). Henceforth,
a *'consulta'* (consultation) with past WSF attendees would lead to a choice
of themes which would constitute the clusters or 'terrains' for debates. This
radical experiment was at least partially successful at the 2005 WSF event
in Porto Alegre, articulating a more purposeful and self-conscious movement for social transformation. The problems of growing size were still,
however, present and it was significant that Venezuela's Hugo Chávez proved
the biggest draw for audiences.

As befits a social movement organization committed to radical transfor-
mation of the existing order, the WSF has been extremely reflexive in regards
to its own experience. Thus, Michael Albert, an active US promoter of the
WSF, would write in the run-up to Mumbai that: 'The worldwide Social
Forum phenomenon is thriving. In contrast, the WSF once-a-year international event has run up against internal limits and needs renovation'
(Albert 2004: 323). That process of renewal could only come, according to
Albert, by rejecting the notion that WSF could become a 'movement of
movements' and, rather, become a venue or facilitator for more local events.
Then, founding WSF member, Chico Whitaker, from one of Brazil's main
NGOs put forward the stark choice of 'Forum-as-space and a Forum-as-
movements' (Whitaker 2004: 111), coming down firmly on the side of a
horizontal space with no leaders. Only by becoming an open space could
the WSF ensure respect for diversity, something he did not see as possible
in a movement. Others posed the choice as one between WSF as 'arena' or
as 'actor' that is perhaps simply a different way of posing that dilemma. In
practice, of course, the WSF could be an arena and actor at the same time.

The myriad attempts to discern what the WSF is or is not, have been
unable to come to a clear-cut conclusion, something that may well be
inevitable given that the movement is still developing. More or less at
random we can examine differing views or definitions of the World Social
Forum:

> the WSF is not the embryonic framework of a new political force but
> rather the catalyst for the variety of assembled collectivities building
> the links between themselves.
>
> (Wainwright 2005: 4)

the WSF is not an entity, but a process – a snowballing momentum that is bringing together forces which, through developing in the same direction, were without mutual contact and often completely unaware of each other.

(Cassen 2003: 59)

the WSF will increasingly become less and less an event or set of events, and increasingly a process based on the work of articulation, reflection and combined planning of collective actions . . .

(Santos 2004a: 30)

So, the WSF is not likely to become the Fifth International, following in the footsteps of the social democratic Second, communist Third and Trotskyist Fourth Internationals. It may, however, reflect some of the characteristics of the First International as envisaged by Marx as a transnational network. It is more of a social process than a social organization and, at most, a catalyst for mobilizations against globalization. While it may preach that 'another world is possible' it is unlikely to gather the forces to make that happen, something that had been the aspiration of the Third International in the heyday of international communism. But, however cautious we must be in assessing the WSF as an agent of global counter-hegemony we might consider the verdict of Glasius and Timms that: 'The national and local social forums can be seen as one of the most significant developments to have come out of the idea of the WSF' (Glasius and Timms 2005: 207) as a suitable conclusion to this section.

Ghosts in the machine

Human rights and women's rights would probably appear to most readers as obvious human goods and their pursuit a generally progressive endeavour, all things considered. We have already seen what achievements NGOs and social movements promoting these rights have been able to accomplish. The World Social Forum, in articulating the simple yet effective slogan that *Another World is Possible*, is also seen by (nearly) all as a progressive antidote to neoliberal globalization and its project for the world we live in. However, we need to reflect critically on the possibility that these reform movements are operating in the terrain of, and replicating the terms of, the neoliberal governance agenda. This is saying much more than the obvious danger of contestatory movements being co-opted by the powers that be. Nor is it a simplistic repeat of the reform versus revolution argument that bedevilled the early socialist/communist movement in nineteenth-century Europe.

In an interesting analysis, André Drainville refers to the 'cosmopolitan ghosts' that are emerging in the field of global civil society, 'created by simultaneously pulverizing humanity into functional bits and reassembling it into an abstract bearer of rights, responsibilities and moralities' (Drainville

2004: 22). From this perspective, 'global civil society' is a political construction that serves to decontextualize real social struggles on the ground. This is a 'politically neutered humanity' (Drainville 2004: 22) taken out of its real, concrete social and cultural context and reconstructed in the language of the UN and the NGOs. Third World women, indigenous peoples, informal sector workers, are all real but take on a spectral character in the international corridors of power as this or that NGO or social movement seeks to (re)present them to the rulers of the world on a social stabilization mission.

To what extent is the new 'civic cosmopolitanism' put forward as an ethical global politics by David Held and others as part of the 'global civil society' project, simply the social wing, as it were, of the dominant neoliberal economic project? Or, to express it differently, if global civil society did not exist, would the World Bank/IMF/WTO not have to create it to have a valid civil society interlocutor? Capitalism, as it expands worldwide at an accelerated pace, *needs* a social interlocutor. It cannot enforce its rule by force alone; it requires dialogue if not consent to achieve a modicum of social legitimacy. This is not an argument for non-engagement with official structures to maintain the solidarity or purity of contestation, but it is a call to recognize its limits. In this regard Drainville rightly notes that when the multilateral economic organizations met with NGOs at 'preconference gatherings they worked to establish relevance and set the limits of possibilities. Problems were selected, circumscribed and classified, policy priorities established and interlocutors gathered together on the basis of their problem-solving relevance' (Drainville 2004: 112). This interaction clearly goes beyond joint agenda setting to establish the parameters of what is and what is not a problem for global governance.

The social interlocutors of the dominant economic agent must be seen as valid and legitimate by the latter if they are to be effective. After the debacle of Seattle 1999 when no agreement was reached and the mob was seen to be baying at the window, even the WTO sought to bring the 'reasonable' and 'respectable' NGOs into the big tent. By the time the WTO met in Cancún in 2004 many of the mainstream NGOs were contributing to the proceedings with their critique of its current policies. But these were, on the whole, the big INGOs of the North, well established and well financed, who were in a position to contribute. Since the 1990s, the voice of the INGO has steadily increased in the UN and other international political fora. Yet, to what extent does this exclude more contestatory voices (especially from the South) who do not share the dominant liberal understanding of global civil society and the virtues of consultation/cooperation?

If the interactions between the economic policy makers and the 'representatives' of global civil society are examined in detail, we see that 'the form, content and eventual outcomes of such gatherings are so heavily circumscribed by the interests of states' (Colás 2002: 153) that it is hard to perceive the voice of an autonomous 'global citizen'. The shared perception of pro-globalizers from the right and the left that the days of the sovereign state are numbered blinds them to this material reality. Furthermore, contrary to the benign yet vague progressive rhetoric of most INGOs they mainly are, as Colás puts it, 'fundamentally pressure groups which do not contest the overall legitimacy of a specific regime but mostly seek to alter a particular policy – on human rights, environmental law, women's rights, and so forth' (Colás 2002: 62). It is the very professionalization of the INGOs and their focused attention to 'their' causes that removes them from a broader contestatory role.

There is another major problem in promoting global civil society and the transnational political fora that are the subject of this chapter. That is, their ability to reflect, let alone deal with, the social conflicts and problems of today's complex, globalized world. We need to reflect on the implications of what Jai Sen wrote on the eve of the Mumbai WSF event, from the inside, as an organizer:

> we in India are so overwhelmed by all that is going on in the country in these turbulent times – communal violence, state-sponsored pogroms, nationalistic war hysteria, a sustained rise of the right, continuing caste discrimination, massive impacts of economic liberalization including suicides by farmers and workers, flagrant corruption, and environmental and social devastation caused by huge 'development' projects, to speak of only some of the scarred landscape – that we have developed a highly insular and parochial view of the world, and whatever little information is available to us on the Forum and on world events gets overwhelmed by the demands of more 'local' and 'national' developments.
>
> (Sen 2004: xxvi)

But is this 'insular and parochial' view of the world that unusual among the losers in the great social transformation wrought by globalization? Is the World Social Forum, for all its professed global outlook and undoubted good intentions, not a little bit too Western, too 'white' to understand the majority world where social, religious and ethnic conflict is quite raw, immediate and overwhelming?

The limits of global civil society are similar to those Marx discerned in the formation of the modern state that sought to abolish non-political distinctions but was, at the same time, based on private property and social rank: 'far from abolishing these real distinctions, the state only exists on the presupposition of their existence; it feels itself to be a political state and asserts its *universality* only in opposition to these elements of its being' (Marx 1844). The false or unreal 'universality' of human rights as dealt with above is central to a continuation of this critique in the contemporary era. Kenneth Anderson and David Rieff have argued that the INGO/social movement engaging with global civil society:

> appeals to universal, transcendental, but ultimately mystical values –
> the values of the human rights movement and the 'innate' dignity of
> the person – rather than to the values of democracy and the multiple
> conceptions of the good that, as a value, it spawns.
>
> (Anderson and Rieff 2005: 32)

It is probably not an exaggeration to draw a parallel between today's NGOs
and the missionaries that Ireland sent to 'Christianize' Africa (think of 'Saint'
Bob Geldof) or those priests and monks who accompanied the Spanish
Conquest of America. Missionary zeal is, ultimately, no substitute for democratic development and cannot short-circuit the fundamental reforms of
global political economy that are needed.

If we retreat from a quasi-religious messianic faith in 'universal' human
rights and the onward march of global civil society we can still focus on
the democratic potential of social engagement with economic power.
Following an exhaustive study of how various social movements have engaged
with the World Bank/IMF/WTO, O'Brien *et al.* conclude that: 'Although
GSM [global social movement] activists are usually disappointed by their
lack of influence upon MEIs [multilateral economic institutions], the shift
of the MEI agenda is a significant accomplishment' (O'Brien *et al.* 2000:
228). In the course of the 1990s, especially towards the end of the decade,
the international managers of globalization were beginning to acknowledge
the social impact of their free market economic doctrines. While internal
contradictions of the dominant order undoubtedly played a role, the contestation from below was also a prime mover in this shift.

While most certainly challenges to the dominant order will be subject
to capture and co-option by the dominant order, this is not the only dynamic
at play. Thus, for example, the 'mainstreaming' of gender policies at the
World Bank in the 1990s, may be viewed as co-option by radical feminists
but it is much more besides. Sanjeev Khagram and co-authors note appo-
sitely that 'once international norms are in place they empower and
legitimate the transnational networks and coalitions that promote them'
(Khagram *et al.* 2002: 16). The 'long march through the institutions' that
many feminists engaged in from the late 1980s onwards paid off with
'gender-sensitive' policies in the 1990s. This allowed women's groups on
the ground to exploit the legitimacy of these international norms and make
real social gains at the national and local levels.

Another very significant progressive effect of the transnational political
fora phenomenon is how it has actually been able to generate and legitimize
new forms of social opposition. Thus, referring to the rise of a transnational
indigenous people's movement, Passy notes that: 'Their grievances, which
are local or at best national at the outset, globalize when they enter the
UN. They leave the specific community, region or national boundary within
which they took origin to reach the whole planet' (Passy 1999: 160). The
UN does, thus, offer excellent opportunities for oppressed groups to organize

towards and express their identity at a discursive level. If the UN might take a more inclusive approach towards social movements than the 'iron triangle' of the World Bank/IMF/WTO, this can only be to the advantage of those social groups seeking to articulate a public voice.

So, while transnational political fora such as those around human rights can be co-opted even as they contest the dominant order, a process of social transformation is under way. Liberal governance strategies may well include a co-option of NGO and social movement opposition discourses. But, as Drainville puts it: 'until global governance has in fact succeeded in fixing hegemonical terms of presence in the world economy . . . global capitalism is taking a risk by dangling global civility under people's noses' (Drainville 2004: 155). If we are, indeed, at a transitional point in world history as a new world order consolidates itself (or not) then there is considerable fluidity, as well as risk, in the global hegemonic order, and we should not simply take a necessitarian view of the situation that sees even concessions to democracy as part of a grand master plan. Maybe history is more open than that, as we shall explore in Chapter 8.

While the outcome of the struggle for global hegemony is most uncertain we need to acknowledge, finally, the extent to which transnational political fora have made their presence felt in recent years. The rise of the 'parallel summits', as Mario Pianta calls them, was an incipient phenomenon in the late 1970s as East–West détente set in, decolonization was completed, and supranational decision-making processes came to the fore. In the 2001 *Global Civil Society Yearbook*, Pianta stressed how, after 1995 (year of the Copenhagen Conference on Social Development and the Beijing Conference of Women) parallel summits really began to make their mark and how they proliferated after 2000 post-Seattle 1999 (Pianta 2001). But when Pianta returned to update this data in 2003 he found that what was once a 'parallel' process was now the main event in 2002 (and the first three months of 2003) when fully one third of the total global civil society gatherings since 1988 took place representing a 50 per cent increase on 2001 (Pianta 2003: 388). The transnational political fora were here to stay.

6 Local transnationalisms

Workers, peasants and environmentalists

Whereas Chapter 5 dealt with the explicitly transnational political fora that sought to democratize globalization, this chapter treats the very local transnationalisms of workers, peasants and environmentalists. The overall theme is the very '1960s' slogan of 'Think globally, act locally' that animates many environmentalists and localized social movements. I consider, in turn, the workers' movement, the peasant and farmer movements and the Green movement as case studies of local transnationalism. These case studies help us reconsider the common preconception that the contestation of globalization must necessarily occur at a global level. Indeed, we need to go further and deconstruct the traditional notions of spatial levels of social activity in the complex and hybrid nature of actually existing social contestation movements.

While the previous chapter took up the general subject of 'cosmopolitan ghosts' this one addresses the equally general issue of 'militant particularism'. Against the a-spatial imagination of the first, the latter pits the particularity of place. Yet the politics of place in the era of globalization are neither obvious nor simple. For some analysts and activists there is a simple schema in which global is bad and local is good. Of course, the cosmopolitan may well look down on the place-bound political imagination of the local activist. Clearly, we need to move beyond the binary opposition between the local and the global. The case studies in this chapter and the concluding theoretical section seek to accomplish this task in taking up the 'local' interventions of social movements that are, of course, often as transnational as those considered in Chapter 5.

Workers united

Labour internationalism has always taken different forms and these have rarely followed the mythical injunction to 'workers of all countries unite, you have nothing to lose but your chains'. In fact, from the period of the First International until 1968 it was, according to Marcel van der Linden, a 'national internationalism' (Linden 2003) that prevailed. That is to say, it was based on a narrow and Eurocentric conception of the 'international working class' and it was a form of solidarity between national trade union movements rather than a genuine transnationalism. In the period since 1968 we have seen the rise of the new social movements, the collapse of communism, and the emergence of globalization as a dominant societal paradigm. What this means in terms of internationalism is that we have probably entered a transitional phase akin to that associated with the formation of the First International, with new political and organizational forms emerging.

Traditional models of internationalism ignore the complex contingencies at play and the very real contradictions underlying its practice. For example, we might have to recognize that there are often narrow sectional interests lying behind 'internationalism', as when US trade unions promote unionism in the South to dampen competition over wage levels with their own members. Also, we might find that the best way to combat globalization is through a form of national alternativist trade union strategy. So, one of the new global unions ICEM, in a document arguing for 'global unionism' concludes that 'priority must be given to supporting organizing at local union level' (ICEM 1999: 25) to build union strength on the ground. There is, in reality, no 'one right way' to practise internationalism and we need to recognize that it is a complex, shifting and transitional phase we are currently experiencing.

The particular form of workers' joint action and solidarity we explore here is that of 'local transnationalism'. Our basic hypothesis is that articulated by Andrew Herod, namely that:

> the global should not be privileged *a priori* as *the* scale at which activities to confront global capital must be carried out. Whereas in many cases it may be necessary for workers to organize, globally, in others it is workers' local activities that may give them purchase upon global political and economic interests.
>
> (Herod 2001: 52)

This is not an argument in favour of the new localism or for labour to enter local 'growth coalitions' with capital and the state. It is simply a recognition that globalization impacts on a range of different social scales and so, likewise, social contestation and transnationalism may also benefit from moving beyond a stark local/global imaginary.

The auto industry led worldwide in the introduction of 'lean production' in the 1980s as neoliberal globalization took shape as dominant management strategy. Originating in Japan it eventually dominated the global auto industry with an emphasis on labour flexibility, extensive outsourcing and the 'just-in-time' (JIT) approach to the assembly line. In the Flint Michigan General Motors (GM) plants there had been bitter strikes in 1994 and 1996 against the consequent 'downsizing' of the workforce. Labour in the capitalist heartlands was beginning to fight back after a long lull imposed by a managerial offensive. Then in 1998 the United Auto Workers (UAW) again launched a strike at GM in Flint over the company's attempt to change local work rules. As Herod recounts, 'GM's reliance upon JIT production and inventory control meant that the Flint strikes had a snowballing effect' (Herod 2001: 111) as component provider plants began to close down.

GM had developed a finely tuned and well-integrated production machine that depended on the whole network functioning and the cooperation of the workforce. Network capitalism was productive and it was flexible but it was also vulnerable. A strike by barely 9,000 UAW members in a small US community in a matter of days had impacted on 27 of the 29 GM assembly plants in North America and 117 component supplier plants in North America, Mexico and Singapore (Herod 2001: 262). The company lost nearly US$2.5 billion and half a million vehicles as a result of this dispute. By successfully mapping the production and supplier chains of the multinational corporations, workers were able to locate the pressure points that they all inevitably possess. A feeling of demoralization and disempowerment at local level was successfully halted in Flint, Michigan, and reinstated the local community as a player in the globalization game.

The power of the local to impact on the new global capitalism is clear from the GM strike. While the spread of capitalism is its strength it is also a potential weakness if there are key nodal points in its network structure. Maybe the GM strike will be difficult to replicate and counter-measures will already be in place, but it does indicate that the local still matters even while globalization tends to obliterate space.

Around the same time as the GM strike in the US, dock workers in Liverpool (UK) were being locked out by an employer keen to enforce the (re)casualization of dock labour. What began as a seemingly traditional defensive and local labour dispute soon burst onto the international stage with the first coordinated global work stoppage by dock workers in 1997. For sympathetic observers such as Kim Moody: 'The Merseyside dockers had given world labor a lesson in how to counter the power, not only of dock, shipping and other transportation firms, but all the TNCs whose vast investments rest on this fragile transportation system' (Moody 1997: 251). As with GM a specific, very local group of workers was impacting on a global industry. The mid-1990s' Liverpool docks strike has been variously seen as the last gasp of traditional male manual labour and the harbinger of a new internationalism. The reality was more prosaic, with many of its features following a pattern set in Liverpool labour history, including a tradition of 'militant particularism'. The workers' own union – the TGWU (Transport and General Workers' Union) – did not support the strike but, whether reluctantly or not, the ITF (International Transport Workers' Federation) did throw its considerable 'official' weight behind the international solidarity campaign in the docks and waterfronts.

In the course of the two year long dockers' campaign various strategies came to the fore, from building support in the local community, pressurizing their national union to support them, to building on existing international links between dockers. The international turn was largely pragmatic and defensive; as one dockers' leader put it: 'The move onto the international scene was taken in some respects out of sheer frustration against unfair and one-side [national] labour laws' (Terry Teague, cited in Kennedy and Lavalette 2004: 216). While this campaign was spectacularly effective in its own terms it did not help the dockers 'win' their struggle. In 1998 Australian dockers were more successful in repelling a similar employer offensive mainly on the basis of much stronger local support. So rank-and-file internationalism may be part of labour's armoury but is not necessarily effective always and everywhere. Liverpool's long drawn-out dispute does, however, well illustrate the complex dynamic of local/global forms of struggle and the basis for local transnationalism.

Our third vignette is not strictly 'local' but also points towards more complex forms of internationalism than those articulated by the global justice movement. In the mid-1990s trade unions in Brazil, Argentina, Paraguay and Uruguay (that formed MERCOSUR – the Common Market of the Southern Cone) recognized that: 'With the globalization of the economy, we will not be able to face problems like unemployment through defensive and corporative actions confined to a national ambit' (cited Munck 2001: 18). While the MERCOSUR governments rejected out of hand the notion of a regional Social Charter they did agree to set up a working sub-group for Labour Relations, Employment and Social Security. The labour voice was further extended in MERCOSUR through the 1994 Ouro Preto Protocol that established, among other structures, a Socio-Economic Consultative Forum. There the regional trade unions, led by the powerful Brazilian CUT (*Central Unica dos Trabalhadores*) made a considerable impression.

The regional trade union umbrella group has taken a strong stance in favour of further regional integration through MERCOSUR and other networks. However, this is posed as a counter-hegemonic form of regionalism against that of the unregulated market integration under the auspices of the US and the multinational corporations. Thus, the unions call for 'the construction of a development model centred on the construction of a society based on a more equal income distribution and the consolidation of social justice' (cited Munck 2001: 19). Rather than seeing regionalism as simply a form of globalization's expansion, the MERCOSUR trade unions have, rather, appreciated its contradictory aspects, in providing some counterbalance and increased regional sovereignty in relation to US imperial designs. It is also a decisive voice in favour of democracy in the region severely threatened by the social impact of neoliberalism.

Labour movements have, on the whole, been slow to appreciate the significance of the regional dimension in contesting globalization. The regional moment is in a liminal situation, lying in a fluctuating position somewhere betwixt and between the national and the global. Yet if the analysis above is generalizable at all then we might expect a resurgence of regional-level labour organizing, agitating and action against neoliberal globalization.

On the basis of these three brief case studies, albeit limited to the Americas and Western Europe, we can now maybe move beyond what some observers call the 'local-global paradox'. This refers to the fact that 'while economic relationships have become ever more *global* in scope and nature, political responses to economic globalization are becoming more *localized*' (Jonas 1998: 325). While this might be the case, it is not, I would argue, incompatible with the emergence of a new labour internationalism. Workers are clearly divided by national, regional, gender, ethnic and other fault-lines. The growing internationalization of capitalist rule may increase competition along national, regional and even city lines, but globalization has also created a more numerous global working class and, arguably, a common focus for workers worldwide (Munck 2002). Some workers and their organizations have responded with a 'new realism' that simply accepts an irreversible change in the balance of forces against workers. In other cases national and regional alternatives have developed along traditional political mobilization lines. What we have explored here is the potential for a local transnationalism based on the notion that workers' internationalism need not mirror the international structures of capitalism of either the multinational corporations or the WTO.

Peasants revolt

Peasant internationalism did not begin with Jean Bové distributing Roquefort at Seattle 1999 in protest against US protectionism and the nefarious role of the WTO in regards to the small farmer in the era of globalization. In 1923 the Communist International had founded the Red Peasant International (better known by its Russian acronym Krestintern) with responsibility for worldwide organization of the peasantry in pursuit of communism. Its organization seemed impressive with a bi-annual International Peasant Congress, a Peasant Information Bureau, an International Agrarian Institute and its own publication. However, in practice, it failed to make significant advances in Eastern Europe where it might have been expected to succeed and in the Third World it served more as a vehicle for opportunist Comintern alliances with right wing peasant parties rather than as organizer of those who toiled the land.

Trotsky carried out an admittedly self-interested critique of the Krestintern in 1928 in the context of the Chinese revolution which has a contemporary ring to it. He argued that from the beginning the Krestintern was 'merely an experiment' given that 'the peasantry, by virtue of its entire history and the conditions of its existence, is the least international of classes' (Trotsky 1928: 33). The peasantry could only become internationalist if torn away from bourgeois influence and by recognition of the proletariat as its leader. Only the peasant poor are likely to choose this path and they will follow their national proletarian leaders. Interestingly, Trotsky argued against international organization of the peasantry 'without regard

to the national Communist parties' (Trotsky 1928: 33) as this could harm
national workers/poor peasant alliances. To be specific, 'it is hopeless to
attempt to forge a direct link between the peasant of Hupei and the peasant
of Galicia or Dobruja, the Egyptian fellah and the American farmer' (Trotsky
1928: 34).

Contemporary peasant internationalism seems to have disproved this view
and shown that the abject failure of the Krestintern was not due to innate
political characteristics of the peasantry. Against traditional Marxist class
analysis of the peasantry there is now a focus on what unites all who work
the land. Thus, a past president of the National Farmers Union of Canada
remarks in an interview:

> If you actually look at what 'peasant' means, it means 'people of the
> land'. Are we Canadian farmers 'people of the land'? Well, yes, of course.
> We too are peasants and it's the land and our relationship to the land
> and food production that distinguishes us . . . We're not part of the
> industrial machine. We're much more closely linked to the places where
> we grow food, and what the weather is there.
>
> (Nattie Weibe, cited Edelman 2003: 187)

Building on this broad peasant category helps us relativize the distinction
between the industrialized farmer and the subsistence farmer, the First and
Third Worlds as it were. As Edelman explains, 'the upsurge in transnational
agriculturalists' movements during the past two decades is a direct result
of a worldwide farm crisis' (Edelman 2003: 188). The steady development
of capitalism in agriculture ('agribusiness') led to a process of capitalization
and concentration to the detriment of the small producer. This was accentuated by the WTO's agriculture policies in the 1990s. Even mainstream
and quite conservative organizations such as the International Federation of
Agricultural Producers (IFAP) began to articulate a critique of the now
dominant neoliberal policies in agriculture. Of course, it was just as likely
that this would take the form of hostility against other national producers
(e.g. 'French farmers') as take an internationalist form. But nationalist and
protectionist tendencies in the early and mid-1990s gradually gave way to
a new form of peasant internationalism.

Vía Campesina (Peasant Road) was formed as an agriculturalists' network
in 1993 through the efforts of a small Dutch NGO but it came to international prominence at the 1995 Global Assembly on Food Security in
Québec where it made a significant intervention. By the late 1990s Vía
Campesina had some 55 peasant and farmer affiliated organizations from 36
countries. As Edelman remarks, this 'represented an unprecedented unity
on a considerable range of political positions and between producers in developed and poor countries' (Edelman 2003: 205). Its main unifying discourse
was centred upon the concept of 'food sovereignty' that posed food as a
human right rather than as a commodity. Vía Campesina articulated the

view – *contra* the WTO dominant philosophy – that farmers and peasants in the North and the South do not need greater access to global markets but, rather, protection of their role in local markets.

For many, José Bové, the French farmer jailed for tearing down a MacDonald's outlet near Millau, symbolizes the new peasant internationalism as an integral element of the anti-globalization movement. Bové was and is very much a product of the French May 1968 events, and, in particular, the Larzac mobilization of the 1970s against the French Army occupation of that plateau. Bové himself refers to being influenced by Spanish anarchists, Martin Luther King, Ghandi and Mexican farm workers organizer César Chávez (Bové and Dufour 2001: 90). The 1980s saw an extension of farmers' networks across Western Europe that then 'went global' in the 1990s, culminating in the formation of Vía Campesina. For José Bové this is 'a fantastic network for training and debate . . . a real farmers' International, a living example of a new relationship between North and South' (Bové and Dufour 2001: 96).

Vía Campesina supporters made their presence visible at Seattle 1999 in a striking way through high-profile protests as well as lobbying. Since the mid-1980s GATT (General Agreements on Trade and Tariffs) and then the WTO had sought to regulate agricultural production and trade along neoliberal lines. At the anti-WTO protests at Seattle the answer was clear: 'Food out of the WTO', a key demand of Vía Campesina. The struggle against biotechnology and GM (genetically modified) food was a related area of intervention that brought the farmers and peasants into alliance with environmentalists. In its campaign for comprehensive land reform, and in dialogue with the World Bank, Vía Campesina declared that 'land is much more than a commodity' (cited Edelman 2003: 207). This echo of Polanyi and the struggle against commodification by social forces is key to understanding the new peasant internationalism.

One of the first rural social movements to target the WTO was the Kainaka State Farmers' Association (KRRS) in India. Opposed to so-called 'Green Revolution' in agriculture it has focused on chemical and capital-intensive agriculture and, more recently, on biotechnology. In India it has mounted very public campaigns against multinationals such as Monsanto and Cargill and, inevitably, the ubiquitous Kentucky Fried Chicken outlets. It has also quite effectively built alliances with other mass movements concerned with the impact of neoliberalism in India such as the anti-dam movement as well as women's, tribal and fisherfolk movements. In the summer of 1999 KRRS organized what was called an 'intercontinental caravan' over to Western Europe to highlight their campaign against agribusiness and to build a real transnational movement over and beyond Internet-based solidarity campaigns.

The Inter-Continental Caravan for Solidarity and Resistance, to give it its full title, brought some 450 representatives from grassroots movements in the Indian sub-continent to Western Europe marking an explicitly transnational orientation. It was based on a genuine North–South solidarity model as against the paternalism often lying behind Northern solidarity movements. The Caravan was effectively 'jumping scales' to use a spatial metaphor, from a local/national scale to the regional/international level. Not surprisingly this event was not devoid of exclusionary nationalism as when the mainly Indian participants objected to the profiting of Nepalese speakers at one event. Overall, though, the Caravan experience is illustrative of what Featherstone refers to as a 'strategy [that] represented a significant shift in the way that the movement constructed maps of grievances, from targeting rural-urban division in India to contesting transnational power relations' (Featherstone 2003: 5).

In Latin America the most visible peasant movement is the Zapatistas but, in fact, they do not play a strong role in the new peasant internationalism. The lead there is taken by Brazil's MST (*Movimento Sêm Terra* – Landless Movement) committed to agrarian reform and an end to free market policies. The hallmark of the MST has been massive land occupations and an astute policy of national and international political alliances. Contemporary peasant movements in Latin America – whether in Brazil, Colombia, Ecuador or El Salvador – tend to share a common anti-imperialist identity that may merge with anti-globalization but is not necessarily the same thing. They are, arguably, more 'classical' social movements than the new ones, committed to modernity (albeit not a free market one) most often within the clear parameters of the nation-state.

The MST strategy has been called 'modernization from below with equity' and it has been effective in national and transnational fora precisely due to such a clear orientation. While they, indeed, believe that 'another world is possible' this is not conceived in utopian or futuristic terms. Rather, as Petras and Veltmeyer explain, this movement and others across Latin America have adopted modern goals, and organizational forms are combined with 'traditional forms of cohesion based on kinship, community and, in many cases, class and ethnic identity' (Petras and Veltmeyer 2003: 103). Thus, we can understand that there may often be a tension between local, national and transnational strategies. Indeed, a number of the Central American peasant organizations who pioneered the new peasant internationalism have since withdrawn and 'retreated' to the national political arena as a priority.

The new peasant internationalism could be seen as completing the mission of the Krestintern under very different conditions to the 1920s. It has effectively unified very distinct rural populations against the effects of neoliberal globalization on agriculture. Outside of an agribusiness that becomes a capitalist enterprise like any other, all agriculturalists are affected by WTO policies negatively. Vía Campesina articulates well the rejection of 'neoliberal policies that push countries into cash crop production at the expense of domestic food production' (Vía Campesina 2005: 1). This movement also articulates clearly what they see as an alternative, namely the sustainable use of *local* resources, the production of food for *local* consumption to overcome the problems arising when *local* production systems are destroyed. Thus, we have here a very clear-cut case of the new local transnationalism.

Reclaiming the Earth

The slogan 'Think Globally, Act Locally' originated in the environmental movement and it is thus an apposite case study of local transnationalism. The environment transcends national boundaries, and issues such as 'global warming' are, by definition, transnational. Yet, as David Held and co-authors put it: 'Despite the global proclivities of the movement, much of the activity has been local and national in its focus' (Held *et al.* 1999: 387). While environmental INGOs such as Greenpeace have been highly visible, their national counterparts are usually much better resourced. Also, despite the early global governance focus on the environment at the Rio environmental conference of 1992, the INGOs have not been particularly successful in terms of inserting themselves in the transnational environmental negotiations and institutions. Nevertheless, environmentalists with the bold mission to reclaim the Earth and transform humankind's relationship to nature have been an effective component of the broad anti-globalization movement.

The environmental movement is widely seen as an exemplar of the new internationalism. The 'global environmental crisis' is addressed through transnational political campaigns addressed to the UN and other global governance institutions. By challenging the dominant industrial mode of production and unbridled corporate interests, the environmentalists bring themselves to the centre of the anti-globalization movement. This is very much at the core of the 'globalization from below' strand that accepts fully the desirability of internationalization but seeks to turn it to people's advantage. There is a strong focus on the desirability of local level, small-scale production and local community politics. As the Irish Green's Comhaontas Glas puts it: 'All political, social and economic decisions should be taken at the lowest effective level' (cited Starr 2002: 85). This philosophy has been mainstreamed now with, for example, the EU's abiding principle of 'subsidiarity' which means precisely the same thing.

Grassroots environmental movements are often seen as exemplars of the new politics of trans-localism. Thus, Friends of the Earth (FOE), according to Neil Washbourne's study, shows 'the importance of translocal and translocalist action . . . that is decentred, connects to other places without having to go to centres, whether of power or geography' (Washbourne 2001: 132). This empowered and empowering form of action helps us break from a single local/global opposition. FOE can thus be well networked globally while also facilitating a decentralized mode of organizing and campaigning at the local level. Information technology has, of course, been a key facilitator for this new mode of organization, helping to bridge the gap between the different locals. Interestingly within FOE there was a strong debate on the rise of information technology which concluded it was, indeed, congruent with environmental globalist views of the world.

Another example of the local–global dialectic was the anti-dam movement in Southern Brazil during the 1980s, focused around local peasant mobilizations against the flooding of valleys by large hydroelectric dams. This movement had both local links (with the agrarian reform movement, the radical sections of the Catholic Church, etc.) and global ones with the international environmental movement. A study by Rothman and Oliver of this particular movement highlighted the continuous interplay between the 'internal' and 'external' actors, with resistance beginning locally and 'interchange among activists and international organizations and movement was always two-way' (Rothman and Oliver 2002: 128). The local activists and the needs of the poor peasants affected by the dams took up the framing ideologies of liberation theology first and then international political ecology, but always in terms of their own very particular situation, traditions and political perspectives.

The dialectics of globalization and local resistance are also played out in the dramatic struggle of the Ogoni against Shell in Nigeria. This was a classic case of a multinational corporation exploiting the ecosystem to the detriment of the indigenous population. Environmental expropriation and degradation in pursuit of oil created fierce local resistance from the Ogoni people of the area. The local resistance movement against Shell, going back several decades, became internationalized in the 1990s with widespread calls to make Shell accountable. In the aftermath of Ken Saro Wiwa's execution in 1995 the issue gained widespread international attention but the local movement of resistance was crushed. The main lesson of this bitter local–global environmental struggle, according to Cyril Obi, is 'the overestimation of the pressure that the global civil society could bring to bear on Shell and the state in Nigeria' (Obi 2000: 291). Perhaps more solid local and national alliances might have prevented the debacle that followed but that is only the benefit of hindsight.

The way Greenpeace operates also demonstrates the keen awareness among environmentalists of local–global interactions. As Amory Starr notes, 'while participating in national and local campaigns, Greenpeace has also built an international presence and constituency, and appears as an international voice for ecological concerns' (Starr 2002: 86). Direct action at a local level, national lobbying activity and a range of international campaigning tactics all provide a subtle range of scalar activity. Interestingly Greenpeace also began to move from a generalized environmental remit to take on specific corporations in the very effective (if controversial) campaign against the Brent Spar oil rig sinking in the North Sea, focused on Shell. This trend continued with the likes of the mainstream Sierra Club environmentalists in the US becoming firmly anti-corporate in the lead up to the large cross-sector mobilizations in Seattle in 1999 (see Chapter 2).

Although the local/global environmental movement has advanced new models of organization and brought many activists into the anti-globalization movement it does suffer from severe limitations. For one, its ecological absolutism might constrain the project of global transformation. As Harvey puts it:

> the right to be free of ecological destruction is posed so strongly as a negative right that it appears to preclude the positive right to transform the earth in ways conducive to the well-being of the poor, the marginalized and the oppressed.
>
> (Harvey 1996: 400)

Whatever the merits of 'deep' ecologism in terms of sustainable development, its tenets often contradict popular development in practice. This may well be part of a broader problem which is the clearly Northern-centred perspective lurking behind the supposedly 'global' programme of environmentalism. Clearly, we are not 'all in one boat' and all the planetary images and globe talk will not dissolve the dilemma of underdevelopment in the majority world.

At another scale of human activity we can point to the continued relevance of the national level in regards to environmental issues. A good starting point, derived from a study of European environmentalism, is that: 'when would-be global movement actors do attempt to think globally, they tend to do so in terms heavily freighted with the assumptions of the culture from which they originate' (Rootes 2002: 423). French farmers, German Greens, Italian anti-globalization activists and Basque nationalists may all share a given European environmental platform but they will do so from very different perspectives. The export of live animals might be an issue coming to the fore among British environmentalists but may have very little impact among their 'continental' counterparts. The cultures of protest are also nationally specific as, of course, are the particular political systems within and against which they operate. If there is no clear European environmentalism, so there is less likely to be a real global environmentalism.

The national question comes to the fore even more when dealing with the Southern reaction to what appear to be Northern environmental concerns. Even beyond this global divide we see the clear effectiveness of nationalism such as in the Australian reaction to the French secret service sinking Greenpeace's *Rainbow Warrior* in Auckland harbour in 1986. Damian Grenfell comments that: 'given the possible global consequences of the French nuclear tests, it is ironic that the protest movement in Australia turned inward to a sense of nation, rather than outwards towards greater acts of international solidarity against the nuclear industry' (Grenfell 2002: 117). Certainly Chinese nuclear tests around the same period did not awaken the same popular or political reaction. But rather than seeing nationalism as a barrier to transnational solidarity perhaps we should understand it as another reaction towards the spread of neoliberal globalization (see Chapter 7) that is effective in its own right.

We really need to foreground the political dimension in unpacking the rhetoric and the social reality of environmentalism. So, for example, to take the case of international toxic waste trade, Greenpeace made a conscious political *choice* to foreground the global dimension of this problem. As Jackie Smith points out:

> from the perspective of national and local groups, efforts to combat local effects of toxics trade may have been more immediately effective if they were focused on national governments accepting waste shipments or at the corporations engaging in the trade.
>
> (Smith 1999: 177)

It was thus a political calculation that a global campaign would, in the long term, be more effective than local campaigns perhaps based on a NIMBY (not in my back yard) type of philosophy or logic. To influence the global governance of toxic waste management is clearly a more ambitious target than stopping a particular shipment to a particular destination. Success at a global level can then empower future local and global struggles on the issue, of course.

Likewise the environmental justice strand of the global Green movement also brings politics to the fore in its discourse and debates. Whether it is the toxification of communities of colour in the US, or indigenous struggles over water rights in Andean America, it is the border or interaction between the environmental and justice elements that prevails and sets the tone of the conflict. It is the imbalance of global power that creates damaging environmental consequences for those who are marginal to, or ejected from, the capitalist development process in the era of globalization. This borderland also includes the very real tensions, but also possibilities, opened up when the environmental movement enters into dialogue with the workers' movement, often perceived to be on the wrong side of the industrial society/sustainable ecology divide. The basic conclusion is that any appeals to 'Mother Earth' as a mystic entity in its own right will fail to address the basic social divisions between its human inhabitants.

The contradictions of environmentalism's local transnationalism are inevitable. But, as David Harvey puts it: 'as a movement embedded in multiple "militant particularisms", it has to find a way to cross that problematic divide between action that is deeply embedded in *place* . . . to a much more general movement' (Harvey 1996: 399). The issue is whether the solidarity based on place can extend and be generalized across space. The basis on which local experience and social interactions in one place build and sustain a particular local campaign may not be the same elsewhere. Whether it is always possible, or even desirable, to move to a higher level of abstraction is, of course, debatable. Harvey still clings to traditional socialist notions of universalism that may not translate readily into viable radical politics today. It might be better to accept the contradiction at the core of local transnationalism rather than to seek to 'resolve' it in favour of a universalist, abstract and transcendental politics.

Militant particularisms

Against the perceived abstract cosmopolitanism of the transnational political fora (see Chapter 5) there has been a concerted move towards '*Reasserting the Power of the Local*' (subtitle of Cox 1997). This research/political strand emphasizes the localizing aspects of globalization as a necessary counter to its 'deterritorializing' tendencies. Thus the transnational corporations need roots in particular places and societies and are not simply 'footloose and fancy free'. Likewise, the local political context is an essential element in any movement seeking to contest the globalization project. This is particularly the case if one adopts the perspective of the 'new' social movements (see Chapter 3) that address the particular grievances of identity-based social groups rather than the grand abstractions of class and nation. A general perspective of 'localized resistance' would take up the post-structuralist vision of Michel Foucault for whom repressive power/knowledge is always resisted in the particular rather than through grand narratives.

David Harvey has, however, recently sought to critique 'militant particularism' as an adequate antidote to the abstract universalism of the 'cosmopolitan' social movements. Workers, peasants and environmentalists are often very 'grounded' in particular places and imbued with communal or cultural identities. The solidarities of place can often be extremely militant, hence the term 'militant particularism', first deployed by the cultural theorist Raymond Williams. While understanding both its appeal and its effectiveness, David Harvey takes issue with the politics of negation he sees at its core. Thus, for Harvey the political philosophy of a Foucault 'urges us to revel in the *fragmentation* and *cacophony of voices* through which the dilemmas of the modern world are understood' and can often end up 'actually celebrating the *fetishisms* of locality, space, or social pressure group' (Harvey 1996: 399) that underlie localized resistance. Harvey warns against identifying simply with the local and the particular and bids us to struggle always 'to achieve sufficient critical distance and detachment to formulate global ambitions' (Harvey 1996: 44).

To seek to reconstruct the 'global ambitions' of traditional socialist and other modernist movements today may not, however, be possible or even desirable. As M.P. Smith puts it in a sympathetic engagement with Harvey's ambitious project, much of it depends on 'inscribing capital accumulation as the central driving force of human existence and class politics as the only universal, and hence the only legitimate form of political struggle' (Smith 2001: 37). It is not a demonic postmodernism that has decentred capital accumulation and social contestation alike but the evolution of capitalism itself beyond its national/modernist classical incarnation. Localized forms of resistance to this new capitalism do not ignore systemic class domination but express the multiple forms of oppression characteristic of capitalist society today. There is not much to be gained, in terms of meeting the contemporary challenges of social transformation, through blaming the localism of identity politics for the political fragmentation that seems to prevail.

Paradoxically or not, the rise of globalization as dominant discourse and contested social reality has also led to what Arif Dirlik refers to as 'the irruption of place consciousness into social and political analysis' (Dirlik 1999: 151). A sense of place has always been with us and it certainly has a connotation of rootedness and groundedness, but places are not pre-ordained, natural locations where humans simply inhabit. Rather, we need to understand place as a product of complex interacting social relations. It is the relations between classes, genders, ethnicities and age groups that shape the seemingly timeless nature and homogeneity of a place-bound 'community'. In the era of neoliberal globalization, an ever-increasing commodification and ever-greater 'freedom' for the self-regulating market, places and communities are on the defensive. They only come to the fore when they are threatened by deindustrialization in the North or 'development' in the South.

Many globalization theorists seem to practically revel in the disappearance of place. Thus Manuel Castells starts from the premise that: 'At its core, capital is global. As a rule, labor is local' (Castells 1996: 475) to derive a very negative prognosis for the latter. Capital is seen to expand endlessly in the smooth space of global financial flows while labour is seen as mired in the particular and the world of culture. Castells refers to how 'the end of history, enacted in the circularity of computerized financial flows . . . overpowers . . . the mechanical time of industrial work' (Castells 1996: 476). In this brave new world the local clearly does not stand a chance. The ontological picture is completed by Castells when he argues that: 'capital and labor increasingly tend to exist in different spaces and times: the space of flows and the space of places' (Castells 1996: 475). This new global apartheid is undoubtedly a tendency but can we really dismiss the role of workers and places with a glib 'end of history' thesis?

There is also now a growing tendency, especially within some sections of the anti-globalization movement, to reaffirm the positive aspect of local places. Thus, Dirlik argues that 'the defence or advocacy of a place-based imagination here is not a product of a utopian project, but a response to a very real systemic crisis' (Dirlik 1999: 175). It is that very crisis of globalization that simply has not delivered on its promise of prospects for all that prompts people to build on the local, a sense of community and shared cultural values. Certainly these may have a backward-looking and reactionary aspect but that does not necessarily prevent a positive impact on 'humanizing' globalization. It goes further than this though because while the local is certainly globalized, the global is also localized (Dirlik 1999: 177) in the sense that it does not exist as some kind of nebula and must, itself, always be grounded to be effective as a capital accumulation strategy and as hegemonic social and cultural project.

While it is necessary to recognize the continued and even accentuated importance of place in the era of globalization it is also important to understand the limitations of the ontological binary opposition often seen dividing the local from the global. Whether it is space versus place or global universalism versus local particularism, we are dealing with debilitating binary oppositions based on an unsustainable ontological dualism. Smith refers in this regard to how 'locality is still often assumed to be a space of nature springing from human sociability' (Smith 2001: 121). If we move beyond naturalistic conceptions of the local we can understand how it is also a socially constructed category as much as class, race or gender. By treating the 'global' as an a priori category the local reacts to, these binary constructs also ignore the complex ways in which the global is always already local in its genesis, development and day-to-day maintenance as hegemonic project.

To move beyond the global/local optic we need to foreground the complex interplay of social scales in the construction of globalization. We cannot operate with the tacit rather simple divide between the global as smooth and the local as the place where difference is generated. Nor is it simply the case that the economy is always global and culture is situated at the local level. The cultural political economy of globalization needs to constantly bear in mind both inextricably linked elements. We also need to foreground all the scales including the regional, the still extremely relevant and the supranational that is not yet global. In terms of political practice, the same way that global managers may 'download' problems to the national level, so the agents of contestation may take local issues 'upwards' in an imaginative 'jumping of scales' as it were.

In superseding the local/global divide we also bring back into the political equation the question of human agency. In its dominant form this divide between the local and the global carries a very strong image of the global as dynamic, thrusting and modernizing in contrast to a local seen as stagnant, passive and backward-looking. It also has a clearly defined gendered image of a male/female divide associated with it. But, to be clear, by foregrounding the local we are not idealizing it. As Probyn puts it: 'the local is only a fragmented set of possibilities that can be articulated into a momentary politics of time and place' (Probyn 1990: 18). To be more specific, 'in thinking of how locale is inscribed on our bodies, in our homes, and on the street, we can begin to loosen its ideological effects' (Probyn 1990: 187). In this way a focus on the local as nodal point of the work of globalization can be seen as a starting point for its deconstruction and not as the ready-made alternative which localist critics of globalization see it to be.

In terms of the politics of the local as a constitutive element of the anti-globalization movement, we can now be clearer why local/good and global/bad (or for that matter, vice versa) are poor guides to progressive political praxis. As Doreen Massey puts it: 'Setting up the question as local versus global is to accede to spatial fetishism. That is: imagining that "space" or "spatial scale" has a political meaning, to assume that the local is always better simply because it is local' (Massey 2000: 2). Not only is that not the case but this perspective ignores the real geography of power developing across the world today. Some 'locals' are empowered while others are disempowered or marginalized, or some locals are more equal than others. These 'locals' are, furthermore, not simply geographical locations but the site of complex, historically derived social interaction and contestation. We cannot simply counterpose a vaguely progressive 'local' to the onward march of globalization that supposedly obliterates space and place.

Finally with Boa Santos we might usefully distinguish between a 'local that has been integrated in hegemonic globalization' and 'what in the local is not the result of hegemonic globalization' (Santos 2004b: 21). Much of what has been referred to under the rubric of 'glocalization' can be seen to reflect that first tendency whereby the processes of globalization absorb the consuming power and creativity of local places. There is a logic here of assimilation that subsumes the local within a new hegemonic global scale of human oppression and emancipation. Yet the movement of contestation does not always, or even often, start at that global level. As Boa Santos recalls:

> most movements involved in the World Social Forum started as local struggles fighting against the social exclusion brought about or intensified by neoliberal globalization. Only later, often via the WSF, have they developed local/global linkages through which they reglobalize themselves in a counter-hegemonic way.
>
> (Santos 2004: 22)

In conclusion then, the local is not a 'pure' place and militant particularism is not the answer to abstract universalism. The local is itself multiscalar, penetrated by transnational economic social and cultural relations in a complex manner. The local provides a space for a new politics that transcends modernist or nation-statist conceptions of the local/global based on a simple inside/outside the nation-state parameter divide. The local is a site for struggle and the agents of neoliberal globalization continuously seek to colonize it, not least through the glocalization strategies of a Sony Corporation or a McDonald's. Those who lack power, or even a voice, may also, in the local spaces of sociability and political interaction, find a platform to contest the 'localized globalization' that is currently the hegemonic modality of local/global interaction. The politics of the local will continue to play a major role in the complex contestation of globalization's current trajectory, dynamic and politics.

7 Reaction and globalization

Nationalists, patriots and Jihadists

Perhaps the overriding characteristic of academic and non-academic coverage of the anti-globalization movement is its focus on movements and protests seen generally as sympathetic, with the odd critical reference to the street violence practised by a minority. Major political phenomena of contestation such as 'Islamic fundamentalism' are simply categorized elsewhere, filed under 'global terrorism' or some other self-contained category. In North America we have the so-called Patriot movement which has millions of followers who all see the 'new global order' as the main enemy. Yet these currents are not seen as in any way part of the anti-globalization movement for reasons that amount, it seems, to political taste. The question that comes to mind is whether we can, or should, seek to distinguish between 'good' and 'bad' social movements. It might be more consistent to simply take social movements for what they claim to be rather than us trying to find their 'true' meaning.

The third political strand we examine in this chapter is that of contemporary nationalism which has, paradoxically, increased in importance while the nation-state has been diminished by economic internationalization. Is nationalism a defensive reaction against globalization, a reassertion of cultural identity in an era of uncertainty? Are nationalist movements also reactionary in a political sense always and everywhere? After considering the role of nationalists, patriots and Jihadists in terms of social counter-movements in the era of globalization we can move towards an answer to the question of whether they are simply the 'dark' side of globalization or society's reaction against the expansion of the unregulated market.

Nationalism resurgent

As Manuel Castells puts it: 'The age of globalization is also the age of nationalist resurgence' (Castells 2004: 30). This seemed counter-intuitive since for over a decade the 'death' of the nation-state had been announced and the birth of a new universal liberal democratic culture celebrated. Nations were now universally deemed to be mere 'imagined communities' (Anderson 1983) and nationalism itself an atavistic throwback to an earlier era. In the aftermath of the collapse of the Berlin Wall in 1989 and the unravelling of the state socialist alternative in the early 1990s, the 'end of history' (Fukuyama 1992) was proclaimed by the optimistic liberal gurus. In these circumstances it was hardly surprising that the national development path would be deemed as obsolete as the state socialist one. However, within a few years it was clear that a new era of cosmopolitan reasonableness under the aegis of the free market had not descended over the world.

In an introduction to a broad survey of the geography of national identity David Hooson would write about 'a new age of rampant and proliferating nationalisms' developing around issues of identity 'in the shrunken, apparently homogenizing, high-tech world of the end of the twentieth century' (Hooson 1994: 2–3). Keynote events were the break-up of Yugoslavia after 1990, the massacre in Rwanda in 1995, and the unexpected national resistance in Iraq to the US–UK invasion in 2003. Were these unfortunate aberrations in an otherwise dominant trend towards a smoother world where the market would override prickly national sensitivities? Were these outbursts merely a reflection of the collapse of communism and the relatively stable bipolar era of the cold war?

To answer these questions we need to delve briefly into the theory and politics of nationalism itself. The modern concept of 'nation' emerged as part of the democratic revolutions that overthrew absolutism. To construct a politics based on the 'will of the people' was as much a national as a democratic mission. Nationalism and internationalism were not incompatible, in fact they most often went hand in hand. However, the inter-imperialist carnage of the First World War severed the link between nationalism and internationalism. National democracies were more than capable of going to war with each other and internationalism became the privileged arena of the fledgling socialist movement. Today, there is a widespread belief that nations that participate fully in the globalization project are not likely to go to war with each other. At a popular level this translates into the belief that no two countries that have a McDonald's outlet have gone to war with each other.

From this globalist perspective, nationalism is seen as basically 'backward', a reflection of the localisms that McDonald's and the juggernaut of globalization will sweep aside. To get around the continued existence of nationalism across the world, and not only in 'backward' regions, some theorists have sought to distinguish between a 'good' nationalism and a 'bad' nationalism as practised by reactionary, backward or simply violent people (see Doob 1964). Of course, at one level this is simply a reflection of a general tendency towards dualism in the dominant view of the world, but in relation to nationalism the illusion is particularly widely held. The liberal view of nationalism, as Calhoun points out, 'took for granted the historical processes that produced relatively consensual national identities, and also typically exaggerated the extent of consensus' (Calhoun 1997: 87). Western liberalism also took a totally Eurocentric view of the world and thus found it hard to understand nationalisms other than its own.

With the coming of the age of globalization many analysts predicted, understandably enough, the end of the era of nationalism. From the right of the political spectrum Kenichi Ohmae wrote ecstatically about the new 'borderless world' (Ohmae 1990) and 'the end of the nation state' (Ohmae 1995). In the new global order nation-states had become for him 'little more than bit actors' or more specifically 'the nation state is increasingly a nostalgic fiction' (Ohmae 1995: 12). From the opposite end of the political spectrum Arjun Appadurai weighs in with a text on the cultural dimensions of globalization where one chapter deals with 'Patriotism and its Futures' from a firmly 'post-nationalist' perspective, arguing that: 'we need to think ourselves beyond the nation' (Appadurai 1996: 158). For Appadurai, 'we are entering a postnational world' that will hopefully allow us 'to free ourselves from the trope of the tribe, as the primordial source of those nationalisms that we find less civil than our own' (Appadurai 1996: 158–64). Whether from the right or the left there seems a basic incomprehension of the basic functions of nationalism and a tendency to miss nuances and contradictions.

Post-nationalism now joined the other 'posts' such as post-colonialism, post-modernism and post-feminism as desirable states of being for a post-ideology era. It was seen as a novel and desirable development of this last turn of century. Post-nationalism was endorsed normatively in the post-cold war period by many Western liberal intellectuals, who saw it as the harbinger of a new civilized cosmopolitanism. It was seen as the democratic antidote to the 'ethno-nationalisms' that supposedly plague the more 'backward' regions of the world. It is often deployed in situations where there is a nationalist resistance to colonialism and imperialism. Thus, Richard Kearney writes on 'postnational Ireland' and takes as his main target what he sees as the narrow and parochial nationalism of Irish Republicanism to which he counterposes 'an abandonment of the obsession with national self-sufficiency and conflict in favour of . . . a transinsular [Ireland and Britain] network of association' (Kearney 1997: 179). What is perhaps naive in this viewpoint is the assumption that to oppose nationalism on behalf of a 'transinsular' pact with the imperial power is somehow not political and more in keeping with the global era of tolerance and cosmopolitanism.

Underlying the post-nationalist interpretation and ideology of the national, lies a particular negative interpretation of nationalism. Ernest Gellner referred to the 'Dark Gods' theory of nationalism that misinterpreted it as pertaining to the past rather than a path to modernity (Gellner 1983). Tom Nairn, borrowing from W.B. Yeats, has coined the title of 'Rough Beast' theory which is seen as something or someone 'out there slouching towards us in the post-2000 darkness, he is mean, he is backward, and it is time he was chained up again' (Nairn 2000: 2). This image was conjured up when Yugoslavia broke apart, civil strife broke out in Rwanda or in relation to resistance against the occupation of Iraq by Western powers. In the case of Yugoslavia and the ex-Soviet Union it was hardly surprising that national politics would reassert themselves after the break-up of multinational states.

In Rwanda the massacre was hardly inseparable from the tribal politics of the imperial power and, more recently, the wild swings in commodity prices such as those of coffee.

When catastrophic conflicts emerge they are rarely attributable solely to the emergence of nationalism as a dark atavistic force emerging out of the mists of a mythical past. Most often these conflicts can be related to international politics and, above all, the failure of democracy. Nationalism cannot be reduced to false consciousness as many Marxists and liberals alike are prone to do. Rather, we need to understand the real cultural and community roots of nationalist movements and the 'sense of belonging' that they create. Nationalism is a way of constructing collective identities in a thoroughly modern way. As Calhoun, no apologist for nationalism, puts it, it 'is a positive source of meaning – and even sometimes inspiration – and mutual commitment among very large groups of people' (Calhoun 1997: 126). Across wide swathes of the majority world, people owe their ability to live under democracy to the existence of nationalist liberation movements, and they now live in nation-states that provide some bearings in a complex global world that is changing very rapidly.

Crucial to an understanding of contemporary nationalism is the dictum that it 'is more reactive than proactive, it tends to be more cultural than political' (Castells 2004: 33). That is to say, it is not the classical modern era construction of a sovereign nation-state that is most often at stake. Globalization has threatened – to a very varied degree of course – the ontological security people might feel through belonging to society in some way and participating in a political order. Paul James describes this process eloquently as a 'violent fracturing of felt security' (James 2001: 18). When this happens all forms of destructive conflicts can ensue with unforeseen consequences. The new nationalisms – part and parcel of globalization – are but one form that this reaction can take along with the new localism, regionalism or ethnic identification.

So globalization has not transcended nationalism as the globalizers had hoped and cultural nationalists had feared. Its resurgence cannot be seen as some primordial return to 'blood and belonging' as commentators such as Ignatieff have claimed (Ignatieff 1993). Nor does the notion of a 'clash of civilizations' (Huntington 2002) understood as nationalist or religious wars capture the complexity and integral nature of the nationalism–globalism relationship. The rise of the new nationalism needs to be seen as both response to, and product of, globalization. The insecurities generated by globalism, and the perceived failure of alternative development paths, have generated new nationalisms. But their reaction to cultural loss and disorientation has taken full advantage of the benefits of globalization in terms of increasingly accessible international travel and the communications revolutions. In this way the new nationalisms are, perhaps, well described as post-modern.

Returning finally to the Polanyi problematic that frames our analysis of globalization and the great counter-movement, we can conclude with Nairn and James that 'the spreading general constraints of a global economy have not dissipated but magnified the importance of the non-economic' (Nairn and James 2005: 12). Economic logic and the new market fundamentalism has, indeed, transformed the world but it has also generated social counter-movements among which nationalism, broadly understood, stands out as a major element. Against the social and existential insecurity created by the 'one big market' that is globalization, nationalism reaffirms the importance of culture, identity and roots. Nationalism can thus be seen not as some unfortunate hangover from an era before the 'end of history' was proclaimed but, rather, as an integral element of the ongoing march of globalization.

Globalism and nationalism are, perhaps, best seen as two sides of the same coin and inextricably linked. They are both equally positive and negative social forces to varying degrees. What is called 'fundamentalism' in the West is more often than not related to the nationalist resurgence we have discussed in this section. While of course religious revivals (as we shall see below) feed into the phenomenon known as fundamentalism, it needs to be related to the broader underlying tendency for nationalist impulses to emerge as counter to the dominant globalizing movement. In terms of political analysis this tendency may well be seen as 'reactive' in relation to globalization but it is not always or simply 'reactionary' in the sense of right wing or conservative political viewpoints. Most certainly this analysis would make us question an understanding of global civil society consisting only of progressive, democratic and non-violent political forces.

Patriots against globalization

If we were to casually surf anti-globalization websites in the US we would come across many describing globalization as 'treason' and railing at the 'new world order' but from a distinctly non-liberal left position. They deploy their movement in a networked, decentralized way and are assiduous users of the Internet. They challenge the legitimacy of the US state and defend the right of the citizen to bear arms against oppression. There are counter-hegemonic moves to create an alternative popular currency and court systems. Yet these political voices, resembling the social movements countering globalization from the perspective that 'another world is possible', are most often religious fundamentalists, fervent supporters of a patriarchal order and unashamed supporters of the 'white man' against the hybridity of multiculturalism they associate with globalization.

The Patriot movement in the US came to prominence in the 1990s with a range of different activities, from the armed militias to reasonably mainstream radio stations. The movement gained maximum notoriety when Timothy McVeigh blew up a federal government building in Oklahoma City in 1995 killing 170 people. Associated with the Michigan Militia,

McVeigh and his co-conspirators had as their inspiration one William Pierce, white supremacist author of the best-selling *Turner Diaries* and *The Patriots* which prefigured the Oklahoma incident. For Pierce:

> In brief, the New World Order is a utopian system in which the US economy (along with the economy of every other nation) will be 'globalized'; the wage levels of all US and European workers will be brought down to those of workers in the Third World; national boundaries will for all practical purposes cease to exist; an increased flow of Third World immigrants into the United States and Europe will have produced a non-White majority everywhere in the formerly White areas of the world; an elite consisting of international financiers, the masters of mass media, and managers of multinational corporations will call the shots; and the United Nations peacekeeping forces will be used to keep anyone from opting out of the system.
>
> (William Pierce in *National Vanguard*, cited in Klanwatch/Militia Task Force 1996: 37).

In the years following the Oklahoma City bombing the Patriot movement declined in terms of numbers as its more 'mainstream' supporters drifted off. However, as a 'hatewatch' intelligence report noted, 'a leaner, harder "Patriot" movement emerged, produced terrorist conspiracies and crimes on a level not seen for decades' (Southern Poverty Law Center 1998: 1). This reactionary wave was driven by far-right militants who were inspired by the Christian Identity religion, and espoused an openly racist theology. However, there was another strand encapsulated by the dramatic performance of Patrick Buchanan in the 1996 US presidential elections. Buchanan's reactionary populism touched a chord in wide layers of the US electorate, with his echoing of the Patriot critique of the New World Order in which the big banks and multinationals would swamp the 'way of life' of the US middle class (that included workers). Buchanan's economic nationalism can also be seen as a reactive anti-globalization impulse.

Now, in analysing the US Patriots it is very easy to focus on its more outlandish elements, and even to take the view that it is a 'paranoid politics' we are dealing with. Thus, a recent review of Patriot periodicals carried out by a 'hatewatch' intelligence report found among others the following positions:

> *The Present Truth* (Oklahoma) featuring 'proof' that concentration camps were being built and that black helicopters roamed the skies spying on patriotic citizens; books on how to form a militia and the coming biological war; and ads on 'the ultimate preparedness, having a like minded mate to survive the uncertainty of the future'.
>
> *The Spotlight* (Washington, DC) published by the anti-Semitic Liberty Lobby as the 'Voice of the American Majority' featuring articles on the

supposed roles of Mossad in the assassination of J.F. Kennedy; feature stories on Mexican immigrants 'stealing' US jobs and ads for a 'White Pride' rally.

(Southern Poverty Law Center 1999: 1)

While this unsteady amalgam of old and new right wing themes might seem bizarre to the outside observer it forms part of everyday 'common sense' for very many ordinary people in the US. Just because a movement chooses to focus on the 'demonic' roots of globalism rather than historical materialist explanations of its causation that does not mean it is irrelevant in terms of the politics of anti-globalization.

The far-right opponents of globalization do have a view of the world that makes sense in terms of their own position in society. As Mark Rupert explains:

> Far-right anti-globalists tap deeply entrenched strains of American common sense, articulating in varying degrees liberal individualism with masculinist, religious, and racial identities in order to construct an image of American exceptionalism as a bastion of white, male, Christian privilege.
>
> (Rupert 2000: 17)

Globalization is seen as the agent undoing this privileged situation, not least through the 'export of jobs' to low-wage locations which has created a sense – and a reality – of downward mobility across wide swathes of the US working class that once would have considered itself to be firmly 'middle class' in terms of lifestyle, differentials vis-à-vis African Americans, and social prospects.

Workers in the US – once secure in a class compromise state that provided reasonable social benefits in return for political stability – need to make sense of their rapidly changing world like anyone else. This discourse draws on long-standing populist traditions and the 'radical' critique of corporations in the US. The articles of Ralph Nader, for example, on the evils of the corporations, appear in the same journals that carry far-right attacks on globalization as the work of Lucifer. Both agree that in the new world order profits prevail over people and power over rights. They have a similar diffuse idea of who 'the people' are. Of course, left and right populists differ in their relationship to democracy (see the section 'Beyond good and evil' below). Chuck Harder of *For the People* refers to US workers as 'the disposable victims of global corporations chasing larger profits and lower labor costs' (cited Rupert 2000: 182), words that could easily find echo in many speeches by progressive US trade unionists.

We can now move beyond a diagnosis in terms of 'paranoid politics' and unstable/intellectually challenged misfits such as Timothy McVeigh. The Patriots do have a recognizable social base, and their support is widespread.

A significant component of the Patriot movement, according to Castells, is 'made up of disaffected farmers in the Midwest and in the West, supported by a miscellaneous cast of small town societies, from coffee-shop owners to traditional pastors' (Castells 2004: 98). These would be classical social sectors displaced by the operation of the unregulated market and ripe for a Polanyi-type social backlash movement. The 'hatewatch' Intelligence Report also refers to Patriot support being based on: 'a world peopled, in part, by the downwardly mobile, those who are struggling to remain in the lower middle class ... and [amid] fears that the modern economy would leave them behind' (Southern Poverty Law Center 2001: 1). Again, this is a classic Polanyian reactive societal movement against the depredations of the free market.

The Patriots cannot, however, be reduced to a particular social base nor can they be ascribed a particular 'class belonging' as orthodox Marxist theories once did in relation to the rise of fascism in terms of a displaced petty bourgeoisie. Rather, we should conceive of US Patriots as a broad-based cultural response to globalization with a diverse set of political answers to the perceived crisis. They are, as Castells puts it, reacting against 'the feeling of loss of control' (Castells 2004: 100) due to a series of factors such as increased internationalization and immigration and the declining effectiveness of sexism and racism. The end of the cold war and the collapse of communism had removed the common enemy: 'The age of information becomes the age of confusion, and thus the age of fundamental affirmation of traditional values and uncompromising rights' (Castells 2004: 100).

Like other contemporary movements organizing against the impact of neoliberal globalization, the US Patriot right has also become internationalized. Racists, anti-immigrant and anti-Semitic networks on both sides of the Atlantic now agree on the common enemy. The US, along with the EU and the UN, are seen as harbingers of the new multiracial and multicultural threats to the 'white race'. The nation is now increasingly defined in terms of race. As one anti-fascist report puts it: 'Across the Western hemisphere, the radical right has become increasingly international in scope, tactics and goals – mirroring the increasingly interdependent global order and its institutions' (Potok 2001: 2). In taking on an anti-globalization rhetoric, and even a critique of US cultural imperialism in relation to national cultures, many of those social layers displaced by neoliberal policies will find attractive a political message that proclaims itself to be 'beyond left and right'.

In case there are any lingering doubts that we are dealing with a movement that appeals to working-class 'common sense' we can briefly recapitulate the history of opposition to NAFTA in the US. When the NAFTA debate in the US began in earnest around 1992, Patrick Buchanan and Ross Perot achieved widespread support for their campaign against it on clearly nationalist, not to say xenophobic and racist, grounds. Perot promoted a famous image of a great 'sucking sound to the South' as jobs left the US for Mexico. Of course, from a Mexican perspective NAFTA was seen in much more classically imperialist terms. But for many US trade unionists the debate was simply about their own jobs and possible job losses so they readily 'bought in' to the nationalist message of 'Buy American' as a counter to the incipient North American free trade zone.

There was no hermetic barrier between the left and right positions in the US as regards to NAFTA insofar as both focused on job losses. Thus, Mark Rupert recalls how he 'encountered those currents of racist anti-globalism when, at an anti-NAFTA rally primarily organized by and for Syracuse-area unionists local neo-Nazis circulated through the crowd distributing audio cassettes' (Rupert 2000: 107) including one produced by William Pierce (cited above). For Pierce and his co-religionists, NAFTA spelled inter-nationalization and de-industrialization and was solely to the benefit of the 'power-elite' (a term first used by progressive US sociologist C. Wright Mills). NAFTA was seen as the thin end of the wedge behind which lay the unification of the globe under the aegis of financial interests and leading to one world government. Far more was at stake here than the loss of jobs, with sovereignty itself being seen as at risk.

Commentators on the left see a big leap forward in terms of attitudes between these early to mid-1990s economic nationalisms and the mood post-Seattle 1999. Thus, Dan Clawson writes of how:

> Instead of 'Buy American', labor's message was resolutely internation-alist. For the early 1990s NAFTA debates the language focused on nation and race . . . By Seattle in 1999 labor as well as others framed the debate in terms of class and rights.
>
> (Clawson 2005: 151)

Of course, there was a seismic shift in attitudes and one cannot neglect the importance of veteran AFL-CIO trade unionist Lane Kirkland stating that 'You cannot be a real trade unionist unless you are an internationalist' (cited in French *et al.* 1994: 1). The sobering reality is that following the conflu-ence of labour and the new social movements at Seattle in 1999, the AFL-CIO took up as its major campaign keeping China out of the WTO in a pro-tectionist move that bordered on conjuring up the 'Yellow Peril' in its determination to 'protect American jobs'.

Islamists and Jihad

There are not many Western observers – or for that matter members of the anti-globalization movement – at present thinking of *al-Qaeda* as part of the broad counter-globalization movement. Such is the hold of the 'war against terror' discourse that no alternative interpretation is allowed space. However, it seems quite clear that *al-Qaeda* – as an element in the broader global Islamic network – is a particular type of social movement. As Castells puts it, *al-Qaeda* is most certainly characterized by 'purposive collective action aimed at changing the dominant values and institutions of society on behalf of the values and interests that are meaningful for the actors of the movement' (Castells 2004: 109). We are witnessing the effects of a multi-ethnic, multinational global network motivated by clear political objectives and organizing its supporters. *Al-Qaeda* is both a product of globalization (as we shall argue) and part of the Polanyian counter-movement against the unregulated free market on a global scale.

This interpretation is not, however, shared by the proponents of global civil society, which is not usually seen to include social or political forces such as *al-Qaeda*. Thus, for example, Mary Kaldor and Diego Muro in an article on religious militant groups for the *Global Civil Society Yearbook* state that: 'By "fundamentalist" we mean groups that are inflexible about their doctrines and try to impose these doctrines on others' (Kaldor and Muro 2005: 152). The definition of what is 'extreme', 'violent' or 'terrorist' is equally normative. Most global civil society advocates would clearly rule out *al-Qaeda* from membership because it is not pro-democracy in a recognizable Western mode. Kaldor and Muro are troubled by such a clear normative ruling against what is called the 'dark' side of global civil society but still ask themselves the question 'Should we tolerate the intolerant?' (Kaldor and Muro 2005: 151). Presumably, the answer is no.

Rather than approach the issue from a political philosophy standpoint I prefer to first contextualize *al-Qaeda*, as emblematic of this so-called 'dark' side, in terms of globalization and its discontents. The rise of what is commonly called 'Islamic fundamentalism' in the 1990s is a complex story, not reducible to resistance to globalization's cultural homogenization tendencies. During the long historical period of Western colonialism most Muslim countries oriented towards a Western development model through 'modernization'. The influence of the state socialist development model was also quite strong given its links with the anti-colonial movement. This national development model along Western lines began to lose its effectiveness after 1968. Egypt's unsuccessful war against Israel in 1973 showed the bargaining power that Arab-controlled oil represented and then the collapse of the Shah's regime in Iran in 1978 saw the Western model wane in attractiveness. The Gulf War of 1991, finally, damaged the credibility of Arab nationalism and thus, according to Williams, 'Islamic solidarity then appears as the correct alternative' (Williams 1995: 203).

Neoliberal globalization in the 1990s began its hegemonic drive at the same time that political Islamism was making its advances internally. As Kamal Pasha puts it, the Islamic movements are not thus simple responses to Western conquest and control 'but a movement against western-centred globalization, promoted by fractions *within* Muslim society, and a movement *for* realizing an alternative to secular nationalism' (Pasha 2000: 241). Thus, for a movement such as *al-Qaeda* there are Muslim opponents, such as the Saudi regime, that have 'sold out' to the West, and secular regimes in Islamic countries that have not embraced true Islam. But the underlying enemy is seen as the state of Israel because of its occupation of Jerusalem and the oppression of Palestinians, and the Western Crusader powers – led by the US – that are seen to exploit, demean and kill Muslims everywhere.

To label this movement as 'fundamentalist' is tempting but ultimately misleading. Mainstream Islamic movements in the 1990s moved away from the aspiration of a transnational Muslim community towards consolidation of national political regimes. Yesterday's fundamentalists are busy creating domestic political legitimacy and becoming reliable actors in the international state system. Even the likes of Hamas in Palestine have become 'nationalized'. The neo-fundamentalists such as the broad coalition led by Osama Bin Laden have moved with a quite conservative version of Islam into a hyper-modern transnational enterprise. They embody the crisis of the nation-state and cannot be reduced to backward-looking traditionalists. In fact, as Olivier Roy explains, 'this new brand of supranational neo-fundamentalism is more a product of contemporary globalization than of the Islamic past' (Roy 2001: 4). Taking full advantage of the communication benefits of globalization, these movements – as with nationalists – are Janus-faced, looking backwards and forwards at the same time.

In the migrant Muslim populations of Western Europe we find strong congregations of so-called 'fundamentalists'. However, what is happening here is considerably more complex than a simple return to 'tradition'. Research on Muslim immigrants in Western Europe shows how they 'are often required to translate their discursive traditions into the dominant language of the nation of immigration in order to educate the generations born in their new societies' (Veer 2001: 10). What to the casual observer in France or Britain is obscurantism, or more politely 'cultural tradition', is in fact a product of considerable ideological work adapting one culture to deal with another cultural environment. Islamic writers point, in this vein, to the 'need of a new set of terms to describe the Islamic system in rhetoric familiar to a Western audience for it is characterised by a distinct set of political ideas and political relationships unfamiliar to Western political theory' (Ashgar 2005: 17).

Al-Qaeda responds to a widespread feeling of injustice and humiliation in many Islamic cultural areas. The legacy of colonialism is still very fresh and the failure of Western development models now seems obvious. Islamic philosophy and politics thus emerge as a plausible alternative development model. In terms of the crisis of the development model we should recall Polanyi's argument that 'a social calamity is primarily a cultural not an economic phenomenon . . . not the economic exploitation as often assumed, but the disintegration of the cultural environment of the victim is then the cause of the degradation' (Polanyi 2001: 164). Certainly, it is the cultural onslaught against 'Islamic fundamentalism' as in Huntingdon's 'clash of civilizations' thesis for example, that can be seen as a prime driver of Islamic resistance.

Kamal Pasha, in a phrase reminiscent of Marx's more positive readings of religion, argues that 'appealing, to those with neither power or privilege, Islamic resistance is primarily a cry of the disinherited' (Pasha 2000: 250). While it is certainly true that the leaders and key operatives of *al-Qaeda* come from relatively privileged backgrounds their appeal lies in the peripheral sectors of Muslim societies, the shanty-towns (including those in the West) and the growing army of unemployed or socially excluded as a result of the ever-increasing expansion of the self-regulated market. While based on a shared religious identity it is important to consider Pasha's conclusion that '*Islamic resistance is not about religion per se*' (Pasha 2000: 251). It is thus entirely plausible to consider these movements as an integral part of the great counter-movement and not as something alien and incomprehensible.

Of course, *al-Qaeda* is at war and it is not a benign democratic political force. This group's attack on symbolic US targets such as the Pentagon and the World Trade Center in 2001 (read '9/11') was widely read as something quite unprecedented and an attack on 'the West' and civilization itself. Seyla Benhabib, in a piece entitled 'Unlikely Politics', writes of how 'These attacks, perpetrated against a civilian population in its own land, and in a country in no state of declared hostility with the attackers, not only defy all categories of international law but reduces politics to apocalyptic symbols' (Benhabib 2001: 2). It seemed incomprehensible in that there were no 'demands' being made. But was this really a holy war of vengeance, a Jihad against the great Satan, and thus quite beyond rational/secular comprehension? In terms of a de-territorialized transnational response to globalization these attacks in 2001 can be seen as part of a broader 'asymmetric war' between the major powers and various social and political groups that oppose their hegemonic projects.

Since the early 1990s counter-insurgency experts at the US Rand Corporation had been predicting a new form of insurgent warfare. The Zapatistas had been seen as epitomizing the new 'transnational social netwar' but even earlier these US strategists argued that:

> The revolutionary forces of the future may consist increasingly of widespread multi-organizational networks that have no particular national identity, claim to arise from civil society, and . . . are keenly adept at using advanced technology for communications, as well as munitions.
> (Arquilla and Rondfeldt 1993, cited Castells 2004: 84)

Most of the various accounts of *al-Qaeda* agree that it is a new network-based organization that gains much of its strength precisely because it can bring together Muslims on a transnational post-state (or perhaps pre-state) basis in pursuit of collective goals.

Western incomprehension of Islamic resistance and collapse into a Crusade-like 'war on terror' owes a lot, one could argue, to the lingering influence of Orientalism. As Sardar argues, 'the achievements of Muslim civilization made Islam an intellectual, social and cultural problem' (Sardar 1999: 18) and Orientalism emerged as Europe's response. Orientalism was the intellectual justification for colonialism and a way of controlling and subordinating a recalcitrant Other. In Edward Said's classic formulation, Orientalism was/is: a 'western style for dominating, restructuring and having authority over the Orient' (Said 1978: 41). In this imperialist logic, the Orient was characterized on the whole as 'backward' and 'traditionalist'. To conquer such a region on behalf of a superior civilization, to bring progress and eradicate backwardness seemed, indeed, a noble enterprise.

Orientalism resurfaced with a vengeance following the *al-Qaeda* attacks in the US in 2001. Islamic fundamentalism was the new 'global security threat' and world peace depended on its defeat. As Zahid puts it: 'the orientalists consider the Islamic culture to be fundamentally responsible for the political, economic and social failures of the Middle East and in the contemporary era' (Zahid 2005: 75). Instead of facing up to its own inherent weaknesses and failures it is seen as an ideology of victimology wallowing in self-pity over colonialism and development failures. Democracy would have to be brought to these troubled lands by the enlightened West through the barrel of a gun, a tradition going back to 1798 when Napoleon invaded Egypt on behalf of the European Enlightenment. In an era of imperial 'regime change' in the non-Western world, clearly 'fundamentalist' counter-movements will continue to be generated.

Beyond good and evil

For Michael Wieviorka 'we can speak of an anti-movement when each of the elements by which a movement may be defined is deformed, inverted and perverted' (Wieviorka 2005: 13). These are 'sectarian' movements that define an 'implacable enemy' that may 'be racialized or made to appear diabolical' (ibid.). This last description fits the American Patriots and the Islamic Jihadists but what makes these 'anti-movements' and what does that actually mean? Just because a social movement conceives of the world in terms of a total war that has no limits, why would that make them an 'anti' movement? Wieviorka acknowledges that this type of movement is generated by globalization but then categorizes them in opposition to social movements because they do not have 'the slightest connection with the "global" approaches of classical social movements' (Wieviorka 2005: 13). Yet both racist/fascist movements and, above all, Islamic movements, are increasingly 'global' in their aspirations.

Manuel Castells starts his analysis with a very different methodological principle: 'First, *social movements* must be understood in their own terms: namely, *they are what they say they are*' (Castells 2004: 73). Of course, some will be revolutionary and others conservative, while some may consider themselves to be a-political. All social movements respond to some kind of societal or political issue and many today are symptoms of globalization in one way or another. The movements we have examined in this chapter all have clear identities reflected in a discursive practice, they define their adversaries clearly and they posit goals they aim for. It is not for us to decide their 'true' purpose and Castells is surely right to argue that 'from an analytical perspective, there are no "bad" and "good" social movements' (Castells 2004: 73). The complexity of the world of social movements is not really a good enough reason to fall into a simplistic moral yardstick for evaluating them.

Rejecting the label of 'anti-movement' for social movements that we do not consider progressive does not mean that we should be indifferent to their politics. We can certainly evaluate some social movements as more or less democratic than others, both in the way they operate and their objectives. But what blanket categorizations prevent us from achieving is an understanding of the complexity and contradictory nature of most contemporary social movements. For example, many influential NGOs and campaigning social movements may be viewed in a far less positive way in the global South than they are in the affluent countries of the North where their mission is simply assumed to be progressive. Likewise, many social movements in the South might be viewed as somewhat nationalist or even authoritarian, by their more cosmopolitan counterparts in the North. If social consciousness is invariably contradictory, so too, inevitably, will be the social movements that it generates.

Moving on now, to my mind the key issue that this chapter drives us to is the question: 'Why has globalization engendered nationalism, instead of transcending it?' (Nairn 1997: 63). This is a crucial question for social theory as much as one for political practice. As the cold war was replaced by the second great transformation brought on by the expansion of the global market in the 1990s, there was a liberal consensus emerging, from left to right, that nationalism would now fade in importance. For the right, the market would now rule supreme, while for the left, cosmopolitanism would now emerge in strength. Both shared a notion that human history was marked by 'Progress' and were theoretically blind to the role played by nationalism in history (except to denigrate it). A strong counter-view is that of Nairn for whom 'nationalism is not now and never was in the past a deviant or accidental departure from what "should have happened". It is no counter-current or side eddy, interfering with the majestic mainstream of progress: nationalism is the mainstream' (Nairn 1997: 48).

This is not at all an argument for nationalism as a universally progressive social and political force. It is simply that nationalism, whether good or bad, provides an 'empty signifier' for a vast range of social hopes, dreams and demands. The nation and nationality remain crucial forms of human social and cultural organization that cannot be reduced to primeval or even 'socially constructed' myths. In the context of this chapter we should stress as Balibar does that nationalism and racism are in a mutually conditioning relation. To be specific: 'nationalism is the determining condition of the production of racism, and although racism is not always equally manifest in all nationalisms, it is nonetheless a necessary element in their constitutions' (Balibar 1991: 48, from Torfing 1999: 202). Racism shapes nationalism through the construction of the fictional 'people' (or *ethnos*) that creates a nation out of individuals. In the era of globalization such boundary drawing is likely to increase, rather than decrease in importance.

If these thoughts help us understand theoretically who the US Patriots are, the relationship between nationalism and religion is equally problematic in the case of political Islam. While the 'clash of civilizations' and Orientalist perspectives may prioritize religious interpellations, nationalism has often been a key factor in many conflicts involving Muslims, from Bosnia to the Lebanon, from Sudan to Palestine. For Brian Beeley, in most cases of conflict involving Muslim groups 'it appears that it is nationalism – as the expression of group identity with territory within the state system – which is stronger than religion as a demarcator of allegiance' (Beeley 1995: 189). This is not to deny at all the importance of *ummah* as a perception of togetherness across billions of Muslims or the role that religion plays as a defensive counter to the uncertainties and distress caused by neoliberal globalization and imperialist aggression.

To better understand the nationalist, Patriot and Islamist movements we have briefly considered in this chapter, it may be opportune to introduce the concept of 'populism'. While populism has long been present as a political concept it has usually been seen as an inferior brand of politics compared to 'proper' democratic politics. Indeed, to call a politician or political movement 'populist' is most often seen as derogatory. For Ernesto Laclau populism has been 'confined . . . to the realm of the non-thinkable, to being the simple opposite of political forms dignified with the status of full nationality' (Laclau 2005: 19). Populism has been demoted and denigrated, seen as a form of anti-politics appealing to irrational forms of mass psychology and inimical to any progressive project of social transformation. Yet if we look at the appeal and discourse of anti-globalization leaders such as José Bové – not to mention political leaders such as Ignacío 'Lula' de Silva in Brazil and Hugo Chávez in Venezuela – there is a distinctive populist air to their appeal.

Students of Latin American populism, in particular, have tended to pursue a more positive interpretation of populism. Thus, Ernesto Laclau has argued, admittedly polemically, that 'a "socialist populism" is not the most backward form of working class ideology but the most advanced' (Laclau 1979: 174). Populism reflects a plethora of basic anti status quo sentiments that only attain political meaning when articulated with particular political discourses. Thus the case studies examined in this chapter – nationalism, right wing US 'Patriots' and militant Islamic movements – might all be populist in different ways. Most successful social movements – Cuba, China, Yugoslavia, etc. – were able to articulate precisely populist feelings within a democratic socialist ideology of change and transformation.

Populism is present in the way the US Patriots have attracted a mass following. Their negative view of globalization chimes with some themes in the anti-globalization repertoire but it is articulated within a xenophobic, anti-Semitic and racist political project. José Bové picks up many populist themes in his appeal to French farmers but he articulates these with a worldview that is firmly anti-capitalist in determining who the 'main enemy' is. Populism is, in Laclau's terminology, an 'empty signifier' that only takes a political direction when articulated with a project of social change. But it is important to retain the notion that 'populism' is not some 'lowest common denominator' and best avoided where possible. In fact, populism can be seen as synonymous with politics insofar as 'the construction of the "people" is the political act *par excellence* – as opposed to pure administration within a stable institutional framework' (Laclau 2005: 154).

Nationalist populism represents in many ways the basic 'common sense' ideology for the majority of the population. Against heroic 'onward march' accounts of the Western labour movement Arrighi notes in a sombre account that:

> Whenever faced with the predisposition of capital to treat labour as an undifferentiated mass with no individuality other than a differential capability to augment the value of capital, proletarians have rebelled. Almost invariably they have seized upon or created anew whatever combination of distinctive traits (age, sex, colour, assorted geo-historical specificities) they could use to impose upon capital some kind of special treatment. As a consequence, patriarchalism, racism and national-chauvinism have been integral to the making of the world labour movement.
>
> (Arrighi 1990: 63)

A Polanyian perspective allows us to make sense of this disturbing analysis, because alongside Marx-type struggles based on proletarian class organizing there are many more defensive Polanyian struggles seeking to protect workers from the onslaught of capitalist modernization. Workers, peasants and artisans will naturally (we might argue) draw non-class boundaries around themselves to shelter themselves from the anonymizing and commodifying onward march of capitalist globalization.

It is not only capitalists that compete with one another in the market-place but so also do workers, and in that process they may shelter behind nationalist, patriarchal and other banners. Non-class forms of identity and consciousness have always been, and will probably continue to be, important in the shaping of workers and their social movements. And it is particularly in 'backlash' resistance struggles – for example, those of US blue collar workers who see their jobs disappearing due to economic internationalization – that these exclusionary dynamics come to the fore. As Beverley Silver writes, 'by Polanyi-type labor unrest, we mean the backlash resistances to the spread of the global self-regulating market, particularly by working classes that are being unmade by global economic transformations' (Silver 2003: 20).

To sum up then, we might recall Antonio Gramsci's dictum in his *Prison Notebooks* that: 'common sense is an ambiguous, contradictory and multi-form concept . . . a chaotic aggregate of disparate concepts' (Gramsci 1971: 423). Certainly the task of progressive political forms is to build a new common sense that will transform society in a democratic direction. But Gramsci recognizes the enduring power of the 'national-popular' dimension of politics, ideology and day-to-day living. We have seen in the pages above how nationalism, far from having been superseded by globalization has seen a resurgence over the last decade. We also advanced a theory of populism as a non-class ideological form that goes some way to contextualizing the progressive and reactive responses to globalization. Finally, we have shown that even in the heart of the 'socialist' labour movement there lie deep reservoirs of exclusionary ideologies that need to be understood as defensive reactions to the homogenizing impact of capitalist development.

8 The great counter-movement

Empire, multitude and social transformation

This book has sought to unravel some of the complexity of the great counter-movement that free market globalization has engendered. We have seen that the counter-movement cannot be reduced to the post-Seattle wave of street protests or the inspiring meetings of the World Social Forum in Porto Alegre and beyond. What we need to do at this stage, is to provide a broad-brush synthesis of the context in which the counter-movements to globalization operate and their prospects for the future. Rather than travel through all the various academic frameworks generated from within particular disciplines over recent years (valuable as these may be in transforming academic discourse) we take as our starting point the emblematic work *Empire* by Antonio Negri and Michael Hardt, widely seen as an inspirational text for the anti-globalization movement.

Put at its simplest, are we entering a new age of Empire in which US hegemony rules supreme and a diffuse 'desire' of the oppressed arises everywhere quite spontaneously? Or is this not a vision as a-historical as Fukuyama's 'end of history' thesis in 1989? And who is to contest the new hegemony: the new figure of the 'multitude', nation-states or social classes? The challenges to orthodox categories and ways of thinking by the concepts of 'empire' and 'multitude' are serious but also welcome. My own narrative then resumes, taking up the Polanyian theme of the broad historical movements of market liberalization and the varied social reactions in response. My conclusion is that while 'another world is possible' it may not necessarily be that dreamt of by the anti-capitalist movement. Finally, I turn to the issue of strategy, namely the diverse paths that the counter-globalization movement may follow, including democratic governance, the human rights path and the new (or not so new) internationalism.

Empire

> No word resonates more strongly today than 'Empire', the title of a literary sensation that has given a name to an enigmatic totality of money, power and culture.
>
> (Balakrishnan 2003: vii)

The impact of Hardt and Negri's *Empire* was, indeed, huge and crossed the entire political spectrum. For the right there was a recognition of the pre-eminent role of the US in world affairs and even a transcendental role for the 'American' Constitution in the new world order. For the left, *Empire* represented hope reborn after the decade of despair following 1989 and the collapse of actually existing socialism. *Empire* appeared at the crucial histor-ical juncture (for the counter-globalization movement) between Seattle 1999 and the first World Social Forum in Porto Alegre in 2001. *Empire* delivered a theoretical framework for a new form of sovereignty in the era of global-ization based on disciplinary bio-power and a new form of resistance based on the immanence of molecular energy.

Empire reinterprets, in an original way, the world revolution of 1968 in an overarching paradigm of empowerment and co-option. For Hardt and Negri 1968 stood for a rejection by the 'multitude' (see next section) of the disciplinary forms of production in the West (Fordism) and the remnants of colonialism (Vietnam). As Sherman and Trichur express this shift: 'it thus creates the context for a peaceless, global, imperial (not imperialist) power (Empire) based on US constituent power (but not reducible to the US)' (Sherman and Trichur 2004: 825). *Empire* as the new hegemonic regime would thus reabsorb all the energy, productivity and subjectivity of the 1968 counter-cultural movement. Colonialism and disciplinary forms of production would be replaced by a more consensual form of subjection to the world market and by workers to the capitalist production regime. Post-colonialism and post-Fordism were the order of the day in the age of Empire.

A post-modernist reading of the rise of neoliberal globalization or Polanyi's world scale self-regulating market would be interesting, but what made *Empire* riveting on the left was, of course, its optimism with regard to the prospects for social transformation. *Empire* is diffuse and everywhere but so also is resistance. Struggles in the new era are 'uncommunicable' (unlike those of the era of working-class internationalism) but because they cannot travel horizontally they must travel upwards according to Hardt and Negri. What this leads to is that: 'the construction of Empire and the globalization of economic and cultural relationships, means that the virtual centre of Empire can be attacked at any point' (Hardt and Negri 2000: 59). Counter-powers emerge at local level that can leap immediately to the global level, becoming immediately subversive of the world order through a bio-political challenge to the construction of Empire in its generality.

What *Empire* provides is thus clearly an ambitious overarching framework for the understanding of globalization and counter-globalization movements alike. Empire's passion, vision and breadth made it noteworthy to a whole range of political forces on both sides that were grappling to understand the new developing world order and how to challenge it. Globalization was discerned as a totally new phase in world history unifying the globe in a homogeneous or 'smooth' new order. Unlike many on the left, Hardt and Negri seemed to welcome this and showed no nostalgia whatsoever for nation-state capitalism. From the other shore of politics, however, this was also an uplifting grand narrative as many of the themes of post-structuralism (the importance of bio-power, the local and culture, for example) were worked into a new challenge to the powers that be, albeit within a still recognizably Marxist account of capitalist production and development.

While *Empire* was hugely beneficial in breaking through the mood of despondency and the general acceptance that 'there is no alternative', it is also profoundly flawed in its diagnosis of the present state of world affairs. It is a profoundly Eurocentric work quite oblivious to the non-Western world except for the odd trite reference to Islamic 'fundamentalism'. Islam does not figure as a major ideological force since the fifteenth century and the current renaissance of capitalism in the East (primarily China) receives hardly a mention. The European Enlightenment – and its subsequent migration to North America and substantiation in the American Constitution – rules supreme in *Empire*. In terms of the world being made by globalization through the dialectical processes of social inclusion/exclusion, *Empire* simply reflects the globalizer's ideology that we are entering a 'smooth' world. As one commentator puts it succinctly, 'If Hardt and Negri had taken African historical examples seriously, for example, they would have avoided the numerous presentist and universalizing flaws that plague – and ultimately undermine – their work' (Dunn 2004: 159).

Empire is also an inherently androcentric text having seemingly missed out entirely on the theoretical and practical revolution carried out by the world's feminisms since 1968. Its millennial tone, prophetic vision and glorifying of the militant is male politics incarnate, something that cannot be said about the post-Seattle 1999 anti-globalization movement as a whole. Lee Quinby writes that: 'Hardt and Negri's gender-blindness renders their concept of resistance to authority rhetorically engorged yet methodologically flaccid' (Quinby 2004: 240). The global political economy has gender relations at its core, from the feminization of poverty through to World Bank development policies. The concrete worlds of work, community and family are only amenable to critical analysis through a gender lens. Both power and resistance in the contemporary world order – be it the invasion of Iraq or the revolt against environmental degradation – require a precise understanding of gender relations and how they are changing.

Nevertheless, *Empire* represents a fundamental challenge to classic theories of imperialism that were no less Eurocentric and androcentric in their day. Since *Empire* appeared in 2000 its analysis has taken a severe practical setback with the emergence of full-blown 'red in tooth and claw' US imperialism in Afghanistan and Iraq. The power-holders and their ideological backers in the US have no problem at all in articulating an openly imperialist project. Extending the neoliberal revolution at home in the US and the UK a range of 'revisionist' writers have sanitized the imperialisms of the past to articulate a civilizing mission for a renewed US imperialism today. A popular example is Niall Ferguson with his *Empire: How Britain Made the World*

(Ferguson 2004) and its sequel, *Collosus: The Rise and Fall of the American Empire* (Ferguson 2005). Imperialism is here rehabilitated as a key element in the expansion of the West and the development of capitalism.

It is a fact that today's division between rich and poor countries roughly mirrors the nineteenth-century division between colonizer and colonized. Uneven development on a global scale remains the most enduring inequality at a global level despite the changing patterns of industrialization and class development, notwithstanding the century that has elapsed since the era of classical imperialism. So are we now witnessing a revival of colonialism, a neo-imperialism as it were? To answer that question we need first to highlight the distinction between the *territorial* and the *capitalist* or economic logics of power. These may, of course, intertwine (as many accounts of current US expansionism show) but as David Harvey notes: 'the literature on imperialism and empire too often assumes an easy accord between them: that political-economic processes are guided by the strategies of state and empire and that states and empire always operate out of capitalist motivations' (Harvey 2003: 291).

This distinction allows us to avoid simplistic accounts from the left announcing an era of new imperialism because US strategic interests and oil drive it to conquer and subjugate. For a global power to become truly hegemonic it must be in a position to hegemonize and lead through consent as well as pure coercion. Britain, in the heyday of its empire, did achieve sporadically and unevenly, precisely such a hegemonic role. The US, as the successor as world power, did seek from the start of the twentieth century 'to mask the explicitness of territorial gains and occupations under the mask of a spaceless universalization of its own values' (Harvey 2003: 47). This culminated towards the end of that century with the discourse of globalization as economic and cultural driver of progress and 'democracy' (as made in the US) as the legitimizing political form of organizing development.

Imperialism is the result of the territorial and economic logics of capitalist power coming into conjunction. It is not at all clear that the hegemonic social forces in the US today are actually interested in recreating imperialism in the classic sense, notwithstanding cheerleaders such as Robert Cooper (one time Tony Blair adviser) who would recreate the nineteenth-century distinction between pre-modern (for which read barbarian) and post-modern states who would be the guarantors of civilized behaviour (Cooper 2002). To go beyond the notion of Empire as metaphor for aggression and imperialistic designs is problematic for a number of reasons: not least because contemporary globalization is quite different from global capitalism in the era of imperialism. While imperialism was a state-centred project of territorial expansion, globalization as per Pieterse, 'is intrinsically multidimensional, involves multiple actors, and is in significant respects decentred and deterritorial, involving multiple and diverse jurisdictions' (Pieterse 2004: 38).

To distinguish globalization from imperialism is not meant to make the first a more benign enterprise. It is simply to recognize the complexity and fluidity of the current world situation where there are multiple and, often, contradictory globalization and counter-globalization projects at play. Taking a long-term historical view we can see empires and imperialism as phases of internationalization that culminate with neoliberal globalization. This is not to say that there are elements in power in the US today that have an imperial project, as articulated by Ralph Peters, a planner for 'future war' for whom:

> We are entering a new American century in which we will become still wealthier, culturally more lethal, and increasingly powerful . . . The de facto role of the US armed forces will be to keep the world safe for our economy and open to our cultural assault. To those ends we will do a fair amount of killing.
>
> (cited Pieterse 2004: 57)

No one can doubt that the overwhelming concentration of military, economic and cultural power in the US today creates something akin to Empire and that its designs are imperialistic. However, there is no reason to believe that this neo-conservative offensive could lead to a situation described by Harvey as one where 'the logic of capital will look to regime change in Washington as necessary to its own survival' (Harvey 2003: 207). We cannot draw a simple equation mark between globalization and imperialism, let alone Empire. The desire of Hardt and Negri to articulate a 'strong' version of Empire over and beyond its use as metaphor, ultimately obscures more than it clarifies the present world order, particularly in its dubious promotion of a new theory of right. Thus, I would agree with Balakrishnan's not unsympathetic conclusion that 'Empire is ultimately a Sorelian myth of empowerment, offering consolation to oppositional desire, in place of sober political realism' (Balakrishnan 2003: ix).

Multitude

For Hardt and Negri, 'the multitude . . . [is] . . . the living alternative that grows within Empire' (Hardt and Negri 2004: xiii). Whereas globalization is a network of hierarchies, the multitude springs from the expansive networks of cooperation, communication and communality. The multitude is not the same as the 'people' (conceived as a more unitary category), the 'masses' (where differences are submerged in the main) and finally the traditional 'working class' because it is not as open and inclusive as the multitude as a concept. Initially for Hardt and Negri the multitude is conceived as 'all those who work under the rule of capital and thus potentially as the class of those who refuse the rule of capital' (Hardt and Negri 2004: 106). But they go much further than broadening the concept of working classes because from their perspective the main issue is not so much the 'empirical existence' of multitude but, rather, 'its conditions of possibility', or more simply: 'The question to ask . . . is not "What is multitude?" but rather "What can the multitude become?"' (Hardt and Negri 2004: 105).

While multitude goes beyond traditional Marxist concepts of working class it is not unrelated to the understanding of working people elaborated under the influence of the new social movements from 1968 onwards where gender, race and other 'non-class' determinations came into play. Even the question of what might the multitude become is not so different from Marxist conceptions of class 'in itself' and class 'for itself' as it becomes conscious and strives for social transformation. However, it can be read as an expression of the contemporary irreducible plurality of social existence as a necessary precondition for effective political action. The multiplicity of experience of oppression and exploitation is well captured by the term 'multitude' which Paolo Virno defines as the 'form of social existence of the many as many' (Virno 2004: 1). Certainly this conception has been very influential in the anti-globalization movement in the West.

Multitude as a concept both reflects and influences the theory and practice of the young street protestors of the post-Seattle 1999 anti-globalization movement. It renews the critique that new social movement theory carried out in the 1970s of all economistic and reductionist conceptions of social and political change. It rejects all narrow and restricted views of political antagonisms as based on pre-established social structures and institutionalized forms of political representation. Where one sees structure the other sees fluctuation as the norm. If market fundamentalism called for deregulation of the economy, the multitude approach calls for a deregulation of all forms of representation. But the danger, as Barchiesi puts it, is that 'multitude' becomes so 'all-encompassing and self-explanatory' that it could 'lose much of its explanatory power when it comes to define how the singularities that comprise the multitude come to articulate their desires and demands in oppositional terms' (Barchiesi 2004: 3).

In 'deregulating' our understanding of social antagonisms and political representation, we are perhaps left with no coherent explanation of their contemporary dynamic. In *Multitude* we are presented with an image of radical immanentism as spontaneous response to Empire, insofar as to revolt is natural to the human condition. The unity of the oppressed in revolt is also unexplained and simply assumed as an innate tendency towards convergence. As Ernesto Laclau puts it:

> The features of this formless but self-defined totality are transmitted to the multitude as Empire's grave-digger – in a way reminiscent of Marx's description of the universalization brought about by capitalism as a prelude to the emergence of the proletariat as the universal class.
>
> (Laclau 2005: 240)

There is no coherent explanation of the sources of social antagonism in contemporary society and no understanding of the complex political mediations lying behind the counter-globalization movements, for example.

Multitude is significant in what it leaves out from this complex picture (peasants and nationalism, for example) and what it foregrounds (migrants, for example) in the making of the new revolutionary subject. Hardt and Negri take a quite stereotypically modernist approach towards the peasantry. For them 'the figure of the peasant has . . . throughout the world faded into the background' and they conclude categorically on 'this disappearance of the figure of the peasant' (Hardt and Negri 2004: 120–1). While there is a plausible argument that the peasant is, as an economic category, becoming less central to the world system, its political importance is still considerable, not least in terms of the broad counter-globalization movement. It is thus inexplicable that in *Multitude* the peasant is seen as a 'nonpolitical figure, disqualified from politics' and, to be more specific, where 'the peasantry is fundamentally conservative, isolated, and capable only of reaction, not of any autonomous political action of its own' (Hardt and Negri 2004: 122).

This unduly negative view of the economic, cultural and political role of the peasantry is reminiscent of the most clichéd phrases of Marx about the French peasantry as 'sacks of potatoes'. While the effects of capitalist expansion across the globe on the peasants are mixed and open to considerable debate, its 'disappearance' is not likely. Nor can we assume as Hardt and Negri do that peasants can only enter the realm of progressive politics when they leave the land, forsake rural traditions and enter into 'communication' with the urban 'multitude'. In the struggles around the remaking of the peasantry by neoliberal globalization we find a whole range of crucial sites of contestation such as the environment, gender and indigenous knowledge. The very Eurocentric and modernist dismissal of the world's peasantry from the scene weakens considerably the understanding Hardt and Negri might develop on the nature of globalization and its contestation today and in the period to come.

Another area of contestation that Hardt and Negri seek to devalue is the whole terrain of the nation-state and nationalist revolts. For them the nation is a concept that sums up the hegemonic bourgeois solution to the problem of sovereignty. They understand the progressive nature of subaltern nationalism for the pre-Empire era when they could serve as a defence against powerful external forces and as a potential source of community. Even then they see a strong element of totalitarianism in nationalist revolts insofar as 'the community is not a dynamic collective creation but a primordial founding myth' (Hardt and Negri 2000: 113). We have already dealt with the weakness of the primordialist approach to nationalism (Chapter 7) but the issue is crucial to Hardt and Negri insofar as they see it as the cause 'blocking the constructive interactions of differences with the multitude' (Hardt and Negri 2000: 113). As with peasants it is only when nationalists forgo the primordial that they can 'communicate' with the multitude.

In the present era of imperial sovereignty Hardt and Negri take an even more categorically negative view of all things national. They argue that 'it is a grave mistake to harbour any nostalgia for the powers of the nation-state or to resurrect any politics that celebrates the nation' (Hardt and Negri 2000: 336). This might read at first as a sensible warning against any belief that the nation-state and nationalist politics are an adequate and progressive answer to the speed of free-market globalization. However, the authors of *Empire* base this assertion on the belief that 'the decline of the nation-state ... is a structural and irreversible process' (Hardt and Negri 2000: 336) that smacks of the 'death of the nation-state' thesis that we have already placed in context (Chapter 2). Whether it is the Group of 20 challenging the WTO from the South or Palestinians taking on the US–Israel power structures, the national question is an enduring element in the making and unmaking of globalization.

While the many millions who work on the land and engage in national struggles of one sort or another are dismissed from the *multitude*, Hardt and Negri argue in *The Communist Manifesto* messianic mode that 'A specter haunts the world and it is the specter of migration' (Hardt and Negri 2000: 213). Following Nietzsche and his quest for the *barbarians* who would invade the Empire, Hardt and Negri raise migration to 'a spontaneous level of struggle' and laud 'the power of desertion and exodus, the power of the nomad horde' (Hardt and Negri 2000: 213–14). Migrants are seen to embody the desire for something more as well as a resolute refusal to accept the present state of affairs. Migrants are seen to embody the geographical hierarchies of the new global order, but in *Multitude* they are granted a privileged position in the construction of 'the general commonality of the multitude by crossing and thus partially undermining every geographical barrier' (Hardt and Negri 2004: 134).

It is certainly the case that the complex waves and flows of migrants, whether legal, irregular or somewhere in between, are a living testimony to the mobilities generated by globalization. Migrants are, indeed, part of the global working class in the making and they have generated a whole range of 'transnational communities' that are part of the social effects of globalization. However, Malcolm Bull is probably correct to refer to an element of self-delusion in the way in which 'migrants have become a potent symbol of the social dislocation caused by globalization and have been invested with some of the left's more romantic aspirations' (Bull 2004: 218). The flight of skilled workers from developing countries to the affluent North is viewed there in anything but romantic terms. Migrants are no more the privileged agents of social transformation than industrial workers, peasants or students were in past futile searches for the golden key to revolution.

In conclusion to this section I would like to take up Laclau's verdict that in *Multitude* Hardt and Negri 'tend to oversimplify the tendencies towards unity operating within the multitude' (Laclau 2005: 243). Even a cursory examination of the different currents, eddies and flows within the broad social counter-movement against the self-regulating market shows the complexity and contradictions that are at play here. Thus, for example, there is a whole history of conflict, confluence and compromise lying behind the Seattle 1999 slogan 'Teamsters and Turtles Unite' that many took to be a signal of labour–environmental alliance. However, as Gould *et al.* note in a review of 'Blue-Green coalitions', 'in many ways forming a coalition at Seattle was easy: this was a short-term marriage of convenience on an issue both groups strongly opposed' (Gould *et al.* 2004: 92). Within a year more usual antagonisms between organized labour (blue) and the environmentalists (green) had resurfaced and were dominant.

Soon after Seattle 1999 the labour–race divide came to the fore in the US as the anti-globalization movement came under fire from anti-racists for its 'whiteness'. The Colours of Resistance Network was formed in 2002 to articulate this critique. Among its criticisms of the anti-globalization movement were the points that it was exclusionary with regards to 'people of color' and that white activists fetishized tactics as against the need to build up a long-term grassroots movement (Starr 2004: 127). There are also serious tensions between, for example, the anti-globalization movement and the diverse indigenous people's movements. For all that the Zapatistas had as a slogan, *'todos somos indios del mundo'* ('we are all Indians of the world') when they marched on Mexico City in 2001, the reality is that indigenous movements for social change (for example, in Andean America) may prioritize recognition issues or agrarian issues that are not those central to the labour movement. Unity must be constructed politically and cannot be assumed.

History

At this stage it is necessary to go beyond the breathless 'presentism' of Hardt and Negri's theorizing of *Empire* and of *Multitude*. They do, of course, open up many new avenues for research and their bold iconoclasm can only be welcomed when contrasted with state academic and political debates. However, if we renew the historical comparative problematic of Karl Polanyi (see Chapters 1 and 2) we can add a much-needed long-term strategic perspective on globalization and contestation. Polanyi's basic theorem is that global history is ruled by a 'double movement' in which two organizing principles of society are dominant, namely the principle of economic liberalism and that of social protection. The first aims at the establishment of a self-regulating market on a global scale (globalization for short) and the second aims at protecting society and nature as well as production, from the deleterious effects of the market (contestation for short).

The counter-movement is dynamic and can be plotted onto the long waves of global history. In Europe, prior to the industrial revolution in the nineteenth century, exchange relations were regulated by principles of reciprocity and the economy was 'embedded' in society. Industrial expansion was characterized by the spread of the free market and the *laissez-faire* state, leading to the 'disembedding' of the economy from society and political control. In the mid-twentieth century, after economic depression and world wars, a compromise system of 'embedded liberalism' began to prevail. Now going beyond the period above analysed by Polanyi, we can apply this same optic to the neoliberal offensive of the 1980s which can be seen as a wave of economic 'disembedding' and deregulating of the market. Our question now then is whether we are witnessing a counter-movement whereby society protects itself from the unregulated market and political forces emerge seeking to regulate, if not control, the free market.

For Silver and Arrighi the last two decades show no lack of outstanding cases of mobilization by 'groups, sections and classes' in response to the dislocations caused by the resurgence of the 'liberal creed' and politics designed to promote a 'self-regulating global market' (Silver and Arrighi 2003). The elements of a great social counter-movement range from the anti-IMF 'food riots' in the South in the 1980s to the anti-globalization street protests in the North after Seattle 1999. But they also include the Group of 20 large developing nations that have challenged the impositions of the WTO and the establishment's moves to create a post-Washington Consensus to succeed the now discredited naked neoliberal model. The counter-movement thus has a facet of revolt 'from below' but also a reform move 'from above' seeking to pre-emptively deal with revolt and potential instability of the global system.

The Polanyi problem – to balance the urge to liberalize with the basic need for some social stability – affects the rulers of the new world order as much as it does the subaltern classes. As yet the social counter-movement is at an early stage of development, and we cannot pretend that the anti-globalization movement, at present, is a serious challenge to the established order. The main challenge to the unregulated market is for now located in the developing countries and nationalist movements of various types across the world. The contradictions from within the system are not yet as severe as they were during the great depression of the 1930s. Inter-imperialist rivalries are also less likely to emerge strongly in the present context and, as Silver and Arrighi argue: 'a more likely source of destabilization of the US-centred process of world market formation is the persistent protectionism of the United States itself' (Silver and Arrighi 2003: 348).

Inconsistencies in the US position are thus a major source of instability, crusading on behalf of a free market and yet retaining strong protectionist elements itself. Nor is the use of overwhelming force to secure US predominance the best way to ensure hegemony over the system as a whole. It is in this context that Joseph Stiglitz, one time chief economist at the World Bank, can take up the Polanyi problematic and read the lessons for today's managers of contemporary capitalism. Stiglitz is keen to contest the common wisdom that 'the end of communism marked the triumph of the market economy, and its belief in the self-regulated market' (Stiglitz 2001: xv). What was occurring was the imposition by force of 'risky doctrines' once the countervailing weight of the state socialist order had collapsed. 'But this perspective is not only uncaring', argues Stiglitz, 'it is also unenlightened: for there are myriad unsavoury forms that the rejection of a market economy that did not work at least for the majority, or a large minority can take' (Stiglitz 2001: xv).

So, precisely in the apparently unconstrained victory for the unregulated market came the unforeseen consequences. This came, for example, in the shape of a dramatic and catastrophic transition to capitalism in Russia in the early 1990s which, in its speed and lack of planning, destroyed social capital and empowered the Mafia. As Stiglitz puts it: 'rapid transformation destroys old coping mechanisms, old safety nets, while it creates a new set of demands, *before new coping mechanisms are developed*' (Stiglitz 2001: xi). Then, towards the end of the 1990s, from 1997 onwards, came a series of economic collapses that represented, individually and collectively, a serious blow to the credibility of the unregulated market model. In his own book on 'globalization and its discontents' Joseph Stiglitz subtitles his chapter on the East Asian Crisis of 1997 'how IMF policies brought the world to the verge of a global meltdown' (Stiglitz 2001: 89). Whether the IMF or the broader economic model was at fault the implications were clear: the winners of the cold war had problems on their hands.

If the winners had problems, the losers in the great free market offensive suffered the most, of course. It is important to bear in mind in this regard that capitalist accumulation has always progressed through exploitation of labour but also through naked dispossession. Today, the ever-expanding, self-regulating market is dispossessing people in diverse forms. David Harvey writes of how 'destruction of habitat here, privatization of services there, expulsion from the land somewhere else, bio-piracy in yet another realm – each creates its own dynamics' (Harvey 2003: 174). This diffuse and often inchoate form of dispossession is yet another manifestation of Polanyi's liberalizing dynamic. The response to this tendency is, itself, most often fragmentary and localized. Sometimes it links up with the more 'traditional' anti-exploitation movements of labour or national liberation but, more often, it remains at the margins, taking on the effects of globalization but not necessarily offering a coherent or noble alternative.

Hardt and Negri, in a not unrelated way, refer to how 'simplifying a great deal, one could argue that postmodernist discourses appeal primarily to the winners in the process of globalization and fundamentalist discourses to the losers' (Hardt and Negri 2000: 160). Mobility, fluidity and indeterminacy might be welcomed by those who benefit from globalization, but they might also translate into uncertainty, constant flux and insecurity for those who are subject to dispossession by the machine of the self-regulating market. Thus different forms of fundamentalism – from the Christian right to Islamic militants, from the French anti-immigrant right to, arguably, ecological fundamentalists – respond to the threat of uncertainty and insecurity of the present era with their own particular versions of certainty and the truth. Hardt and Negri may well be prophetic when they tell us that 'the losers in the process of globalization might indeed be the ones who give us the stronger indication of the transformation in progress' (Hardt and Negri 2000: 150).

The question that now arises is whether a Polanyian counter-movement can protect humanity from a self-inflicted demise. At one level Polanyi can be read simply as a humanist appeal to resist the commodification of the human and natural ecologies now under way. But it is a perspective that also offers an alternative vision of globalization in terms of its inextricable links with the local and its communities. Whether it is a mining site, a financial market or a sweatshop, the globalization project necessitates local grounding. And as a result, as Adaman and colleagues write: 'the local becomes the site of encounter, contestation and possibly resistance' (Adaman *et al.* 2003: 7). As local identities proliferate so do diverse projects of contestation and even accommodation that represent different faces of a social counter-movement that is an integral element of the globalization project.

While we need to appreciate the breadth and diversity of the great counter-movement now emerging to contest globalization and its envisaged smooth world, it does not mean we value them all equally. Harvey quite rightly draws our attention to how many movements are struggling against the dispossession that globalization brings in its wake:

> The danger lurks that a politics of nostalgia for that which has been lost will supersede the search for ways to better meet the material needs of the impoverished and repressed populations; that the exclusionary politics of the local will dominate the need to build an alternative globalization . . .; that reversion to older patterns of social relations and systems of production will be posited as a solution in a world that has moved on.
>
> (Harvey 2003: 177)

The next section deals with political strategies more explicitly, for now we just note how the combined but uneven nature of capitalist development will inevitably produce such effects.

The great counter-movement, then, is essentially about a return of the 'political' which the de-regulationist offensive had sought to evacuate from economics. This politics, as we have seen, does not necessarily take what used to be called a 'progressive' form. Indeed, it is always good to recall that for Polanyi, the cataclysm-triggered transformations of the 1930s saw societies taking control of the economy in very different ways, including the New Deal in the US, Stalin's Russia and Nazi Germany. If classical fascism can be seen as a perverse, reactionary social and political response to the chaos of the crisis-ridden capitalist system, so today, we can imagine very many less than attractive responses to the social crises unleashed by globalization. However, as Polanyi advised in relation to the period he observed, it is necessary for us 'to detach the poignant national histories of the period from the social transformation that was in progress' (Polanyi 2001: 80).

What we are witnessing today – if we abstract from the particular situations of chaos and conflict – is the 'inability to regulate markets at the international level [that has] created social dislocations beyond the ability of "normal" domestic politics to resolve' (Evans 2000: 238). If Polanyi's concerns and verdicts on the problem of reconciling free markets with social and political stability were correct in the 1930s and 1940s they are doubly so in the 1990s and 2000s as the global casts its particular glow across the regional, national and local domains of life. It is inevitable that politics will now come to the fore to seek social control, or at least influence, over this process. This response of the 'lifeworld', as Habermas famously calls it, will be diverse and not necessarily effective. It will also be countered by serious moves 'from above' seeking to co-opt or even to create a 'global civil society' to match global capitalism.

Strategy

In the age of *Empire*, following Balakrishnan, 'revolutionaries no longer need to distinguish tactics and strategy, position and manoeuvre, weak links and vulnerable ones; they can now rely on a pervasive, if diffuse popular desire for liberation and an episodic intuition of friend and enemy' (Balakrishnan 2003: xv). As an ethos of liberation this approach captures well a dominant strand in the Western anti-globalization movement, but since its bursting onto the world scene in 1999 many of these classical political categories have come back into play. The strategy of a given movement is clearly distinguished from the specific tactics it might follow in the streets or in negotiations with the powers that be. The distinction between what Gramsci called a 'war of manoeuvre' (classical early twentieth-century revolutionary strategy) and a 'war of position', typically of the entrenched positions of those who now struggle for hegemony, is well understood. And all parties are aware of where the weak links of the system may be, where there are contradictions, and where pressure might most readily lead to reform.

Whether it is the 'global governance' or 'global civil society' discourses there is a strong tendency within 'globe-talk' to adopt a 'neutral' political stance. Now, while not everything in society is political, as Laclau puts it: '*all* struggles are, by definition, *political*' (Laclau 2005: 154). Society, the way we view it and the 'people' are being constantly reinvented in the political domain. There is no a-political stance towards a neutral globalization process that we should just seek to administer better to the benefit of all. Developing this theme, Laclau argues that:

since the construction of the 'people' is the political act *par excellence* –
as opposed to pure administration within a stable institutional framework – the *sine qua non* requirements of the political are the construction
of antagonistic frontiers within the social and the appeal to new subjects
of social change.

(Laclau 2005: 154)

The various political projects that seek to offer an alternative to the unregulated free market of globalized capitalism are all constructing their subjects
through discursive operations that urgently require deconstruction.

With politics back 'in command' in terms of determining the future
direction of the broad counter-globalization movement(s), we can consider
the various broad options in the struggle. One of the most ambitious political projects in the era of globalization is that of 'cosmopolitan democracy'
based on the notion that for global issues, such as protection of the environment or the regulation of migration, to be subject to democratic control:
'democracy must transcend the border of single states and assert itself at
a global level' (Archibugi 2003: 7). This project seeks to give a voice at the
global level to people who may be disempowered at a national level. It is
a perspective that does not shy away from the question of force, arguing
unambiguously for 'humanitarian intervention' where necessary. For British
Prime Minister Tony Blair, NATO's air raids on Yugoslavia at the close of
the twentieth century were justified because: 'It's right for the international
community to use military force to prevent genocide and protect human
rights, even if it entails a violation of national sovereignty' (cited Archibugi
2003: 10).

The new 'cosmopolitan' is unapologetically West-centred. For Martin
Shaw, still professing a left politics:

> This perspective can only be centred on a new sense of purpose among
> Western peoples and governments, since only the West has the
> economic, political and military resources and the democratic and multi-
> national institutions and culture necessary to undertake it. The West
> has a historic responsibility to take on this global leadership.
>
> (Shaw 1994: 180–1)

There is a direct lineage here with the justification of colonialism as the
'white man's burden' and the European social democratic support for 'social
imperialism' to bring lesser peoples to the light. National sovereignty is
seen as a quaint anachronism in the era of globalization as the movement
for 'global justice' must take precedence. The new liberal cosmopolitanism
has its own 'right' and 'left' exponents but, overall, it seems to offer little
to the majority world or those seeking social transformation.

There is no reason why we should accept that the alternative to liberal
cosmopolitanism is illiberal nationalism or various dark forms of funda-

mentalism. At best cosmopolitan democracy is a cosy complacent ideology for those privileged to be born in the 'safe zones' of the new world order. At worst this call to go 'beyond' the confines of the nation-state is simply an apologia for the most powerful nation-state on earth as it goes about the business of world domination. In all versions the leftist language of universalism masks a denial of genuine attempts at popular sovereignty. The answer, from a social transformation perspective, should not merely be one of critique. As Timothy Brennan puts it:

> We should be encouraging popular efforts in Southern Mexico, Colombia, Indonesia or Palestine – and so many other parts of the world – to establish a modicum of real sovereignty, rather than constructing intricate theoretical edifices liable to weaken the very ability to imagine it.
>
> (Brennan 2003: 49)

The Polanyian counter-movement is based precisely on initiatives such as these that build up aspects of the social counter-power to the unregulated free market.

The human rights movement might, one could suppose, provide a more universal construction of the 'people' than the new liberal cosmopolitanism, and its supporters include many (if not most) INGOs. The idea of human rights and their global institutionalization are integral elements of the globalization discourses in most of its political variants. As Roland Robertson, one of the pioneers of globalization theory puts it: 'although the principle of human rights is in one sense applied to individuals, its general significance has to do with the consolidation of humanity' (Robertson 1992: 184). The human rights of the individual are seen to be 'above' the sovereignty of nation-states and are thus important markers of the extra-territoriality that globalization ushers in. From Bosnia to Rwanda it was precisely this theme of human rights that prevailed in Western debates on the conflicts. It is also the justification for the 'international community' to bring the likes of Augusto Pinochet and Slobodan Milosevic in front of international law tribunals.

Now, we should not neglect the importance that the international arena has gained as a strategic alternative for opposition activists seeking to bring national state atrocities to light. The Pinochet arrest in 1998 sent shock waves throughout the human rights community in Chile and transnationally. It did seem that 'global civil society' was able to make dictators accountable for their crimes against humanity. Yet a closer look at the Pinochet case shows that it was domestic pressure and Chilean judicial processes that carried more weight in the end than the international action. As Cath Collins argues: 'one might conclude that external enthusiasts of accountability would do better to seek to support and resource domestic prosecutions than to attempt to replicate the increasingly precarious Pinochet precedent in third-country courts' (Collins 2005: 21). This is an argument that takes full cognizance of the politics of scale in the making and unmaking of globalization, and alerts us to the dangers of automatically prioritizing the global in contesting power today.

The third discourse to consider here is that of 'internationalism', long the main weapon of the left in constructing a global response to capitalism. In much the same way that human rights have become a major instrument of hegemonic power so also has internationalism come to mean something quite different from its Enlightenment origins. The worker's cause, from its origins until at least the Second World War, was always internationalist in rhetoric if not in practice. Even the nationalist revolts in the colonial world after that war were bathed in the glow of internationalism. Yet, since the rise of globalization, internationalism has acquired a quite different connotation, precisely in the US, the hegemonic power, where internationalism once meant simply the opposite of isolationism. Today, as Perry Anderson puts it: 'internationalism . . . is no longer coordination of the major capitalist powers under American dominance against a common enemy, the negative task of the Cold War, but an affirmative ideal – the reconstruction of the globe in "the American image", *sans phrases*' (Anderson 2002: 24).

Where does this leave internationalism and transnationalism as discourses of contestation? The broad transnational movement in solidarity with the Zapatistas shows that another meaning of internationalism is still in existence. Internationalism should, maybe, be seen as an 'empty signifier' that constructs the 'people' in very different ways. We need to return to the history of internationalism as a process rather than a state concept, as Micheline Ishay argues, and distinguish it from the realist paradigm in international relations. For Ishay, 'unlike the realist paradigm, which focuses on economic, military, or any other instrumental links between nations, internationalism includes both an instrumental *and* a normative view of social and global unity' (Ishay 1995: xxi). Internationalism is not the simple opposite of nationalism but, rather, the register of progressive actions in pursuit of global objectives.

Finally, while this is not the place to articulate the new politics of social transformation that has been emerging in recent years across the globe we must point out that another world is, indeed, possible. It is as true today as it was in the 1980s. Arrighi, Hopkins and Wallerstein, in examining the 'dilemmas of anti-systemic movements', concluded that:

> We are massively, seriously in urgent need of reconstructing the strategy, perhaps the ideology, perhaps the organizational structure of the family of world anti-systemic movements; if we are to cope effectively with the real dilemmas before which we are placed.
>
> (Arrighi *et al.* 1989: 51)

Since then we have witnessed the end of the cold war, the rise of globalization and the emergence of the counter-globalization movement. There is nothing automatic about the advance of progressive social movements today, any more than in the mid-1980s when these cataclysmic changes in world history were hardly foreseen.

What we are witnessing in today's 'family' of global anti-systemic movements is an ongoing and profound debate on the 'new politics' that are required. This is focused not least on the nature of the 'democratic counter-power' that is necessary to counter and offer an alternative to free market globalism. Hilary Wainwright uses the word 'counterpower' to 'describe the many sources and levels of power through which it is possible to bring about social transformation' (Wainwright 2005). As with the post-1968 'new' social movements this counter-movement is challenging the positivist paradigm of knowledge and the sanctity of what are deemed to be scientific laws. We should not forget, however, in looking forward that accumulation by dispossession is, as Harvey puts it, 'the primary contradiction at the core of globalization to be confronted' (Harvey 2003: 177). While there is no easy way to reconcile those looking backwards and those looking forwards it is a necessary precondition for social transformation.

Taking a broad view we can say that the governance agenda that the agents of globalization are constructing in the post-Washington Consensus era depends on questions of politics and power being removed from the equation. Against this project the social counter-movements will bring back in political contestation and resistance to domination in all its forms. I would argue, finally, in agreement with Sousa Santos, that 'in the womb of this alternative counter-hegemonic globalization, another governance matrix is being generated, an insurgent counter-hegemonic governance' (Santos 2005: 16). In this battle of the governances, the outcome of the Polanyi problematic we now face will be decided. At the very least the counter-movement and its alternative globalization project have placed back on the broad political agenda questions of equity and justice within the context of a sustainable global development model.

Bibliography

Abdel-Malek, A. (1981) *Social Dialectics*. Albany, NY: State University of New York.

Adaman, F., Bulut, T. and Madra, Y.M. (2003) 'The Global-Local Clash. Embedding the Global Economy in the Local Society', Ninth Karl Polanyi Conference, Istanbul.

Albert, M. (2004) 'WSF: Where to Now?', in J. Sen, A. Arnaud, A. Escobar and P. Waterman (eds) *The World Social Forum. Challenging Empires*. New Delhi: Viveka Foundation.

Althusser, L. (1969) *For Marx*. London: Allen Lane.

Altvater, A. and Mahnkopf, B. (1997) 'The World Market Unbound', *Review of International Political Economy*, 4 (3): 448–71.

Alvarez, S. (2000) *Advocating Feminism: The Latin American NGO 'Boom'* (www.antena.nl/~waterman/alvarez2.html).

—— (1998) 'Latin American Feminisms "Go Global": Trends of the 1990s and Challenges for the New Millennium, in S. Alvarez, E. Dagnino and A. Escobar (eds) *Culture of Politics, Politics of Culture: Re-Visioning Latin American Social Movements*. Boulder, CO: Westview Press.

Alvarez, S., Dagnino, E. and Escobar, A. (1998) 'Introduction. The Cultural and the Political in Latin American Social Movements', in S. Alvarez, E. Dagnino and A. Escobar (eds) *Culture of Politics, Politics of Culture: Re-Visioning Latin American Social Movements*. Boulder, CO: Westview Press.

Amin, A. (1997) 'Placing Globalization', *Theory, Culture and Society*, 14 (2): 123–37.

Amin, S. (1989) *Eurocentrism*. London: Zed Books.

Amnesty International (2004) *Why Do Human Rights Matter to Business?* (http://web.amnesty.org/).

Anderson, B. (1983) *Imagined Communities: Reflections on the Origins and Spread of Nationalism*. London: Verso.

Anderson, K. and Rieff, D. (2005) 'Global Civil Society: A Sceptical View', in H. Anheier, M. Glasius and M. Kaldor (eds) *Global Civil Society Yearbook 2004–05*. Oxford: Oxford University Press.

Anderson, P. (2002) 'Internationalism: A Breviary', *New Left Review*, 14, March–April: 5–25.

Anheier, H., Glasius, M. and Kaldor, M. (eds) (2001) *Global Civil Society 2001*. Oxford: Oxford University Press.

Appadurai, A. (1996) *Modernity at Large: Cultural Dimensions of Globalization*. Minneapolis, MN and London: University of Minnesota Press.

Archibugi, D. (2003) 'Cosmopolitan Democracy', in D. Archibugi (ed.) *Debating Cosmopolitics*. London: Verso.

Arrighi, G. (1990) 'Marxist Century, American Century: The Making and Remaking of The World Labor Movement', *New Left Review*, 179, Jan–Feb: 29–63.

——, Hopkins, T. and Wallerstein, I. (1989) *Antisystemic Movements*. London: Verso.

Ashgar, A. (2005) 'New Caliphate, New Era', *New Civilisation*, 4: 10–17.

Ayres, R. (2004) 'Framing Collective Action Against Neoliberalism: The Case of the "Anti-Globalization" Movement', *Journal of World-Systems Research*, X (1): 11–34.

Balakrishnan, G. (2003) 'Introduction', in G. Balakrishnan (ed.) *Debating Empire*. London: Verso.

Barchiesi, F. (2004) *Classes, Multitudes and the Politics of Community Movements in Post-Apartheid South Africa*. Bloemfontein, South Africa: Annual Congress of the South African Sociological Association.

Baxi, U. (2003) *The Future of Human Rights*. Oxford: Oxford University Press.

Beck, U. (2001) *What is Globalization?* Cambridge: Polity Press.

Beeley, B. (1995) 'Global Options: Islamic Alternatives', in J. Anderson, C. Brook and A. Cochrane (eds) *A Global World?* Oxford: Oxford University Press.

Benhabib, S. (2001) *Unholy Politics* (http://www.ssrc.org/sept11/essays/benhabib.htm).

Bernstein, E. (1978) La Segunda Internacional y el Problema Nacional, Colonial (Vol. I), Mexico DF: Siglo XXI.

Bhagwati, J. (2004) *In Defence of Globalization*. Oxford: Oxford University Press.

Block, F. (2001) 'Introduction', in K. Polanyi, *The Great Transformation*. Boston, MA: Beacon Press.

Bob, C. (2002) 'Globalization and the Social Construction of Human Rights Campaigns', in A. Brysk (ed.) *Globalization and Human Rights*. Berkeley, CA: University of California Press.

Bové, F. and Dufour, F. (2001) *The World is Not For Sale: Farmers Against Junk Food*. London: Verso.

Brennan, T. (2003) 'Cosmopolitanism and Internationalism', in D. Archibugi (ed.) *Debating Cosmopolitics*. London: Verso.

Broad, R. (2004) 'The Washington Consensus Meets the Global Backlash: Shifting Debates and Policies', *Globalization*, 1 (2): 129–54.

Bruce, I. (ed.) (2004) *The Porto Alegre Alternative: Direct Democracy in Action*. London: Pluto Press.

Brysk, A. (2000) 'Introduction: Transnational Threats and Opportunities', in A. Brysk (ed.) *Globalization and Human Rights*. Berkeley, CA: University of California Press.

Bull, M. (2004) 'Smooth Politics', in P. Passavant and J. Dean (eds) *Empire's New Clothes: Reading Hardt and Negri*. London and New York: Routledge.

Burawoy, M. (2003) 'For a Sociological Marxism: The Complementary Convergence of Antonio Gramsci and Karl Polanyi', *Politics and Society*, 31 (2): 193–261.

Burke, J. (2004) *Al-Qaeda: The True Story of Radical Islam*. Harmondsworth: Penguin.

Buttel, F. and Gould, K. (2004) 'Global Social Movement(s) at the Crossroads: Some Observations on the Trajectory of the Anti-Corporate Globalization Movement', *Journal of World-Systems Research*, X (1): 37–66.

Bygrave, M. (2002) 'Where Did All the Protestors Go?', *Observer Worldview: The Globalisation Debate* (http://www.observer.guardian.co.uk/comment).

Calhoun, C. (1997) *Nationalism*. Buckingham: Open University Press.

Caruso, G. (2005) *Report on the World Social Forum in Mumbai 2004* (www.signofourtimes.org/UK/WSF/html).

Cassen, B. (2003) 'On the Attack', *New Left Review*, 19: 41–60.

Castells, M. (2004) *The Information Age Vol. II: The Power of Identity* (Second Edition). Oxford: Blackwell.

—— (1998) *The Information Age Vol. III: End of Millennium.* Oxford: Blackwell.

—— (1996) *The Information Age Vol. I: The Rise of the Network Society.* Oxford: Blackwell.

Cerny, P. (1999) 'Globalization, Governance and Complexity', in A. Prakash and J. Hart (eds) *Globalization and Governance.* London: Routledge.

Chakrabarty, D. (2000) *Provincializing Europe.* Princeton, NJ: Princeton University Press.

Clarke, M. (1985) 'Transnationalism', in S. Smith (ed.) *International Relations. British and American Perspectives.* Oxford: Basil Blackwell.

Claudin, F. (1975) *The Communist Movement From Comintern to Cominform.* Harmondsworth: Penguin.

Clawson, D. (2005) *The Next Upsurge: Labor and the New Social Movements.* Ithaca, NY and London: Cornell University Press.

Cohen, J. (1987) *Class and Civil Society: The Limits of Marxian Critical Theory.* Amherst, MA: University of Massachusetts Press.

Cohen, R. and Rai, S. (eds) (2000) *Global Social Movements.* London: The Athlone Press.

Colás, A. (2002) *International Civil Society. Social Movements in World Politics.* Cambridge: Polity Press.

Collins, C. (2005) *Grounding Global Justice: International Networks and Domestic Human Rights Accountability in Chile and El Salvador.* Paper to Society for Latin American Studies, Norwich (April).

Commission on Global Governance (1995) *Our Global Neighbourhood.* Oxford: Oxford University Press.

Conner, W. (1993) *Ethnonationalism. The Quest for Understanding.* Princeton, NJ: Princeton University Press.

Cooper, R.A. (2002) 'Why We Still Need Empires', *Observer*, 7 April.

Cox, K. (ed.) (1997) *Spaces of Globalization: Reasserting the Power of the Local.* Oxford: Guildford Press.

Dalton, G. (ed.) (1971) *Primitive, Archaic and Modern Economics: Essays of Karl Polanyi.* Boston, MA: Beacon Press.

Dicken, P., Peck, J. and Tickell, A. (1977) 'Unpacking the Global', in R. Lee and J. Wills (eds) *Geographical Economies.* London: Arnold.

Dirlik, A. (1999) 'Place-based Imagination: Globalism and the Politics of Place', *Review*, XXII (2): 151–87.

Doob, L. (1964) *Patriotism and Nationalism: Their Psychological Foundations.* New York: Yale University Press.

Douglas, I. (1999) 'Globalization *as* Governance: Towards an Archaeology of Contemporary Political Reason', in A. Prakash and J. Hart (eds) *Globalization and Governance.* London: Routledge.

Drache, D. (1999) 'Globalization: Is There Anything to Fear?', CSGR, University of Warwick, Working Paper No. 23.

Drainville, A. (2004) *Contesting Globalization: Space and Place in the World Economy.* London and New York: Routledge.

—— (2001) 'Cosmopolitan Ghosts and Resistance Communities: Québec City's Summit of the Americas and the Making of Transnational Subjects', in L. Panitch and C. Keys (eds) *Socialist Register 2001.* London: Merlin Press.

Dunn, K. (2004) 'Africa's Ambiguous Relation to Empire and *Empire*', in P. Passavant and J. Dean (eds) *Empire's New Clothes: Reading Hardt and Negri.* London and New York: Routledge.

Edelman, M. (2003) 'Transnational Peasant and Farmer Movements and Networks', in H. Anheier, M. Glasius and M. Kaldor (eds) *Global Civil Society 2003*. Oxford: Oxford University Press.

Epstein, B. (2001) 'Anarchism and the Anti-Globalization Movement', *Monthly Review*, 53 (4).

Evans, P. (2000) 'Fighting Marginalization with Transnational Networks: Counter-Hegemonic Globalization', *Current Sociology*, 29: 230–41.

Evers, T. (1985) 'Identity: The Hidden Side of New Social Movements in Latin America', in D. Slater (ed.) *New Social Movements and the State in Latin America*. Amsterdam: CEDLA.

Fanon, F. (1969) *The Wretched of the Earth*. Harmondsworth: Penguin.

Featherstone, D. (2003) 'Spatialities of Transnational Resistance to Globalisation: The Maps of Grievances of the Inter-Continental Caravan', Department of Geography, University of Liverpool.

Featherstone, M. (1995) *Undoing Culture: Globalization, Postmodernism and Identity*. London: Sage.

Feffer, J. (ed.) (2002) *Living in Hope: People Challenging Globalization*. London: Zed Books.

Ferguson, N. (2005) *Colossus: The Rise and Fall of the American Empire*. New York: Basic Books.

—— (2004) *Empire: How Britain Made the World*. New York: Basic Books.

Forman, M. (1998) *Nationalism and the International Labor Movement: The Idea of the Nation in Socialist and Anarchist Theory*. Pennsylvania, PN: Pennsylvania State University Press.

Foweraker, J. (1995) *Theorising Social Movements: Latin American Perspectives*. London: Pluto Press.

Francis, H. (1984) *Miners Against Fascism: Wales and the Spanish Civil War*. London: Laurence & Wishart.

French, J. and James, D. (1997) 'Introduction', in J. French and D. James (eds) *The Gendered Worlds of Latin American Women Workers: From Household and Factory to the Union Hall and the Ballot Box*. Durham, NC: Duke University Press.

——, Couric, J. and Littleman, S. (1994) *Labor and NAFTA: A Briefing Book*. Durham, NC: Duke University Press.

Fuentes, C. (1994) 'Chiapas: Latin America's First Post-Communist Revolution', *New Perspectives Quarterly*, 11 (2).

Fukuyama, F. (1996) *Trust: The Social Virtues and the Creation of Prosperity*. New York: Free Press.

—— (1992) *The End of History and the Last Man*. London: Hamish Hamilton.

Fuss, D. (1989) *Essentially Speaking: Feminism, Nature and Difference*. London: Routledge.

García Canclini, N. (1999) *La Globalización Imaginada*. Buenos Aires: Paidós.

Garretón, M.A., Cavarozzi, M., Cleaves, P., Sereffi, G. and Hartlyn, J. (2003) *Latin America in the Twenty-First Century: Towards a New Sociopolitical Matrix*. Miami, FL: North-South Centre Press.

——, ——, —— and —— (2002) *Latin America in the Twenty-First Century*. Washington, DC: The Brookings Institute.

Gellner, E. (1983) *Nations and Nationalism*. Oxford: Blackwell.

Giddens, A. (2001) 'Anthony Giddens and Will Hutton in Conversation', in W. Hutton and A. Giddens (eds) *On the Edge. Living with Global Capitalism*. London: Vintage.

Gill, S. (2003) *Gramsci, Modernity and Globalization* (www.italnet.nd.edu/gramsci/resources/online_articles/index.html).

—— (1997) 'Gramsci, Modernity and Globalization', Gramsci and the Twentieth Century Conference, Sardinia.

Gilly, A. (1998) 'Chiapas and the Rebellion of its Enchanted World', in D. Nugent (ed.) *Rural Revolt in Mexico: US Intervention and the Domain of Subaltern Politics*. Durham, NC and London: Duke University Press.

Glasius, M. and Timms, J. (2005) 'The Role of Social Forums in Global Civil Society: Radical Beacon or Strategic Infrastructure', in H. Anheier, M. Glasius and M. Kaldor (eds) *Global Civil Society 2005/6*. London: Sage Publications.

Goodwin, J. and Jasper, J. (2003) 'Editor's Introduction', in J. Goodwin and J. Jasper (eds) *The Social Movements Reader*. Oxford: Blackwell.

Gould, K., Lewis, T. and Timmon-Roberts, J. (2004) 'Blue-Green Coalitions: Constraints and Possibilities in the Post-9/11 Political Environment', *Journal of World-Systems Research*, X (1): 91–116.

Gramsci, A. (1971) *Selections from the Prison Notebooks*. London: Laurence & Wishart.

Grenfell, D. (2002) 'Environmentalists, State Power and National Interests', in J. Goodman (ed.) *Protest and Globalisation: Prospects for Transnational Solidarity*. Australia: Pluto Press.

Habermas, J. (1987) *The Philosophical Discourse of Modernity*. Cambridge, MA: MIT Press.

Halliday, F. (2000) 'The Romance of Non-Place Actors', in D. Josselin and W. Wallace (eds) *Non-State Actors in World Politics*. London: Palgrave, pp. 21–37.

—— (1999) *Revolution and World Politics: The Rise and Fall of the Sixth Great Power*. Basingstoke: Palgrave.

Harding, J. (2001) 'Globalisation's Children Strike Back', *Financial Times* (http://www.specials.ft.com/countercap).

Hardt, M. and Negri, A. (2004) *Multitude*. Cambridge, MA: Harvard University Press.

—— (2000) *Empire*. Cambridge, MA: Harvard University Press.

Harman, C. (2000) 'Anti-capitalism: Theory and Practice', *International Socialism*, 88: 3–60.

Harvey, D. (2003) *The New Imperialism*. Oxford: Oxford University Press.

—— (1996) *Justice, Nature and the Geography of Difference*. Oxford: Blackwell.

—— (1989) *The Condition of Postmodernity*. Oxford: Blackwell.

Hay, A. (2003) 'What if There Were a Mass Mobilisation Movement?', *World Link: The Magazine of the World Economic Forum* (http://www.worldlink.co.uk/).

Held, D. and McGrew, A. (2003) *Globalisation and Anti-Globalisation*. Cambridge: Polity Press.

——, McGrew, A., Goldblatt, D. and Perraton, P. (1999) *Global Transformations: Politics, Economics and Culture*. Cambridge: Polity Press.

Hellman, J. (1999) 'Real and Virtual Chiapas: Magical Realism and the Left', in L. Panitch and C. Keys (eds) *Socialist Register 2000*. London: Merlin Press.

Herod, A. (2001) 'Labor Internationalism or the Contradiction of Globalization, or, Why the Local is Sometimes Still Important in a Global Economy', *Antipode*, 33 (3): 407–26.

Hertz, N. (2001) *The Silent Takeover: Global Capitalism and the Death of Democracy*. London: Arrow.

Higgott, R. (2000) 'Contested Globalization: The Changing Context and Normative Challenges', *Review of International Studies*, 26: 131–53.

Hirst, P. and Thompson, G. (1999) *Globalization in Question* (Second Edition). Cambridge: Polity Press.

Hobsbawm, E. (1988) 'Opening Address: Working Class Internationalism', in F. van Holhoon and M. van der Linden (eds) *Internationalism and the Labour Movement*. Leiden: Britl, pp. 1–18.

—— (1959) *Primitive Rebels*. Manchester: Manchester University Press.

Hooson, D. (1994) 'Introduction', in D. Hooson (ed.) *Geography and National Identity*. Oxford: Blackwell.

Huntington, S.P. (2002) *The Clash of Civilizations and the Remaking of the World Order*. New York: Free Press.

ICEM (1999) *Facing Global Power: Strategies for Global Unionism*. Durban: Second World Congress.

Ignatieff, M. (1993) *Blood and Belonging: Journeys into the New Nationalism*. London: BBC Books.

Ishay, M. (1995) *Internationalism and its Betrayal*. Minneapolis, MN: University of Minnesota Press.

James, P. (2001) 'Relating Global Tensions: Modern Tribalism and Postmodern Nationalism', *Communal/Plural*, 9 (1): 11–31.

Jessop, B. (2003) 'Polanyi on the Social Embeddedness of Substantively Instituted Economies', Research Paper, Department of Sociology, University of Lancaster.

Jonas, A. (1998) 'Investigating the Local-Global Paradox', in A. Herod (ed.) *Organising the Landscape: Geographical Perspectives on Labor Unionism*. Minneapolis, MN: University of Minnesota Press.

Kaldor, M. (2003) *Global Civil Society: An Answer to War*. Cambridge: Polity Press.

—— and Muro, D. (2005) 'Religious and Nationalist Militant Groups', in M. Anheier, D. Glasius and M. Kaldor (eds) *Global Civil Society 2005*. Oxford: Oxford University Press.

Kaplan, C. (1994) 'The Politics of Location as Transnational Feminist Critical Practice' in C. Kaplan and I. Grewal (eds) *Scattered Hegemonies: Postmodernity and Transnational Feminist Practices*. Minneapolis, MN: University of Minnesota Press.

Kayatekin, S. and Ruccio, D. (1998) 'Global Fragments: Subjectivity and Class Politics in Discourses of Globalization', *Economy and Society* 27 (1): 74–96.

Keane, J. (2001) 'Global Civil Society', in H. Anheier, M. Glasius and M. Kaldor (eds) *Global Civil Society 2001*. Oxford: Oxford University Press.

Kearney, R. (1997) *Postnationalist Ireland: Politics, Culture, Philosophy*. London: Routledge.

Kennedy, J. and Lavalette, M. (2004) 'Globalisation, Trade Unionism and Solidarity: Further Reflections on the Liverpool Docks Lockout' in R. Munck (ed.) *Labour and Globalisation: Results and Prospects*. Liverpool: Liverpool University Press.

Khagram, S., Riker, J. and Sikkouk, K. (2002) 'From Santiago to Seattle: Transnational Advocacy Groups Restructuring World Politics', in S. Khagram, J. Riker and K. Sikkouk (eds) *Restructuring World Politics: Transnational Social Movements, Networks and Norms*. Minneapolis, MN: University of Minnesota Press.

Klanwatch/Militia Task Force (1996) *False Patriots: The Threat from Antigovernment Extremists*. Montgomery, AL: Southern Poverty Law Center.

Klein, N. (2002) *Fences and Windows: Dispatches from the Front Lines of the Globalization Debate*. New York: Picador.

Korten, D. (1995) *When Corporations Rule the World*. San Francisco, CA: Kumarian Press.

Laclau, E. (2005) *On Populist Reason*. London: Verso.

—— (1979) *Politics and Ideology in Marxist Theory*. London: Verso.

Legrain, P. (2003) *Open World: The Truth about Globalization*. Oxford: Oxford University Press.

Levi, M. and Olson, D. (2000) 'The Battle of Seattle', *Politics and Society*, 28: 309–29.

Linden, M. van der (2003) *Transnational Labour History: Explorations*. Aldershot: Ashgate.

itz, R. (1992) 'Reconstructing World Politics: The Emergence of Civil Society', llennium, 21 (3): 389–420.

, M. (1998) 'Sources and Resources of Zapatism', Monthly Review, 49: 10.

s, F.S.L. (1963) Internationalism in Europe 1815–1914. Leyden: A.W. Sythoff.

Carthy, J. and Zald, M. (1973) The Dynamics of Social Movements: Resource Mobilization, Social Control and Tactics. Cambridge, MA: Winthrop Publishers.

cIver, I.M. (1957) 'Foreword' in K. Polanyi, The Great Transformation (First edition). Boston, MA: Beacon Press.

Martínez, E. (2000) 'Where was the Color in Seattle?', Colorlines, 3 (1), Spring.

Marx, K. (1844) On the Jewish Question (www.marxists.org/archive/marx/works/1844/jewish-question).

Massey, D. (2000) 'The Geography of Power', Red Pepper, July.

Mayo, M. (2004) Global Citizens: Social Movements and the Challenge of Globalization. London: Zed Books.

Melucci, A. (1998) Challenging Codes: Collective Action in the Information Age. Cambridge: Cambridge University Press.

—— (1989) Nomads of the Present: Social Movements and Individual Needs in Contemporary Society. London: Radius.

—— (1988) 'Getting Involved: Identity and Mobilization in Social Movements', in B. Klandermans, K. Hanspeter and S. Tarrow (eds) From Structure to Action: Comparing Social Movements Across Cultures. Greenwich, CT: JAI Press.

Miles, A. (1996) Integrative Feminisms: Building Global Visions, 1960s–1990s. New York: Routledge.

Mohanty, C.T. (1991) 'Under Western Eyes: Feminist Scholarship and Colonial Discourses', in C.T. Mohanty, A. Russo and L. Torres (eds) Third World Women and the Politics of Feminism. Bloomington, IN: Indiana University Press.

Moody, K. (1997) Workers in a Lean World. London: Verso.

Munck, R. (2005) Globalisation and Social Exclusion: A Transformationalist Perspective. Bloomfield, CT: Kumarian Press.

—— (2002) Globalisation and Labour: The New 'Great Transformation'. London: Zed Books.

—— (2001) 'Globalization, Regionalism and Labour: The Case of MERCOSUR', Labour, Capital and Society, 34 (1): 8–25.

—— (1986) The Difficult Dialogue: Marxism and Nationalism. London: Zed Books.

Munson, C. (2004) Five Years after WTO Protests, Counterpunch (http://www.counterpunch.org/).

Murphy, G. (2004) 'The Seattle WTO Protests: Building a Global Movement', in R. Taylor (ed.) Creating a Better World: Interpreting Global Civil Society. Bloomfield, CT: Kumarian Press.

Nairn, T. (2000) A Tom Nairn Essay. (http://members.tripod.com/GellnerPage/NairnEssay.html).

—— (1997) Faces of Nationalism: Janus Revisited. London: Verso.

—— and James, P. (2005) 'Introduction: Mapping Nationalism and Globalism', in T. Nairn and P. James, Global Matrix: Nationalism: Globalism and State-Terrorism. London: Pluto Press.

Notes From Nowhere (2003) We Are Everywhere: The Irresistible Rise of Global Anticapitalism. London: Verso.

Obi, C. (2000) 'Globalization and Local Resistance: The Case of Shell Versus the Ogoni', in B. Gills (ed.) Globalization and the Politics of Resistance. London: Palgrave.

O'Brien, R., Goetz, A.M., Scholte, J.A. and Williams, M. (2000) *Contesting Global Governance: Multilateral Economic Institutions and Global Social Movements*. Cambridge: Cambridge University Press.

Oeleson, T. (2005) *International Zapatismo: The Construction of Solidarity in the Age of Globalization*. London: Zed Books.

Ohmae, K. (1990) *The Borderless World*. London: Collins.

—— (1995) *The End of the Nation State*. New York: Free Press.

Olson, M. (1965) *The Logic of Collective Action*. Cambridge, MA: Harvard University Press.

Packard, V. (1957) *The Hidden Persuaders*. New York: Random House.

Pasha, M.K. (2000) 'Globalization, Islam and Resistance', in B. Gills (ed.) *Globalization and Resistance*. London: Palgrave.

Passy, F. (1999) 'Supranational Political Opportunities as a Channel of Globalization of Political Conflicts: The Case of the Rights of Indigenous Peoples' in D. della Porta, H. Kriesi and D. Rucht (eds) *Social Movements in a Globalizing World*. London: Macmillan.

Paulson, J. (2000) 'Peasant Struggles and International Solidarity: The Case of Chiapas' in L. Panitch and C. Keys (eds) *Socialist Register 2000*. London: Merlin Press.

Petras, J. and Veltmeyer, H. (2003) 'Peasant-based Socio-political Movements in Latin America', in J. Petras (ed.) *The New Development Politics*. Aldershot: Ashgate.

Pianta, M. (2001) 'Parallel Summits of Global Civil Society', in H. Anheier, M. Glasius and M. Kaldor (eds) *Global Civil Society 2001*. Oxford: Oxford University Press.

—— and Silva, F. (2003) 'Parallel Summits of Global Civil Society: An Update' in H. Anheier, M. Glasius and M. Kaldor (eds) *Global Civil Society*. Oxford: Oxford University Press.

Pieterse, J.N. (2004) *Globalization or Empire?* New York and London: Routledge.

—— (2000) 'The World Trade Organization After the Battle of Seattle', *Review of International Political Economy*, 7 (3): 465.

Piven, F. and Cloward, R. (1978) *Poor People's Movements: Why They Succeed, How They Fail*. Oxford: Blackwell.

Pizzorno, A. (1978) 'Political Exchange and Collective Action in Industrial Conflict', in C. Crouch and A. Pizzorno (eds) *The Resurgence of Class Conflict in Western Europe Since 1968 Vol. 2*. London: Macmillan.

Polanyi, K. (2001) *The Great Transformation: The Political and Economic Origins of Our Time*. Boston, MA: Beacon Press.

—— (1957) 'Our Obsolete Market Mentality', in G. Dalton (ed.) *Primitive, Archaic and Modern Economics: Essays of Karl Polanyi*. Boston, MA: Beacon Press.

—— (1945) 'Universal Capitalism or Regional Planning?', *The London Quarterly of World Affairs*, January: 86–95.

Potok, M. (2001) 'The New Internationalism', Southern Poverty Law Center Intelligence Report (http://www.splcenter.org/intel/intelreport/article.jsp?aid=175).

Probyn, E. (1990) 'Travels in the Postmodern: Making Sense of the Local', in L. Nicholsen (ed.) *Feminism/Postmodernism*. New York and London: Routledge.

Quinby, L. (2004) 'Taking the Millennialist Pulse of *Empire's* Multitude: A Genealogical Feminist Diagnosis', in P. Passavant and J. Dean (eds) *Empire's New Clothes. Reading Hardt and Negri*. London and New York: Routledge.

Robertson, R. (1992) *Globalization: Social Theory and Global Culture*. London: Sage.

Rondfeldt, D. and Arquilla, J. (1998) *The Zapatista Social Netwar in Mexico*. Santa Monica, CA: RAND.

᠁es, C. (2004) 'Global Civil Society and the Lessons of European Environmentalism',
. R. Taylor (ed.) *Creating a Better World: Interpreting Global Civil Society*. Bloomfield,
⸗T: Kumarian Press.

᠁thman, F. and Oliver, P. (2002) 'From Local to Global: The Anti-Dam Movement
in Southern Brazil From 1979–1992', in J. Smith and H. Johnston (eds) *Globalization
and Resistance*. Boulder, CA: Rowman & Littlefield.

Roy, O. (2001) 'Neo-Fundamentalism' (http://www.ssrc.org/sept11/essays/roy.htm).

Rupert, M. (2000) 'Globalization and American Common Sense: Struggling to Make
Sense of a Post-Hegemonic World', in B. Gills (ed.) *Globalization and the Politics of
Resistance*. London: Palgrave.

Said, E. (1978) *Orientalism*. London: Routledge.

St Clair, J. (2000) *Seattle Diary, Counterpunch* (http://www.counterpunch.com/).

Santos, B. de Sousa (2005) 'Beyond Neoliberal Governance: The World Social Forum
as Subaltern Politics and Legality', mimeo.

—— (2004a) 'The WSF: Towards a Counter-Hegemonic Globalisation', in J. Sen,
A. Arnaud, A. Escobar and P. Waterman (eds) *The World Social Forum: Challenging
Empires*. New Delhi: Viveka Foundation.

—— (2004b) *The World Social Forum: A User's Manual* (http://www.ces.uc.pt/bss/
documentos/fsm_eng.pdf).

Sardar, Z. (1999) *Orientalism*. Buckingham: Open University Press.

Sartre, J.P. (1969) 'Foreword' in F. Fanon, *The Wretched of the Earth*. Harmondsworth:
Penguin.

Sassoon, D. (1996) *One Hundred Years of Socialism: The West European Left in the Twentieth
Century*. London: I.B. Tauris.

Scholte, J. (2005) *Globalization: A Critical Introduction* (2nd edn), Basingstoke: Palgrave.

—— (2000) *Globalization: A Critical Introduction*. Basingstoke: Palgrave.

Sen, J. (2004) 'A Tale of Two Charters', in J. Sen, A. Arnaud, A. Escobar and
P. Waterman (eds) *The World Social Forum: Challenging Empires*. New Delhi: Viveka
Foundation.

——, Arnaud, A., Escobar, A. and Waterman, P. (eds) (2004) *The World Social Forum:
Challenging Empires*. New Delhi: Viveka Foundation.

Shaw, M. (1994) *Global Society and International Relations: Sociological Concepts and Political
Perspectives*. Cambridge: Cambridge University Press.

Sherman, S. and Trichur, G. (2004) '*Empire* and *Multitude*: A Review Essay', *Journal of
World-Systems Research*, X (3): 819–45.

Silver, B. (2003) *Forces of Labor: Workers' Movements and Globalization Since 1870*.
Cambridge: Cambridge University Press.

—— and Arrighi, G. (2003) 'Polanyi's "Double Movement": The *Belle Époques* of British
and US Hegemony Compared', *Politics and Society*, 31 (2): 325–55.

Smith, J. (2002) 'Globalizing Resistance: The Battle of Seattle and the Future of Social
Movements' in J. Smith and H. Johnston (eds) *Globalization and Resistance:
Transnational Dimensions of Social Movements*. Lanham, MD: Rowman & Littlefield.

—————— (1999) 'Global Politics and Transnational Social Movement Strategies: The
Transnational Campaign Against International Trade in Toxic Wastes', in D. della
Porta, K. Kriese and D. Rucht (eds) *Social Movements in a Globalizing World*. London:
Palgrave.

——, Pagnucco, R. and Chatfield, C. (1997) 'Transnational Social Movements and
Global Politics: A Theoretical Framework', in J. Smith, C. Chatfield and R. Pagnucco,
Transnational Social Movements and Global Politics: Solidarity Beyond the State. Syracuse,
NY: Syracuse University Press.

Smith, M.P. (2001) *Transnational Urbanism: Locating Globalization*. Oxford: Blackwell.

Soros, G. (1998) *The Crisis of Global Capitalism: Open Society Endangered*. London: Little, Brown.

Southern Poverty Law Center (2001) 'Youth at the Edge' (http://www.splcenter.org/intel/intelreport/article.jsp?aid=302).

—— (1999) 'Patriot Periodicals' (http://www.splcenter.org/intel/intelreport/).

—— (1998) *The Patriot Movement. Fewer, but Harder*. (http://www.splcenter.org/intel/intelreport/article/).

Starr, A. (2004) 'How can Anti-Imperialism not be Anti-Racist? The North American Anti-Globalization Movement', *Journal of World-Systems Research*, X (1): 119–51.

—— (2002) *Naming the Enemy: Anti-Corporate Movements Confront Globalization*. London: Zed Books.

Stevis, D. (1998) 'International Labor Organizations, 1864–1997: The Weight of History and the Challenges of the Present', *Journal of World-Systems Research*, IV (1): 52–75.

Stiglitz, J. (2001) 'Foreword', in K. Polanyi, *The Great Transformation*. Boston, MA: Beacon Press.

Tarrow, S. (2002) 'The New Transnational Contention: Organizations, Coalitions and Mechanism', APSA Annual Meeting, Chicago.

—— (1998) 'National Politics and Collective Action: Recent Theory and Research in Western Europe and the United States', *Annual Review of Sociology*, 14.

Taylor, P. (2000) 'Izations of the World: Americanization, Modernization and Globalization', in C. Hay and D. Marsh (eds) *Demystifying Globalization*. London: Palgrave.

Thiong'o, N. (1981) *Decolonizing the Mind: The Politics of Language in African Literature*. London: James Currey.

Tichelman, F. (1988) 'Socialist "Internationalism" and the Colonial World', in F. van Holthoon and M. van der Linden (eds) *Internationalism in the Labour Movement 1830–1940*. Leiden: Britl.

Torfing, J. (1999) *New Theories of Discourse: Laclau, Mouffe and Žižek*. Oxford: Blackwell.

Törnquist, O. (1984) *Dilemmas of Third World Communism: The Destruction of the PKI in Indonesia*. London: Zed Books.

Toro, M.S. (2004) 'Draft Criteria for a Proposed Women's Summit About the State of the World', in J. Sen, A. Arnaud, A. Escobar and P. Waterman (eds) *The World Social Forum: Challenging Empires*. New Delhi: Viveka Foundation.

Touraine, A. (2001) 'Marcos; el demócrata armado', *La Journada Semanal*, 22 December.

—— (1985) *The Voice and the Eye: An Analysis of Social Movements*. Cambridge: Cambridge University Press.

Trotsky, L. (1928) *Leon Trotsky on China: Summary and Perspectives of the Chinese Revolution. Its Lessons for the Countries of the Orient and for the Whole of the Comintern* (www.marxists.org/archive/trotsky/works/1928-3rd/3rd.pdf).

Urry, J. (2003) *Global Complexity*. Cambridge: Polity Press.

Veer, P. van der (2001) *Transnational Religion*. Princeton University Conference on Transnational Migration: Comparative Perspectives.

Vía Campesina (2005) 'The Challenge of Building our own Vision and Proposal' (http://www.viacampesina.org/en/).

Virno, P. (2004) *A Grammar of the Multitude*. New York: Semiotext(e).

Wainwright, H. (2005) 'Why Participatory Democracy Matters, and Movements Matter to Participatory Democracy', TNI Website (http://www.tnc.nl/).

—— (2002) 'Notes Towards a New Politics', TNI Briefing Series No. 2.

...erstein, I. (1984) 'Nationalism and the World Transition to Socialism', in Wallerstein (ed.) *The Politics of the World Economy*. Cambridge: Cambridge University Press.

...alton, J. and Seddon, M. (1994) *Free Markets and Food Riots: The Politics of Global Adjustment*. Oxford: Blackwell.

Washbourne, N. (2001) 'Information Technology and New Forms of Organising? Translocalism and Networks in Friends of the Earth', in F. Webster (ed.) *Culture and Politics in the Information Age: A New Politics?* London: Routledge, pp. 91–113.

Waterman, P. (2003) *Second Thoughts on the Third World Social Forum: Place, Space and the Reinvention of Social Emancipation on a Global Scale* (www.antenna.nl/~waterman/).

—— (1998) *Globalisation, Social Movements and the New Internationalism*. London: Mansell.

Weiss, L. (2003) 'Is the State being "Transformed" by Globalisation?', in L. Weiss (ed.) *States in the Global Economy: Bringing Domestic Institutions Back In*. Cambridge: Cambridge University Press.

Whitaker, C. (2004) 'The WSF as Open Space', in J. Sen, A. Arnaud, A. Escobar and P. Waterman (eds) *The World Social Forum: Challenging Empires*. New Delhi: Viveka Foundation.

Wieviorka, M. (2005) 'After New Social Movements', *Social Movements Studies*, 4 (1): 1–20.

Williams, J. (1995) 'The World of Islam', in J. Anderson, C. Brook and A. Cochrane (eds) *A Global World?* Oxford: Oxford University Press.

Wolf, M. (2004) *Why Globalization Works*. New Haven, CT and London: Yale University Press.

Young, R. (2001) *Postcolonialism: An Historical Introduction*. Oxford: Blackwell.

Zahid, M. (2005) 'Critiquing Orientialist Perceptions', *New Civilisation*, 4: 72–7.

Index

An environmentally friendly book printed and bound in England by www.printondemand-worldwide.com

#0403 - 021111 - CO - 234/156 - PB